TWENTIETH-CENTURY
STAGE DECORATION

TWENTIETH-CENTURY
STAGE DECORATION

WALTER RENÉ FUERST

AND

SAMUEL J. HUME

WITH AN INTRODUCTION BY ADOLPHE APPIA

VOLUME ONE: TEXT

BENJAMIN BLOM, NEW YORK

Library of Congress Catalog Card Number (paperbound): 65-24021
Library of Congress Catalog Card Number (clothbound): 67-28846

Manufactured in the United States of America

THIS EDITION IS DEDICATED
TO THE MEMORY OF

Walter René Fuerst
(DECEMBER 8, 1884 — APRIL 20, 1948)

AND

Samuel J. Hume
(JUNE 14, 1885 — SEPTEMBER 1, 1962)

FOR THEIR CONTRIBUTIONS
TO THE THEATER AND THEATER EDUCATION

CONTENTS

LIST OF ILLUSTRATIONS

IN VOLUME ONE

INTRODUCTION

ART IS AN ATTITUDE

THIS attitude ought to be humanity's collective heritage. Instead, we have narrowed it down, made it the personal attribute of the " artist " alone, of the creator of the work of art. Histories of art thus made to consist of chronological lists of such works and of their different methods. We have music, architecture, sculpture, painting, as though art must necessarily consist of carven stones, sounds, colours, even words. Our museums, concerts, and libraries seem to confirm this view. Not twenty years ago, these institutions appeared to us unshakable ; they stood for art, as its glorious trustees and guardians.

To-day, they are so no longer.

We have left our chairs. We are erect, we want to be " of it," we shrink from no violence to reach our goal, we seek for art and we wish to find it in ourselves. We break the barriers asunder, surmount in a stride the steps that separate us from the stage, descend unflinching into the arena.

This assertion cannot be omitted at the opening of a work devoted to the theatre.

But it implies the gift of our intelligences, and the gift of our bodies. To be " of it," we must search, like neophytes, for the point of meeting between the work of art and our whole personalities. In the theatre, this gesture, a novel one indeed, yields us up the key of the scenic problem.

Here is a solution of which we may justly be proud ! What, indeed, should our body do with the painted drops ; and why hamper it with them when it offers itself to us without reserve ? But again, in what way can we ask scenery to heighten the effect of the body, now become an artistic factor, and never again to abandon that position ? If we know the answer, why not assume the situation ?

Games and the conquest of space have made us conscious of the objective existence of the body. We know our debt to it now, and we wish to extend this obligation to the space over which we move, to the earth which we endow with so burning a reality. Can we go on sitting quietly in our stalls in front of a space in which bodies like to our own are enslaved and degraded ? For such are the scenes of our theatres still ; the supreme object of art, the living body, our body, is outraged and debased by our scenic decorations.

The problem of the mise en scène, placed in its true light, is thus solved. It remains to determine the technical consequences of this process of evolution, and their influence on our social life.

Let us take two opposite poles: on the one hand dramatic art, pure and unalloyed; on the other any spectacle intended solely to please the eye.

The more dramatic art approaches pure spectacle, the less its dramatic value. Similarly, the spectacle will lose in richness and in variety if it contains any dramatization whatever.

If dramatic art renounces the weakness which purely representative art can allow itself, what has it left? This is left: the actor's living body. Now, this body is tri-dimensional; it is also capable of movement. Painted drops are bi-dimensional and consist of conventional representations of objects, lights, and shades. The actor is a *living* reality which is untouched by these painted lights and shades, and cannot enter into organic relations with painted objects. The lighting whose purpose is to make the painting visible is not intended for the actor, and yet this lighting affects him. The lighting intended for the actor falls on the painting and falsifies its pictorial values.

These obvious contradictions make it necessary to place the mediums of scenic expression in their proper order of precedence.

The *actor* will take the first place, with full right. After him will come the *setting*, or general arrangement of the scene; to place it here indicates that it is concerned solely with the actor, that tri-dimensional, mobile figure. Next comes all-powerful light, the *lighting*. Last, the *painting*, whose functions are definitely subordinated to those of the three elements which rank above it.

The question of colour is not one for the painting alone. Colour is no less the concern of the actor, the setting and the lighting; the last-named, *a priori*.

There are certain principles, deriving from this order of precedence, to which the producer's imagination and liberty of choice must be subordinated. First and foremost, there is the setting; its lines and rigidity must contrast with the living figure of the actor. For it is its resistance to this figure and its mobility that gives life to space, and makes it a factor in the harmony of representation.

These principles cannot be given hard and fast forms; they are no dogmas; on the contrary, they are pliable, adaptable to the varying intentions of the playwright. But one law will always dominate them: that of the indisputable supremacy of the actor in the scenic space. Everything must be offered to him, everything else sacrificed to him. If this principle is abandoned, proof is requisite that the play in question allows or demands such departure as a necessity. In any case, it will never be to the credit either of the playwright or of his public.

At the beginning of this Introduction I said that we wanted to be "of it"; that we had made the rediscovery of our bodies, lost these many centuries, and that we were feeling a new consciousness, a sentiment of solidarity like some suddenly-revealed categorical imperative. *We have ceased to be spectators.* In the stage which we had now reached, this rather undignified rôle was growing irksome to us. So we are trying to give ourselves a change of air, and our old formulas have been scattered to the four winds of free Heaven. Dance and living statuary now form part of an undefined repertoire, which merges at last into games. Music, words, different kinds of spectacles, simplifications and stylization alternate and blend with one another. This anarchy makes us search our souls ; we feel what its issue will be : its last stage *depends on ourselves*, on an æsthetic purpose which must be unrolled as an organic whole, without hiatus or abrupt transition.

That we wish to be " of it " means that we propose to be free ; but we have become free ! This is undeniable. Let us see to it that we make worthy use of our liberty.

A time will come when professionals in the theatre and the plays written for them will be a thing of the past, never to return. When mankind, free now, will sing in living symbols, more or less dramatic, and adopted by all, their joys and their sorrows, their harvests, their labours, their struggles, their defeats and their triumphs ; and they alone will be spectators whom age or infirmity will gather round us in common, living sympathy.

The time when we shall be artists—*living* artists—because we willed it so.

With all my heart I pray for that time to come !

Adolphe Appia

TWENTIETH-CENTURY
STAGE DECORATION

CHAPTER I

CLEARING THE GROUND

IN undertaking to review the development of stage decoration during the last quarter of a century, it is essential that we have some belief in what constitutes an æsthetic of the art of the theatre, for without some basis for our judgments our work becomes a mere chronicle of events rather than the critical examination of the manifestations of the period that we propose. In giving order to this material, and in attempting to clarify it, we have tried to keep our personal preferences out of the discussion in so far as such a withdrawal is consistent with a critical attitude.

" Twentieth - Century Stage Decoration " should have as a sub-title, " First Phase." Otherwise, it might appear that we consider the book closed ; that the future holds nothing more, and that no new ideas or developments in this field are to be expected. This is far from our thoughts. The theatre, like life, is moving and changing with what seems to be a constantly increased acceleration. That it is progressing may be open to doubt, but that it is a going concern is unquestionable. The theatre that we know to-day will be something different to-morrow, and even before this book appears some new development will have necessitated a new chapter. We close our essay here, leaving it to the prophets to predict what the next chapter will contain.

Since so much confusion and misunderstanding grow out of the fact that the meanings of words are not always definite and clear, we wish here, at the outset, to say a word concerning terminology. The " Société Universelle du Théâtre " has proposed that something like an international code of technical terms and expressions employed in the theatre be established. Such a standardization would, undoubtedly, be of great advantage, not only to those writing on the subject, but to the workers in the theatre as well. At present, the English terminology is extremely loose, the same word being often used to describe quite different functions, while the Germans, on the contrary, with their much more highly organized theatre, often have several terms. In the following table we have tried to show the correspondence which exists between some of these terms in German, French, and English.

German.	*French.*	*English.*
Direktor	Directeur	Manager or Director
Regisseur	Metteur en scène	Producer or Stage Director
Inspizient	Régisseur	Stage Manager
Inszenierung	Mise en scène	Production as a whole
Ausstattung	Mise en scène	Staging, Mounting
Inszene	Mise en scène	Production

German.	French.	English.
Dekoration	Décor, Mise en scène	Stage Decoration, Stage Setting
Bühnenbild	Décor, Mise en scène	Scenery, Setting
Bühnenbildner	Décorateur	Scene Designer, Stage Designer
Dekorateur	Décorateur	Scenic Artist
Bühnenmaler	Décorateur	Scenic Artist
Ausstattungsleiter	None	Art Director
Künstlerischer Beirat	None	Art Director

By " Inszenierung " and " Mise en scène " we understand the completed production as a whole made up of all its constituent elements as setting, costumes, properties, light, etc., together with the actors who contribute the spoken word, gesture, movement, and so on. We propose to use " mise en scène " in place of the cumbrous expression " production as a whole " or " staging " or " mounting," both of which are inadequate. For " Régisseur " and " Metteur en scène " we shall use " Producer," although as now used in English it may mean almost anything. For " Bühnenmaler " and " Décorateur " we shall use " Scene Designer." For that type of stage decoration executed in elaborate perspective and for the manner in which it was painted, characterized by false high-lights and shadows, we propose to use the French word *trompe l'œil*.

By " stage decoration " we mean whatever environs the action of the drama on the stage of the theatre. The forms taken by the stage decoration in its evolution have been of every imaginable kind and have run the whole gamut from the photographically realistic to the completely abstract ; from the ponderous and complicated settings of a Drury Lane melodrama to a bare stage with no setting at all. We propose, here, to deal with some of the most recent manifestations and to glance at what took place before. In doing this it is facile and a little malicious to sneer at earlier attempts to solve the problem of the stage setting. It is only honest and just to recognize that all these efforts, no matter how far they may fail to satisfy us to-day, produced stage decorations which corresponded satisfactorily to the demands and sensibilities of the public to which they were addressed.

A tendency should not be declared false because it appears false to our eyes to-day. In all times in the past as well as in our own, employing all the means at their disposition, producers have believed that they were adequately rendering the world of the drama. A different attitude toward the theatre and a different sensibility demand different forms of expression. Each period has had the theatre it needed, and in the final analysis the difference between the theatre of one generation and that of another consists principally in a more or less developed receptivity on the part of the audience for visual forms. If to-day we reject certain forms of expression in the theatre it is not that they are in an absolute sense false, but only that our sensibility demands of the art of the theatre others more appropriate.

In 1894 Adolphe Appia published, in Paris, his first brochure, entitled " La Mise en Scène du Drame Wagnerien," in which he states briefly the theories which are elaborated in his large book, published by Bruckmann, Munich, in 1899. Craig's first brochure, entitled " On the Art of the Theatre," was published by Foulis, London, in 1905. We have taken the appearance of Appia's larger work *Die Musik und die Inszenierung* as the starting point for this study. This is, of course, purely arbitrary, since the history of stage decoration prior to that date would fill many interesting volumes. Different periods and phases of it have already been treated by students here and there. What we wish to make clear is that what has happened during the last thirty years inevitably rests on, and is linked with, what went before. The theatre, like life, is continuous and consecutive, and hence there can be no real separation, no real break. Appia and Craig, following him, were first condemned as mad theorists and, later, with less justification, hailed as prophets and saviours. Both criticized the theatre as they found it, and both offered solutions for the evils they felt were afflicting it. But Appia and Craig were by no means the first men to be fired by a desire to improve the theatre, nor the first to be shocked by what they saw there. Let us glance at one or two of these protests in passing.

In 1771 Giambatista Pasquali published in Rome a book entitled *Del Teatro in Venezia*, which was republished in Venice in 1773. From the Venice edition we quote the following in free translation :

" If, instead of illuminating the entire stage equally, the lights were concentrated on one part in such a way as to leave the other darker, one could then be able to admire in the theatre that same force and vivacity of light and shade which one sees in the paintings of Titian and Giorgione. And, first of all, let us abolish that triple and quadruple series of lights which encircle the proscenium arch. What a barbarous invention it is ! And those ugly gutters, full of light, placed at the foot of the stage and seen by all the spectators ! What an outlandish idea ! What monstrous unnaturalness to light from below ! Worse still, to confound these lights from below with those from above which are behind the scene ! There is no longer any effect of light and no distribution, but merely a battle between them all, producing only an ugly confusion in everything."

Recall that this was written before the introduction of gas and electricity.

At bottom, we have here one of the proposals of Appia : to use light as a means of expression in the theatre, to give it a significance reaching beyond mere illumination. Again, we have this from Becq de Fouquières in 1884 : [1]

" Since the stage decoration must have only

---

[1] *L'Art de la Mise en Scène*, L. Becq de Fouquières, Paris, 1884.

a general influence on the mind of the spectator, it should be treated with great moderation in its tones and with great simplicity in its details. It must not draw the eyes of the spectators away from the action, and if the eye does rest on it, it must present no traits susceptible of producing a feeling of special excitement."

This is the reformer's plea for the elimination of unnecessary detail, for simplification, the relative importance of the setting in the ensemble.

Before the war, it was comparatively easy to write on the art of Stage Decoration. New ideas were being realized, a great will toward reform dominated the theatre, definite direction seemed to have been given to it, and generally recognized principles ordered and guided creation in this field of the arts. Fifteen years ago, in examining its manifestations, it could be stated with what seemed like certitude that stage decoration had three ends to achieve : to produce a proper environment for the action of the drama, to create the fitting mood or psychological atmosphere for the unfolding of the story, and to establish a three-dimensional relationship between the actor and the space which surrounds him.

Immediately after the war it was still comparatively easy to write on the subject. Scenic means had been simplified and the question of environment or " milieu " had passed into the background, and to express, by visual means, the psychological essence or inner mood of the play had, at that time, become the principal concern of the stage setting, so that again it could be said that stage decoration had two ends to achieve : to create the appropriate mood, and to establish the spatial relation.

But to-day, in the midst of conflicting and contradictory tendencies, to write of the art of stage decoration has become a much more difficult matter. We are in the presence of decorative, expressionist, and cubist painting ; severe and simplified architecture ; constructive dynamism and, pervading it all, we are conscious of the lure of the machine.

On the one hand we find a great richness of fantasy, and on the other, an impoverishment of the stage, almost to the point of anæmia. All these diverse manifestations appear to be in conflict, to be engaged in a struggle in which no tendency seems sure of its supremacy, no theory of its victory, and nothing certain for to-morrow. And now, in the latest phenomenon in Germany, the " Neue Sachlichkeit," we are confronted with an astonishing return to Neo-Realism. We cannot wonder at this condition if we realize that after all it is the reflection of our restless, feverish, speed-intoxicated life of to-day— a life with its technical beauty, with its ephemeral, urgent desires demanding immediate and facile pleasures that the arts gratify with a simplification almost naïve in its precision ; a life filled with brutality and nervous exhaustion, with passionate questions and pitifully inadequate responses, with inextricable problems and provisional solutions.

It is a little depressing to read to-day the books written some years ago on the subject of stage decoration. These books, once young and fresh, announcing principles which seemed at the time immutable, have faded and grown old with startling swiftness ; a swiftness which gives us the measure of the mutability of our conceptions concerning the theatre. In 1914, H. K. Moderwell, in his excellent and comprehensive book, *The Theatre of To-day*,[1] grows almost ecstatic as he writes of the new technical means then in the full flood of development in Germany. He envisaged a mystic union, as it were, between art and technique. The participation of the technician and the technical means in the labour of creative art seemed to him, at that time, to realize a new human relation. " Technical progress," he writes, " does not mean the mechanization, but the humanization of the stage." A short eight years later, Kenneth Macgowan in his book, *Continental Stage-*

craft,[2] heads a chapter " The Twilight of the Machines," and begins by saying that all the past of the new stagecraft is over. A new simplicity has entered the theatre which has no need of the old technical means. The new artist-producer takes the place of the mechanician. It is now a question of the work of art and the creation of feeling, the elimination of technical means, the brain of the producer—these are to be the saving means.

This new art of the theatre and, in general, all that is not realism, Macgowan calls "Expressionism," and indeed expressionist art was so preponderant in the theatre in 1922 that Macgowan proposed the term " Expressionist " for all non-realistic productions. To-day, a bare four or five years later, we are not at all astonished to meet in an essay on the art of the theatre such a statement as this : " Expressionism, or at any rate what usually goes by that name, has fortunately come to a speedy end as far as the theatre is concerned, and we are rid of all the private confessions taken from war diaries, and all the plays full of shrieks and ' O, Mankind '—let us hope for ever." [3]

It seems to-day that in the domain of art every manifestation born swiftly, full of hope, and with pretensions to a durability reaching to eternity, dies with equal swiftness. Appia and Craig already belong to the long past, Craig perhaps more than Appia, who can with justice claim some share in the development of modern stage lighting. Georg Fuchs and his Munich theory of the two-dimensional relief stage is, for us, a prehistoric fossil. The creation of a plastic three-dimensional scenic ensemble threw two-dimensional painting into the discard, although it is a curious fact that with the advent of cubism and expressionism, painting—in a new dress— again entered the theatre. Of the plastic

[1] *The Theatre of To-day*, H. K. Moderwell, John Lane Co., New York and London, 1914.

[2] *Continental Stagecraft*, Kenneth Macgowan and Robert Edmond Jones, Harcourt, Brace & Co., New York, 1922.

[3] *Gebrauchsgraphik*, Vol. III. No. 11, Berlin, 1926.

organization of the stage setting there remain to-day only some stairs and parallels and platforms. Thus, in its course from the first realism of the 1900 period to the stylized realism of the Reinhardt epoch, and from that point, by a constantly increased synthesis, to the architectural setting, then on to expressionism, to scenic dynamism, to constructivism and, finally, to a return to Neo-Realism, as exemplified in the " Neue Sachlichkeit," the stage setting seems to have completed a cycle.

In order better to comprehend this evolution in its entirety, let us glance back and consider in what state the first reformers found the theatre, and briefly recapitulate the history of stage decoration during the last century. We will then be better prepared to discuss what has occurred in the twentieth. We have already pointed out that no real break occurred, and that what we have chosen to call modern stage decoration rests inevitably on what went before. It is in order to preserve this continuity that we hastily review the conditions preceding our point of departure.

The decadence of the Italian Renaissance found painters engaged in a search for the means of deceiving the eye through the development of an elaborate perspective, this *trompe l'œil* becoming constantly more and more complicated and refined. Perspective was an obsession. Recall those vast alignments of columns and vaults through the openings of which were shown glimpses of still further alignments of colonnades and monumental stairways. In an epoch of such great pomp and ostentation, the theatre, far from resisting this tendency of painting, abandoned itself to it with whole-hearted joy. The " bella prospettiva," which was the first concern of the painters, completely conquered and overran the stage, and it was in the theatre that its vogue continued longest, reaching even to our own day.

There is, however, a profound difference between the settings of Bibiena and those which the romantic theatre produced and perpetuated. The epoch itself imposed a certain style on Italian stage decoration, and many of these settings, with their imposing allure, their often great beauty, deserve to be appreciated. There were three recurring types: tragic, comic, and bucolic. These settings were palpably non-representative, for they never pretended to give the illusion of reality, but rather their own illusion—an illusion, so to speak, of stage decoration itself. In the same way, the classic theatre never pretended to give a complete illusion. This, however, was due largely to its arrangement, for the actors were forced to give the performance between balustrades which separated them from the spectators admitted on to the stage, and, as a result, we see the actor playing not *in*, but rather in front of, a stage setting or decoration. The wings of this setting were fixed for the most part, and only the back-drop was changed. This back-drop, hanging between the columns, represented by the wings, pictured a street, a park or a room, as the scene required. The same cut-glass chandeliers illuminated this scene indiscriminately, whether room or street, interior or exterior. Obviously, under these conditions the stage setting was limited to a mere pictorial indication of the place of action, the locale, and while this canvas might be more or less successful as painting, the work of creating the illusion was left almost entirely to the spectator.

As we approach modern times conditions change ; the spectator is banished from the stage, the setting closes around the actor and presents both player and ambience in the celebrated stereoscope. This stereoscopic decoration pretended to produce complete illusion, but it aimed at creating it through the medium of the old " bella prospettiva."

The closer we come to modern times, the more incoherent this setting becomes. First of all, the severe symmetry of the older stage decoration—an element quite non-illusionist— is rejected by the taste of the romantics who were seeking above all else the " picturesque " and with it the natural. They set about to achieve this end by creating settings which were as asymmetrical as possible. Their inadequate ideas of history produced a terrifying pot-pourri of styles, and in the incomprehensible environment which resulted, the figures of melodrama dressed in opera costumes of scintillating velvet and satin, of every conceivable period, moved and had their being. Hence it is no surprise to find a Prince of the Renaissance leading warriors of the Middle Ages, or to see a joyous sixteenth-century scene unfold in a flamboyant Gothic hall. Strange as it may seem, these gaudy anachronisms for melodrama and grand opera have survived with astonishing persistency even to our own day, and still have a tenacious hold on life. No matter to what capital you may go, in Madrid as in Budapest, in Paris as in Buenos Aires, opera, ballet, and even drama, are often mounted in settings which directly continue this tradition of Barocco. In Italy there are houses which on call furnish ready-made stocks of scenery, and thereby continue to inundate the world with these worn-out settings of melodrama and the romantic theatre.

By the middle of the last century, however, an interest in research finally imposed on the settings and properties a greater historical accuracy and a greater verisimilitude. Although this new tendency did not bring with it a satisfying solution of the problem, it at least put the problem—and this is important—of the realization of " environment " on the stage.

This is the period in which Viollet-le-Duc was reconstructing everything closer to the heart's desire in the Gothic manner. There was great activity, which often produced bizarre results, for in Vienna, an entire monumental boulevard is lined with buildings in every known style, one beside the other : a Gothic city hall flanked on one side by a Renaissance university, and on the other by a Parliament building which is a copy of an antique temple. Literature, architecture, painting—all the arts were obsessed by the desire for historic reconstruction. In the field of applied art, it is the period when the Henri II

buffet invaded the dining rooms of the middle classes, and, in Germany, the houses were dressed out in " Renaissance " furniture. In the field of literature, it is the time of Walter Scott and the historical novel, the novel in which dress was meticulously described from head to foot, no detail being left untouched. In this way these enthusiasts deluded themselves, firmly believing that by the accumulation of unessentials they could give life to their historic figures. This is the time of the great paintings representing historic events ; paintings full of pomp, costumes and pretentiousness ; immense canvases covered with cold reconstructions ; unnumbered coronations ; untold square yards of the bacchanalia of Sardanapalus, and Antony and Cleopatra.

It was inevitable that this tendency should invade the theatre. It was the Duke of Meiningen, fanatically devoted to the theatre, general director and producer as well, who in his little court theatre, faithful to the spirit of his time, inaugurated the historical production, or better the historically and archæologically accurate production. However amusing the results of his efforts may seem to us to-day, it must be admitted that these productions had a real merit for their own time. He was the first to drag the theatre out of the impossible routine into which it had fallen, and the first in his time to put the question and pose the problem of the mise en scène, the production as a whole. It was he who discovered the importance of the supernumeraries, which, up to his time, had remained immobile, and by breathing life into these figures, attempted in his way to create an ensemble. So if we find this tendency appearing in the work of stage producers of a later period, we must not forget where the idea originated, nor who it was who first laboured to realize it. In the case of Reinhardt, for example, some critics have reproached him with being too " meiningenlike."

The archæological and historical reconstruction of the settings, as it was practised at Meiningen, devoted itself with slavish fidelity to the reproduction of details based on extensive documentation. It was not by the choice of characteristic and carefully selected elements that the impression of an epoch was to be evoked, but by the juxtaposition of a mosaic of these details. As for the stage decoration itself, all this confusion of unessentials was executed in the old false perspective, the old *trompe l'œil*, with its painted high-lights and shadows.

It is interesting to note, in passing, that for all this Karl Friedrich Schinkel—first precursor of Gordon Craig—had already proposed a radical simplification of the scenic ensemble, even praising the use of curtains in place of the old wings. He was ahead of his time, for we find the theatre still under the domination of *trompe l'œil* when the second experiment which interests us here was made.

This preoccupation with archæological verisimilitude had engendered a historic romanticism of which the work of the Duke of Meiningen was only a partial expression, and it remained for Richard Wagner to push romanticism to its extreme limits in the field of the theatre. The work of Wagner is, nevertheless, important for us, because it posed for the first time the postulate of unity in the mise en scène, the finished production in the theatre, the " Gesammtkunstwerk." Let us say at once that this " Gesammtkunstwerk " was not concerned with the creation of a plastic unity between the actor and his environment, as we understand it to-day, but with a composite whole, to which poetry, the art of acting, music, painting and the art of the stage machinist and technician were all to contribute equally. In the Wagnerian theatre, the art of the machinist above all was of primary importance in the realization of the romantic concept. It is, moreover, complicated machinery—the fire of the Walküre, the collapse of the palace of the Nibelungen, apparitions in the clouds, brilliantly lighted grottoes, gauze veils, changes taking place before our eyes, and the unfolding of panoramas that lead from Walhalla to Nifelheim, or accompany the march of Parsifal through the forest. It must be remembered that in these synthetized creations in the theatre, such as Wagner dreamed them, the stage settings were not invented (as in the case of romantic opera before Wagner), for the mere pleasure which they gave to the eye, for with Wagner the setting has become for the first time an actor in the drama. Here the stage decoration acts, it plays a part ; something which it had never done before. Moreover, we can find in it a tendency toward psychological expression, toward the creation of a mood. Recall the first act of the " Walküre ": first there is the uncouthness of the hut, which reflects the coarseness of Hunding ; then there is the well-known—should it be called ?—stage entrance of the spring night which accompanies the pair of lovers, and again there is the sun which, in the second act of " Siegfried," plays across the leaves of the forest. Is this not the scenic expression of the mood of the music ? Once again, the garden of Tristan and the mourning landscape of the third act, which reflects the complaint of the " Klagendes Lied "—all are attempts to express the mood, experiments in scenic expression. Besides these, there are the elements of Nature : fire, water, storm, lightning—all are mobilized that they may accompany the movement of the music and express in terms of the stage the mood of the music. Later, Adolphe Appia attempted to reform the presentation of Wagnerian opera in modern terms and with a feeling more in keeping with modern ideas, but the only reason he could do this was because the problem had already been posed by Wagner himself. No matter how erroneous or naïve the " Gesammtkunstwerk " may seem to us, it announced two important problems for the theatre : the problem of an organic ensemble of the arts of the theatre, and, though still in rudimentary form, the problem of the creation of mood through the medium of the stage setting.

The reply which the naturalism of the 1900 period gave to this question of scenic unity is well known to every one. We are still too close to that time to dwell on it. Every country had its practising high priest of this school; America its Belasco; Germany its Otto Brahm; Russia its Stanislavsky; France its Antoine. Every one to-day is pretty well agreed on the errors of naturalism; on the mistaken idea of trying to represent the true by the true, "to represent," as it has been said, "a hardwood stairway by a hardwood stairway." On the other hand, we must, in justice, recognize the undeniable progress which naturalism realized in its own period. It forced the actor to abandon the heroic gesture and the buskined manner and to enact ordinary human beings based upon observation of their manners, carriage, gestures, speech, their customs and everyday dress. At the same time, it insisted that the production, as a whole, and the stage setting in particular, should realize characteristic " environment " for these people.

But stage decoration did not immediately cross the bridge into this new field. The idea of the painted setting was too deeply rooted to disappear at once.

To-day we cannot help smiling a little when we look at those stage decorations which characterized the naturalistic revolution headed by Stanislavsky. Take for example the old-fashioned setting for " The Seagull," shown in pl. 2. Think for a moment with what extreme care all the naturalistic details have been set down in this setting for " A Doll's House," with its painted high - lights and shadows (pl. 1). And what are we to say of those frightful settings for " King Lear " (pl. 3, 4)—one of Antoine's greatest successes —settings which date from a comparatively recent period—in fact one year prior to the Reinhardt reforms.

It is only gradually and under the influence of a more refined naturalism that we see— particularly in the case of interiors—the painted doors and windows, with their false high-lights and shadows, give place to solid practical constructions in wood (pl. 5). It was not long, however, before Stanislavsky brought to his service artists like Benois and Dobujinsky, under whose influence the stage decoration gained in style and expression (pl. 7–10). This is particularly true in so far as it concerned the treatment of interiors; as for the exteriors, even artists of the first rank continued for some time to make use of a pictorial language. Although in the end this concern for the true and the real led to exaggerations which were ridiculous, it should be quite clear, nevertheless, that the inability to endure a real piece of furniture in an unreal setting marked a progress in scenic sensitiveness. In fact, naturalism, in its way, developed a better understanding of stage requirements and a better comprehension of the function of the stage setting, thus opening the road to modern experiments. In the period which followed, the men of the theatre, in attacking the new problems presented, began by making use of those means which the naturalist theatre had bequeathed to them. It is from Antoine, Brahm and Belasco that Reinhardt and his followers have sprung.

While these later producers were beginning with a conception which was essentially *of the theatre* in order to attain to a complete visual realization, the theorists were rising up and establishing, or attempting to establish, dogmas which envisaged the creation of quite another form of theatre. Attacking the problem of the mise en scène from the outside, and proceeding on the basis of a preconceived æsthetic, radical reformers like Georg Fuchs and Gordon Craig, to mention only two, devoted themselves to giving to the mise en scène a visual form, each in accordance with his own particular and preconceived system.

It is important to note that while these reformers were trying to make a clean sweep of the contemporary theatre in order to make room for their own special brand of the new, the great producers in the actual working theatre, men who were the products of the naturalistic school, more supple and sensitive and, at the same time, more conscious of the universal character of the theatre, were bringing to the creation of the mise en scène new experiments in stylization and synthesis.

By such eclecticism they placed all the possibilities of the modern theatre at the service of this new conception of the mise en scène.

This brings us to the threshold of the modern phase. One part of its manifestations has sprung from the naturalist school ; another tendency has come from the reformers—Appia, Craig, Fuchs, and the rest. There are then, at the beginning of the modern movement, two sharply defined currents : one, represented by Reinhardt, starts with an essentially scenic concept—a concept grounded in the theatre and *of* the theatre, and moves toward the achievement of a visual realization of the mise en scène ; the other, considering the problems of the theatre, deals with them in terms of a preconceived æsthetic, establishing dogmas based on different systems of simplification and synthesis.

CHAPTER II

THE NEW IDEAS AND THE NEW MEN

DURING the evolution which we have just outlined, different problems were successively put to the creator of stage decoration. First, and for a considerable time, it was the question of " environment " only which occupied him. Drama had created real human beings, more or less well characterized, and the theatre was called upon to create an appropriate setting for them—the problem was still close to reality.

But there was no stopping at this point. There is a multiple soul in drama, compounded of conflict, of joy and of sorrow. It has scenes of abounding gaiety, others altogether lyric, still others sombre and tragic, and often, as in the case of Shakespeare, all appear one beside the other. Again, we have whole plays written throughout in a tone of melancholy or of joy, and yet others built up on violent contrasts. Therefore it is not sufficient to give an approximately adequate suggestion of the environment of the action, unless at the same time we are made aware of the psychological phases of the specific play. The stage decoration must reflect the inner soul of the drama, the atmosphere of the play as a whole, as well as that of each scene, and by visual stage means it must carry over to the spectator this psychological atmosphere, this mood. Thus the second and the most important problem, reaching to our own time, is that of the realization of the psychological atmosphere, the " Stimmung," the mood:

Elsewhere we have seen how the question of scenic unity put by the Wagnerian ideal was transformed by naturalism into a question of unity, realized in terms of physical reality. After that it no longer sufficed to create a stage decoration, no matter how expressive in itself, independently of other scenic factors, above all of the actor. No longer was it enough to hang a back-drop behind this actor and arrange a setting around him. From the moment that it was understood that the actor must move, advance, retire, and design his gestures in space, the sharp contrast began to be felt between the apperception of the actor, a living being, together with the plastic objects which surrounded him on the one hand, and on the other, the apperception of the stage setting as a flat surface in one plane. It was necessary to find the means of creating a unity between the actor and the space which surrounded him, the ambience, of such a nature as to preserve this unity of apperception. It must be understood that in achieving this, an even more profound unity is created, for man—the actor—is then related to the ambient space, and the stage becomes a world containing the characters of the drama. To achieve this end, a setting had to be produced that was of the same world as the actor, that is to say, plastic and three-dimensional. Thus we see how the plastic stage setting developed logically from naturalism itself, while, at the same time, reformers like Appia and Craig, starting from certain given theories of æsthetics, arrived by different roads at the same goal.

So at the beginning of the modern movement we find the art of the stage faced with three problems : environment, mood, and plastic unity. This triumvirate ruled the stage for about ten years, but with the progress of expressionism the eldest, environment, retired discreetly into the shadows of history ; then the constructivists assassinated the second, leaving only the youngest in the form of three-dimensional constructions. It remains for the future to reunite the three members of this scattered trio, and that perhaps is the next phase in the development of stage decoration.

In any case, the modern movement from the beginning realized the existence and the importance of this triple problem, and consequently envisaged the mise en scène in a new light. In fact, up to this time the naturalist theatre, as well as the romantic, had placed its best at the service of the dramatist, and had laboured as faithful servitors to translate the work of the author into terms of the stage. With the birth of the new conception of the mise en scène, the difference which exists between the written drama and the acted drama became apparent. It was seen that in producing a play on the stage an altogether new organism is of necessity created, an organism belonging not only to the world of drama, but constituting in itself quite another world, born under other conditions—the conditions of the stage. These new conditions are not those of the book. It is a different world, with its own laws, its possibilities, its limitations, its own means of expression, an organism which is essentially *of the theatre*. Henceforth, it became a question of giving life to this entire organism, including all the elements which belong to it. This does not mean that the producer meant to supplant the dramatist, even though later extremists courageously proposed that the author be done away with as an embarrassment too difficult to support. But in general they did not go so far. The producer became conscious that in realizing the work of the dramatist on the stage he at the same time brought into being a new creation, different from that of the author, a creation which carried its life within itself.

With the growth of this new consciousness, the theatre tended to become what it should always have been—a creation of the imagination, functioning in terms of the stage. It was no longer important to interpret the drama in a manner more or less true ; it was impera-

tive to recreate it in an entirely new world. The drama—that is, the acted drama—could no longer be a phenomenon which the spectator sensed solely through the medium of the ear. It is clear that the spectator perceives the play as much through the gesture and movement of the actor as he does through the spoken word, and, what is equally important, he must also perceive it through the scenic ensemble in its entirety. The play was now expressed by the entire scene, as well as by gesture and movement, and the spectator became conscious of entire images which themselves contained the drama. The new mise en scène was addressed to the eyes as well as to the ears, thereby creating a spectacle which carried the dramatic action within itself.

Consequently we have the question of the unity of the creation in the theatre under a new aspect. Wagner envisaged it from the point of view of music-drama, but the solution which a musician proposes must necessarily be dominated by his musical bias. The naturalist theatre attempted to produce this unity by the perfection of the ensemble and by a meticulous concern for the truth of details. The new mise en scène emerging from the naturalist school, saw the production in the theatre as a symphonic work, all the elements of which, the word, the gesture, the movement, the music, the costumes, the setting, the colour, the light—in short, the least accessory—contribute by the same right to the realization of a complete and homogeneous spectacle.

With such conceptions, it became logically apparent that for all these factors to function as members of a single organism, they must be submitted to a single directing will. This will is represented by the producer. Thus the importance of the producer became manifest from the beginning of the new movement, and two types of producers had to be discriminated.

We must remember that the producer, even the good producer, cannot necessarily make a good stage setting. Quite special faculties, such as a visual imagination above the ordinary, and some experience of the crafts of the theatre, are indispensable. These gifts have generally been lacking in the great producers. Many among them have come from acting to producing, moving from actor to stage director, while others have come to it from literature. The latter are often men capable of organizing the broad lines of the scenic spectacle and even the details of the acting, but it rarely happens that they have at the same time the ability to organize the details of the visual representation.

This type of producer might be called the producer-orchestra-leader. It is in the manner of an orchestra conductor that he directs those who make up the ensemble, in appealing to the special faculties of each. Moreover, the important producers, Reinhardt above all, have always turned for assistance to a collaborator who has specialized in realizing the visual side of the spectacle. The appearance of this collaborator, this new artist, architect or painter, is a distinctive phenomenon of the twentieth-century theatre.

Ordinarily, the producer first tries collaborating with different artists, as Reinhardt first tried working with Karl Walser, Emil Orlik, Ludwig von Hoffmann and others, fixing his choice finally on an artist with whom he felt a perfect affinity—Ernst Stern. Thus Reinhardt doubled himself so far as everything on the visual side of production was concerned. The same was true later with Jessner and his Pirchan, or Jurgen Fehling and his Strohbach, with Barker and Wilkinson, with Hopkins and Jones, to name only a few. Thereafter the scenic creation became the result of the intimate collaboration of two men, and the producer became in a way a double star, but with this difference : that double stars in general revolve about each other in such a way that the trained observer sees them both distinctly, while for the ordinary observer on the earth the star of the producer almost always covers that of his collaborator and only allows the light from his own person to shine forth. Kenneth Macgowan, as a wise observer, saw this at once, and rendered justice to this second star in comparing this collaboration to the situation of " pilot-fish and shark."

Macgowan pointed out how difficult it often is to separate the share of the artist from that of the producer. He says : " It is ordinarily very hard to say what share the artist or director has had in the scheme of a setting, or whether the director has bothered his head at all about the setting after confiding it to what he considers competent hands. It is an interesting speculation just how much the physical shape of Reinhardt's productions has been the sole creation of his artist Stern. Certainly Stern delighted in the problems which the revolving stage presented, and only in a single mind could the complexities of these sets, nesting together like some cut-out puzzle, be organized to a definite end. It is entirely possible that except for a conference on the general tone of the production, and criticisms of the scheme devised by Stern, Reinhardt may have given no thought at all to the scenery." And this new artist of the theatre, whom modern conditions have developed, is usually a very special and complex being. He has nothing in common with the old designer or scene painter from whom sketches and models for a play were ordered.

If it does not follow that a good stage director or producer can make a good stage setting, it is equally true that a good architect or painter cannot necessarily produce one.

Those qualities which make a good architect or painter are not sufficient of themselves to make of him a man of the theatre. Much more is necessary. First of all, he must have an innate sense of the theatre ; and, secondly, since his creations must correspond to the needs of the stage, he must have something of the actor in him—an actor whose potential talents have never been expressed in acting. No matter what his other talents may be, no man who is a complete stranger to the art of acting can fully serve the theatre. Again, this artist must be sensible not only to the art of the actor, but to the dramatic intent of the author as well. He must be able in reading a play, to see it in action before him on the stage ; that is to say, the drama must leave the printed page and walk upright before his eyes.

It is this faculty which explains why the modern scene designer so often suppresses the stage setting ; it is because he " has his eye on something else besides being an artist." And this man, mirror of the author, a composite of actor, architect and accomplished painter, must in addition have the gift of changing from one play to another, of solving different problems in different and appropriate ways, of being, as it were, an impersonal personality.

During the last twenty years, all that is important in the English and American and, particularly, in the German and Russian theatre, has been the result of the collaboration of this strange artist with the producer-director. But at the same time the ghost of another producer-director has stalked the earth and been discussed at length. Every one knows the ideas of Gordon Craig on this subject. According to him the creation in the theatre, a work born of the theatre itself, must be the product of the same brain which realizes the work in terms of the stage, and hence it follows that one and the same artist must regulate the acting, the movement and gesture, design the costumes and stage decoration, compose the music and even write the play itself. It goes without saying that this author - poet - composer - producer - régisseur-architect - painter - decorator - costumer - machinist-electrician has not yet been seen. But that has not prevented the appearance of certain producers who do not hesitate to set themselves up as embodiments of the Craig theory. Generally, however, they are courteous enough to leave the work of writing the play to the author, merely undertaking to do all that remains.

While we do not wish to say that it is impossible to find men who unite in themselves all the qualities required by the Craig theory, we cannot help noticing that they are extremely rare, and if certain ones seem to succeed in this rôle, it is because of the reduced scale of their productions. It requires a man who combines in himself the qualities of a Reinhardt and of a Stern to realize on a large scale the ideal producer. If the ideal is not realized it is because ideals never are, and because the quality of not-being-realized is inherent in the ideal.

After all, there seems to be a danger in this concept of the super-director who falls short of the ideal figure just described. In questions dealing with the visual realization of the play, he often does not feel it necessary to consult the artist, the man who really knows. Being a super-director, he is convinced that he himself must know, since otherwise he would not be what he is. But in far too many cases he knows only one thing : one little system. One producer has pylons, another steps, another combinations of blocks ; all employ draperies in some form or other ; and, the system being once adopted, every piece is compelled to conform to it.

This forcing of the play into a particular system must often mean injury to the play itself and distortion of the idea of the author. The play is pressed a little here, disarticulated a little there ; a little is cut out in one scene and, if necessary, a little added in another. With goodwill and conviction the piece can somehow always be made to fit the procrustean bed. Much is said of " scenic unity." Everything, we are told, from the realization by the word and the gesture of the actor to the atmosphere of the setting, has issued from an unique conception. And so it has, in truth—a conception that is unique, the same conception for every piece. It is this fact that has produced much of the impoverishment of the modern theatre. It is not in this manner that the great producers of the Reinhardt type have envisaged the problems of production.

The ideal producer-director must possess other gifts which, though more prosaic than those we have discussed, are equally important. We are too prone to think of him in his capacity as artist of the theatre without remembering that, no matter how prolific his ideas or inspired his vision, he will be frustrated without the mechanical means to actualize his dreams. It is a physical impossibility for one man to realize alone an exacting mise en scène, that is if the stage spectacle is to be fully realized. To do this he must know men and women, and be able to get the best out of them ; he must recognize and then develop all the talent at his disposal in all the activities which constitute his theatre. This applies not only to the acting group but to all the others as well. The man who has no experience in human contacts cannot do this. People may be employed to do a specific work, but how they do it will depend on the extent to which they have been fired by belief in, and admiration for, the man who directs it all. Such an organization can never be built by the inferior personality, for, jealous of his prerogatives, vain and fearful, he tends to surround himself with inferior people who gratify his petty egoism. The great producer will always try to find the strongest and most talented associates for himself he can find, realizing that his strength lies not so much in himself as in the combined power of his associates. This potential strength is at his disposal, and can be called forth and exerted when the mise en scène is to be realized. Although it is apparent that the mise en scène is in a way the result of co-operative effort, we believe that a certain amount of despotism is necessary in the theatre if the best results are to be achieved. Obviously there must be discipline and one directing will, but too much regimentation and too much despotism may result in alienating talent and initiative and in producing only a group of marionettes. If there is no co-operation, no willingness on the part of the individual to serve the ensemble, the machinery jams and the mise en scène is compromised.

Unity in conception can only become unity in realization through a perfected organization, a unified group. All the important theatres we know have achieved distinction because of such a group. In the remarkable company of Stanislavsky we have seen the results. Here, of course, we were more conscious of the results as they affected the acting group, but the same principle holds good for all other branches which support them. Reinhardt, who built up before the war one of the finest organizations in Europe, had a highly developed talent for this practical side of the theatre ; and a great part of his success before the world is due to the fact that his perfected theatre-machine made possible the complete realization of his projects. Reinhardt was fortunate in his family. His brothers, although they received very little recognition, were important factors in holding his organization together.

It must be remembered that no theatre organization such as we have discussed can be created over-night. Human material is the most intractable in the world, and it requires time to shape it in such a way that it can fulfil its purpose. People must be together and work together in a common cause before they can function as a whole. The organization of the theatre in England and America makes this impossible. An organization is created to-day, a theatre is leased, the company rehearsed, the settings and the rest of the accessories arranged for, and then the play is on. It may run for months, or weeks, or years, and whatever the organization is, it becomes stale and mechanical through lack of incentive. On the other hand, the play may fail, in which case the organization is usually dispersed, with the result that whatever has been given in time and effort and imagination is wasted. It is all ephemeral and transitory. On the continent of Europe the conditions are not so generally bad, and in Germany before the war they were quite different. There the theatre life was not centred in the capital, and throughout the country there were theatres supported by either the State or the municipality. The theatre had in a way a Governmental standing, and was something of a public institution supported by the citizens of the State. This naturally made for greater permanency, and eliminated to a certain extent the speculative element which is inseparable from the organization of the theatre in England and America. It also made possible permanent organizations and encouraged experimentation. Under these conditions it is not surprising that the modern movement was born in Germany and that most of its most important manifestations are to be found there.

In America the only theatre which approximates these conditions, and by consequence has succeeded in creating a more or less permanent organization, is the Theatre Guild. In spite of a constantly changing personnel—directors and scene designers often having only a temporary association—the Theatre Guild organization has produced the most important series of plays presented by any single management.

In the period before the war Granville-Barker made such an organization for his Savoy Theatre productions. Granville-Barker came to his work as an actor, a playwright and an organizer, and combined distinguished personal qualities which we have seldom seen in others, with the possible exception of Stanislavsky. The sort of thing, we mean,

neither Reinhardt nor any American producer possesses. They are qualities which go with character and a distinguished mind, but, unfortunately, they are incompatible with the immature minds and fluid characters found in our theatre in this generation. Granville-Barker had both knowledge and vision, and if the war had not interrupted his work, he would unquestionably have realized the project for a national theatre which he had so carefully and fully elaborated in association with William Archer. He was the first to introduce and put into practice modern production methods in England, and no one has appeared since to take his place. Since the war Norman Macdermott is practically the only man who has attempted to create a theatre organization on modern lines, and his effort failed for lack of public support. Craig's diatribes against the English theatre seem well-founded.

CHAPTER III

REINHARDT AND STYLIZED REALISM

THE day on which Max Reinhardt presented his first Shakespearean production marked a milestone in the history of the modern theatre. That event was the production of Shakespeare's 'A Midsummer Night's Dream," at the Neues Theater, Berlin, on the 31st of January, 1905. With this first master-stroke Reinhardt completely revolutionized the theatre of his time. Here was an old, old piece, known to all the world, played and replayed to the point of tedium, appearing in Reinhardt's mise en scène, in all the flower of eternal youth. Reinhardt had already shown, in his production of Gorky's " Lower Depths," gifts as a naturalistic producer which placed him beside Stanislavsky, but never before had one seen a classic piece take on a life so intense and so new and, at the same time, present a stage spectacle so complete and so homogeneous.

How had Reinhardt proceeded in order to recreate this play in all its parts and render it fresh and living ? Evidently he had read it as if it had never been played before, and asked himself the question : What is the crucial element in the piece ? What is the element that renders Oberon, Titania, Puck, and all these elves and fairies comprehensible ? What must be rendered on the stage to give plausibility to these beings and their relations with men ? The element which explains them is the forest ; then the forest must be created. The life of these beings must sprout as a plant from this forest itself. It must be realized as visible and palpable, with its grass, its moss and its springs. The spirits of Nature must truly live in their natural environment and be of the same stuff with it. The forest must live and breathe and seem infinite and inexhaustible. Hence, Reinhardt placed a forest on the stage ; he created it in its entirety with great trees, springs, moss and grass ; a wood wherein the fireflies danced about the water and elves emerged from the bushes ; a forest in which all these beings seemed to be the personification and the breath of Nature itself.

Veritable trees, not painted but plastic ones, were placed on the stage, and the space below was covered, not with a painted ground-cloth, but with what seemed to be palpable grass, in which the feet sunk among the flowers ; while here and there were seen bushes and little beeches growing between the trees, and in the midst of all a little lake mirrored between two hills.

And now (constructed on the revolving stage) all this forest began slowly and gently to move and to turn, discovering new perspectives, always changing its aspect, presenting ever new images inexhaustible as Nature. And while the stage turned and changed, the elves and fairies ran through the forest, disappearing behind the trees, to emerge behind the little hillocks. These beings with their green veils and leafy crowns seemed, in their appearance, to form a part of the forest itself. Puck, who up to that time has been usually dressed in the costume of the fantastic ballet or opera, was covered only with grass and became at last the true elf, who rolled with laughter like a child in the green of the forest.

This was a revelation. Never had such unity between actor and stage decoration been seen. Never before, and in a manner so justified, had one seen the stage setting become an actor of such importance in the play. A new impetus had been given and a new and intense life henceforth entered the modern theatre.

However, this first decisive manifestation of the genius of Reinhardt was, so to speak, astride of two epochs. It revealed the spirit that was to animate the new stage spectacle from that moment on; but, when the form under which this spirit manifested itself in this first production is considered, it is clear that it was still closely attached to the naturalism which preceded it. One might even say that it was the apotheosis of naturalism, for the idea of rendering the entire forest in palpable form is evidently nothing more than naturalism pushed to the limit. And while this " Midsummer Night's Dream " contained all the germs of the future, it at the same time marked the culminating point of the naturalistic misé en scène. This statement is not an easy confession that this conception, with its excessive reality, its too " true," is shocking for us to-day; that our sensibility revolts against these " true " trees, these bushes and palpable foliage. Certainly, we demand that the theatre realize an inner truth with less external verisimilitude and, in general, with a greater economy of means. That is not the question. The important thing is that, at the very moment when stage realism in Reinhardt's " Midsummer Night's Dream " reached its height, the epoch itself was already demanding from Reinhardt other forms of expression. And this first essay of Reinhardt, though revealing the new spirit was not final as to the form under which that spirit was to manifest itself.

At this time a tendency toward stylization was seen budding in architecture, in decorative art and in painting. It was impossible for the theatre long to resist a feeling which was beginning to dominate all Germany in every branch of life, from the poster at the street corner to the flower-vase on the middle-class table. As soon as it allied itself with this new movement, the theatre was quickly reinforced by the whole tendency of the epoch, by the

new movement in architecture, decorative art, and every expression of culture by which public taste is educated. So we see Reinhardt calling in as his helpers the very men who were at the head of the decorative movement in Austria and Germany, such as Alfred Roller, Director of the Decorative Art School in Vienna ; Emil Orlik, Professor at the Decorative Art School of Berlin ; Ernst Stern ; Karl Walser ; Ludwig von Hoffmann—all intimately connected with the modern movement.

Under their influence and with their aid, we see the modern mise en scène, hardly yet emerged from the naturalist school, enriched by the stylistic elements of the epoch and, refined through experimentation, crystallize and assume the characteristic aspects of the Reinhardt production, which may be called a stylized realism.

In reviewing the Reinhardt productions, we get the very clear impression that the style, the degree of stylization or of naturalism in his mise en scène does not depend only upon the style of the play in question, but to a very large extent on the artist with whom he collaborated. Only in this way can we explain how the same Reinhardt could produce " The Merchant of Venice," first in naturalistic settings (pl. 11, 12) and then later the same piece in the stylized stage decorations of Stern ; or again, how he could show side by side with these highly stylized productions such excessive naturalism as we see in Roller's settings for " Faust " (pl. 19–21). If we consider the productions which Reinhardt has made in Vienna since the war, it seems probable that his personal leaning is toward a naturalistic conception of the mise en scène. It may be rather because of the genius of certain artist-collaborators like Stern than because of any feeling on his part that the movement toward a stylized stage decoration remains associated with his name.

It is not easy to say whether or not in the early settings of Reinhardt we must recognize an influence coming from the reformers, such as Appia and Craig, then hardly known, but we think it sufficient to associate the Reinhardt movement, at least in its beginnings, with the æsthetic and intellectual feeling of the time. On the other hand, it might be said that naturalism itself, pushed to its extreme manifestation, was forced to end in another form of art. Moderwell recognized this in the work of Stanislavsky. " In trying to become ' more realistic,' the typical Stanislavsky play cast off even the convention of dramatic movement ; in Tchekoff's and Gorky's plays nothing remained but the ceaseless ' interplay of souls.' For these deepest things ordinary realism was insufficient." Thus it was not a reaction against realism that led the Moscow theatre to imaginative vigour, for, in Moderwell's happy expression, " They did not recoil from the mountain that opposed them, they burrowed through it and came out on the other side."

Perhaps it could be equally well said of Reinhardt that with the production of the " Lower Depths " he had already begun " to burrow through the mountain," and that, with the poetry of " A Midsummer Night's Dream," he had emerged on the other side towards a new scenic expression. In fact, one can discern in this mise en scène an element of poetry, of Nature, which, in spite of the fact that it was actualized by realistic means, reached beyond common reality. Henceforth, the concern for the purely realistic had to give place to a concern for expression produced by means of a stylized realism, by imitation plus imagination. This stylized realism tended toward simplification of the setting, at least in the greater part of the stage decoration, at the same time preserving its character of illusion. Thus we have had an " Othello " by Reinhardt and Stern in which the atmosphere of Venice and Venetian Cyprus was produced by a few characteristic traits. A meeting of two enemy parties is the opening of the drama. With Reinhardt this became a sudden and intense vision of all Venice. A meeting at night in gondolas, in a narrow canal by the light of torches ; a section of bare wall, a window, a narrow street revealing at its end a patch of Italian sky—Venice is there, in all its beauty, a living thing. The port of Cyprus, but not a detailed description of the port—nothing more than an enormous dyke between two houses, behind which are seen some masts with their great sails. And the hall in Cyprus, with its colonnaded platform. The arcades open to the sky, lighted with torches, which are too crude for Venice torches, give the note of a Cyprus more barbarous than Venice, placed in an Italian frame. The same Venice is seen again in " The Merchant of Venice," first with settings, by Orlik, close to reality, with many details, but shortly after, in a setting by Stern, in which the street before Shylock's house was suggested by an angle of the building, an arcade carried by heavy columns, a little bridge and another wall ; thus he evoked the environment by means of a few significant traits. This is far from naturalistic beginnings. Even landscape is realized in the same way, as, for example, the Trojan plain in " Penthesilea," where different aspects of the hills covered with high grass, two cypresses, and a bridge of cyclopean stones present the whole frame of the drama.

We have had stylized stage settings in " Gyges und sein Ring," and in " Judith." We have had a " King Lear " (pl. 17, 18), in which a barbarous epoch was evoked by costumes and draped settings decorated with motives in geometric designs. We have seen Reinhardt—or rather, Ludwig von Hoffmann—adopting an extreme stylization, suggesting the garden of Aglavaine and Sélysette through the rhythm of green gauze draperies (pl. 15, 16). Henceforth the whole gamut of possibilities inherent in the stylized stage decoration were at his disposition.

Perhaps the chief merit in the composer lies in his confining himself in these productions to an eclecticism which makes it possible for his collaborators to realize their conceptions. Such eclecticism in a producer is of the very highest value since, possessed of this gift, it is possible for him to give to his work all its amplitude, all its variety, all its richness.

Because of it he will never approach the play with a preconceived and consequently rigid system, but will seek in the play itself the style best suited to express it.

In the other camp of the radical reformers we see experiments and proposals which are pushed further toward the realization of a new æsthetic of the theatre. These are important enough from the point of view of principle, but, to all of them, there seems to adhere a certain dogmatism, a certain sectarianism: they lack the fullness, the amplitude, the expansive life and the richness of imagination which characterize the work of the accomplished producer and director.

The memories of the Reinhardt productions extend themselves indefinitely. There was a camp in "Die Räuber" placed on a hill under the trunks of six great trees silhouetted against the sky, and the hall of old Moor, with its high windows, through which you saw the people, the picture gallery and the length of the entrance corridor, all built on the revolving stage under the hill (pl. 13).

Again, there was "The Winter's Tale," with the tiny flags of the ships topping a green hill; the deafening entrance of the comedians setting up their stage in the great hall of the lord, in order to play "The Taming of the Shrew" before Christopher Sly; and the bright garden of Olivia with Moissi as the Clown seated on the steps, singing with a melancholy voice "the rain it raineth every day"—and so on through the whole list.

If ever it were necessary to consider a stage reform from two different points of view, namely, that of its importance for its own time, and that of its value for us to-day, it is so in the case of the work of Reinhardt; and for the simple reason that this producer-director does not yet belong to history, since he has continued to work and create even down to the present. Yet it must be said with regret that he often gives the impression that he has not sufficiently evolved with his time, and that through all the later revolutions in the theatre he has continued more or less his conceptions

of twenty years ago. He rarely seems to pass beyond a stylized realism; worse still, his latest creations shown at the Josefstädtertheater in Vienna seem to indicate a retrogression reaching to his very earliest realizations. Though Reinhardt may disclaim the production of Unruh's "Bonaparte" at the Deutsches Theater (pl. 31), he cannot fail to accept responsibility for this "Oesterreichische Komödie" which we show in plate 30. This disconcerting setting, overcharged with useless details, might well belong to a period ten years before "Don Carlos" (pl. iv, 22, 23) but it represents his latest work, having been produced in 1927. All the 1927 productions at the Josefstädtertheater—the "Schwierige" of von Hofmannsthal, "Peripherie" of Langer—were conceived in a similar spirit. The new mise en scène for "The Merchant of Venice" is encumbered with three small revolving platforms carrying settings which are cluttered with annoying details (pl. 32, 33). The excuse might be made that the lack of technical installation at the Josefstädter necessitated this cumbersome procedure—two revolving platforms for "Peripherie," three for "The Merchant of Venice," and one setting fitted into another for "Der Schwierige," but it should be clear that this restriction imposed on the artist by the limitations of the stage should have led him, not to a series of complications, but toward a salutary simplification.

In this regard, it is perhaps worth while to examine his creations in the Redoutensaal in Vienna. This hall, with its platform taking the place of a stage, demands a mise en scène in which the stage decoration is almost abstract. But it seems that Reinhardt has not been able to adapt himself to this idea, nor to abandon the "illustrative" setting for the action. Thus he required Professor Roller to create little settings to be placed on the platform, in order to evoke the environment of "Il Barbiere di Siviglia." Sometimes these worked well, but more often badly, as when he put in the middle of a purely architectural setting, already in existence, decorations which signified the open air. This is evidently a deplorable lack of a sense of style.

Moreover, in all that directly concerns the play of the actors, we may again notice this lack of feeling for style. It has always been Reinhardt's intention to give to the play of the actors the greatest possible freshness, and an impression of direct and immediate life, but in approaching dramatic action in this way, must he not of necessity be far from the dramatic style demanded by " Tragedy," and even from the " comedy of style " exemplified, for instance, in a Molière play ? One might certainly think so, after witnessing the performance of " Le Malade Imaginaire " given at the Reinhardt Château at Leopoldskron in 1923. Here was a performance mixed with ballets and pantomimes, which should have been treated in a style removed from reality. In it we saw the comedian, Max Pallenberg, play the part of Argon, in old Yiddish jargon, and with improvisations in the language of our own day. What the comedy may have gained in the way of life, it certainly lost in manner and style, and it cannot be denied that to-day we are much more sensitive to questions of style than we were at the beginning of the Reinhardt epoch, when the new, intense life of his ensembles, hardly emerged from naturalism, carried us off our feet. It is only after leaving performances like the one at Leopoldskron and passing in review Reinhardt's first creations that one realizes that the same faults existed even in the early days. Those early productions, for all their splendour, in a certain way lacked grandeur, the great classic manner. Reinhardt's mise en scène breathed a new life into tragedy, but at the expense of the grandeur which is appropriate to tragedy. He made drama more comprehensible by pulling down the heroes and diminishing them to the stature of the men about us, but what the drama gained in intensity by this means it lost in style. It might be said that there was not only an incompatibility between the style of the tragedy and the too direct acting of the players, but also between the realism of this acting and the stylized realism of the ambience, the stage setting. But on the other hand, it must be admitted that between the old buskined manner of the " tragedian " and that of the Reinhardt hero the choice was simple, and that if to-day we are seeking a new style in acting more fitting for the modern mise en scène, we are far from having found it. There is perhaps to-day much more incompatibility between the synthetic style of the modern stage decoration and the acting of the players who appear within it than there ever was between the acting of Reinhardt's company and the stylized realism of the setting which environed them.

Nevertheless, this acknowledgment of lack of feeling for style and a tendency to relapse into realism will be painful for all those who lived through the first years at the Deutsches Theater. We would like to believe that Reinhardt is to-day a living force in the modern theatre, but unfortunately he is not. He belongs neither to the future nor to the present of the theatre, but only to the past. However, none of our reservations regarding his productions of to-day affect his early contribution to the theatre. He was the first to reunite all the factors of the theatre in a close collaboration for the purpose of creating a scenic equilibrium which later experiments have again upset in one way or another.

If modern stage decoration has followed any line at all it is only in responding to the blows of successive theories, each one of which has brought about a new upset. When stage setting becomes too important, the art of the actor is encumbered and suffers. On the contrary, when the setting, as often happens to-day, contents itself with a few summary indications (however we may admire the ingenuity of the simplification) of the spectacle, the scenic equilibrium is again disturbed. The simplified spectacle is perhaps the only one we can fully grasp. The simplification accords with our receptivity for things of the theatre, and the synthetic modern conception satisfies perfectly the demand of our senses and our nerves, but it can scarcely pretend to satisfy equally our ideal of the complete stage spectacle, since by its very nature it reduces or suppresses certain scenic factors in favour of others. In fact, many productions in the theatre to-day give us a working drawing of a new edifice of the theatre, rather than the edifice itself. But, no matter what objections one may find to the work of Reinhardt, it can never be denied that he presented (with all his faults and errors) a complete and organic edifice such as has not been seen since.

For the history of modern stage decoration there remains the fact that the " Stylized Realism " of the Reinhardt epoch introduced the custom of stylizing the setting by plastic means, and this result was bound to remain a definite acquisition for the theatre. Although the concept of the plastic stage setting was modified during the course of the years, yet, from the production of " A Midsummer Night's Dream " up to very recent times, it formed the basis of stage decoration.

There are many who are so repelled by all which seems " real " on the stage that they believe, and try to make others believe, that the principle of the plastic setting itself implies realism. That is, of course, an error. Not only has the work of Stern shown us the stylized plastic setting but later we see this plastic stage decoration becoming an element in the synthesis of the mise en scène as well. The fact is that the plastic stage decoration is not in itself either realistic, stylistic or synthetic, but adapts itself to this or that interpretation, as the case may be. It is certainly true that in the Stern-Reinhardt interpretation we still meet elements which are more or less " true." Thus, in order to present a stylized garden, Stern reduces the setting to a few sections of hedge, but this hedge is made of flats which his seamstress has spent weeks in covering with artificial leaves. It is certainly a stylized surface, but it is conceived in the realistic spirit (pl. 26). To-day we are content to suggest the hedge by indications further removed from reality. In the same way, the walls which Stern so often employed on the stage of the " Deutsches Theater " are the result of a fairly complicated procedure :

first, the canvas is given a coat of size, then a coat of sand, and finally a coat of heavier gravel (pl. 27). On this ground the painting begins. Papier-mâché had an important part in all this new technique, and in almost all the stylized interiors of Reinhardt one saw glass doors with real glass (pl. 13). To represent grass, the stage floor was not covered with a painted ground-cloth, but with one sewn full of raffia or some other similar material dyed the desired colour. The forest in " Die Räuber " was certainly stylized, since it was represented simply by the trunks of a few trees whose foliage was too high to be seen, but these trunks were realized with the greatest care, even down to the bark and moss. Hardly a stylized exterior at the " Deutsches " but contained the same inevitable little birches, with their carefully executed and perfectly naturalistic trunks, bark, and foliage, (pl. 21).

What then, it may be asked, constitutes the innovation realized by the Reinhardt mise en scène when compared to the mise en scène of the old naturalist theatre ? This stylization consists in the choice of certain characteristic scenic elements. The mise en scène of Reinhardt—or, rather, of Stern—stylized by eliminating and reducing the stage setting to a few suggestive and significant features. A section of hedge represents a garden ; the corner of a house, a street ; a column against the sky a public place ; and, as in the case of " Faust," two columns against a background mounting upward, to be lost in the shadow, suggest the church in its entirety. These elements are selected in accordance with the style of the play and also following the requirements of the epoch, and are realized in a manner more or less " true " ; but the principle itself— the choice of the elements of scenic expression —remained as a definite acquisition to the theatre from that time on.

And this principle of the choice of scenic elements is allied to the plastic execution of the setting. The plastic stage decoration is not only adapted to the execution of the setting in the naturalist manner ; it is still better adapted to stylization, even to synthesis, and often goes beyond.

The advocates of the painted setting claim that painting knows no limits and that it may or may not be stylized. A landscape or a portion of architecture can be depicted in all its details on a decorative panel. But the essential difference between a plastic and a painted setting consists in this : the simplification in the case of the latter is only concerned with the pictorial form and remains always a question of painting, and not of the theatre. On the contrary, the plastic execution of the setting in many cases is only possible if the setting be reduced to its essentials.

If we order a painter to carry out a stage decoration representing a garden, or an antique Greek landscape, he accomplishes nothing in stylizing his forms, because the greater part of the time he gives us, in the painting, Nature in its entirety. This was made evident by the so-called " stylized " settings in the first Russian ballets, notably the settings of Bakst—settings in which he presented rocks, trees, sky and clouds all painted on the back-drop. The plastic representation of the same landscape with all its details, no matter how naturalistically it were treated, would be impossible. Thus it is in part the plastic execution itself which compels us to eliminate, to cut, to reduce the details — to make a choice of the scenic elements to be employed. And by this selection the required expression is accomplished. To this a second degree of stylization is added by a greater or lesser simplification of the stage decoration.

Later, the plastic organization of the setting made use of elements placed on the stage floor and more especially by the employment of different levels and of stairs. Afterwards, as the setting continued to develop, these scenic elements grew in importance, until finally they became one of the principal resources of the mise en scène. It must not be forgotten, however, that it was the mise en scène of Reinhardt which first made use of them. Before talking of " Jessnertreppen," one must speak of Reinhardt's stairways. Later we shall discuss the æsthetic possibilities inherent in this scenic means, but in the meantime, let us remember that with all the novelty that it brought to the stage spectacle, it dates from Reinhardt and his stylized stage decoration.

It must also be noted that this style of stage decoration, by the very fact of its plastic execution, threw into prominence another essential factor in the modern mise en scène, namely, light. Up to this time light on the stage had served, so far as the setting was concerned, to illuminate plane surfaces. On these surfaces the direct light of projectors, torches or candles produced a spot more or less bright, tinted red or blue, but it could not animate these surfaces, since life can only be given to illuminated objects through the play of light and shadow. The plastic setting for the first time furnished three-dimensional bodies which caught light and projected shadows. Thus a whole gamut of expressions by means of light could be developed—and this is the next important element in the modern mise en scène. Like these other elements, the kernel of it is contained in the setting of this period of stylized realism. So it can be justly said that these elements, so important for the modern production—expression by the choice of essential elements, expression by means of different levels, expression by means of light—had already been set forth ; and, more or less independently of the theories of innovators like Appia and Craig, are to be found in the mise en scène of Reinhardt, whence they follow later the evolution of the setting toward synthesis, expressionism and even constructivism.

CHAPTER IV

ADOLPHE APPIA

REINHARDT was, above all, a man of the theatre and, thanks to his eclecticism, reunited all the elements capable of composing the complete stage spectacle. It must be remembered that his point of departure was in no way associated with a search for an æsthetic of the theatre. Yet at the same epoch other men, seeking to establish certain principles, approached the problem of the mise en scène from the outside and from the direction of a personal theory of æsthetics. Although this group of theorists is in strong contrast to that abundance of life, and of errors, which characterized the work of Reinhardt, nevertheless the primary results of the studies made by such men as Appia and Craig are of the highest importance to the modern theatre.

We are accustomed to name Appia and Craig together as the two torch-bearers of that one-time new æsthetic of the theatre. The fact is, however, that there are many who know Craig's books and his projects for the mise en scène, to whom Appia is no more than a name. It is not unusual to find men of the theatre who, on hearing his name pronounced, ask : " Appia ? Who is he ? " This is not after all so strange, because to a very large extent Appia and his work have been overshadowed by Craig, who is an active figure, creating talk about himself, broadcasting his paradoxes by means of his publications, and in general conducting himself in a way to draw attention and create a stir about his person. He is, after all, the actor turned man of letters.

However, the irrefutable dates are always present. Appia's first publication dates from 1894 ; his first designs were published in 1895–96, and his most important book, *Die Musik und die Inszenierung*, in 1899. Before this latter date Craig had been known only as an actor and wood-engraver ; it was not until after 1900 that his activities in the new theatre commenced, and only in 1905 that he began to publish his theories.

If Craig attracted attention immediately, it was probably due to his revolutionary attitude : extremists are always more readily heard than reformers. For it must be remembered that Appia was only proposing certain reforms, and did not wish, as Craig did, to raze the contemporary theatre in order to build something else in its place. Appia takes as his basis those elements which are found in the existing theatre, in the theatre of music-drama in particular, and applies to them his new conception of scenic beauty. It is only later, as we shall see, that he moves toward the creation of a new form of stage spectacle.

Again, it is to be noted that the books of Appia are extremely difficult to read, while Craig, on the contrary, presents his ideas and even his paradoxes in a form which, though at times cryptic, makes on the whole unusually light and easy reading. The works of Appia are to a certain extent hermetical. In him we find a profound thinker, penetrating to the bottom of things, who in all his work reveals both moral and æsthetic beauty. Nourished on German philosophy, he adopts its language to such an extent that his writings baffle all superficial perusal, only becoming clear after several readings. And this language is as difficult in his French texts as in his first book, which appeared in German. To understand

Appia it requires an effort of will—it requires an equal effort of will to resist Craig.

Moreover, for the last twenty years Craig has had what Appia lacked, a personal organ of publicity almost exclusively devoted to propaganda for the extension of the Craig cult. This official organ, *The Mask*, founded in 1908, has now with the last issues reached " Vol. 12 *bis* " (strange how the actor-mind can never rid itself of superstition). Here, in the pages of this interesting magazine, Craig has been free to express his personal views on all matters pertaining to the theatre and on many others much less relevant. All the world loves a fight and in *The Mask* Craig has given it to them. Sometimes in person and sometimes behind the transparent veil of some bizarre pseudonym he has turned his verbal guns on battleships and non-combatant rowing-boats alike. So long as he has stuck to the rowing-boats and lighter craft he has come off excellently, but now and then some heavily armed battleship like Shaw, or an armoured cruiser like Ervine, turns and takes a pot at him, with the result that the guns of Rapallo are temporarily out of commission. All this has produced a continuously amusing and entertaining show for the side-lines, and the world of the theatre has talked and laughed and, more important still, has read.

There is still another reason why Appia has produced relatively less reverberation than Craig. Son of the greatest English-speaking actress of the last generation and raised in the theatre, Craig, in all his proposals, embraces the stage spectacle in the completest sense ; while Appia, profoundly the musician, communicating with his God through sound and rhythm, establishing his ideas on music, and envisaging hitherto no other complete art except one raised on these foundations, has inevitably addressed himself to a much more limited public. His point of departure was the visual reform of Wagnerian music-drama, a reform which must have been considered a heresy in the circles of Bayreuth and by other men interested in revising the theatre ; and this restriction definitely confined the spread of his ideas. Thus it may be said that, from the beginning, Appia at bottom had no public, while Craig, even in jostling everything and proclaiming revolution for the entire theatre, was bound to attract the interest of every one concerned in the fate of the modern stage.

Appia's ideas are contained in two principal works, the first being, *Die Musik und die Inszenierung* (1899), the other, *L'Œuvre d'Art Vivant* (1921). Between the two an important road has been travelled. The starting point of the second, while it is no longer precisely music-drama, is nevertheless a form of spectacle based on music.

In the life of Appia two distinct experiences are to be seen, each of which influenced him profoundly. First it was the music-drama of Wagner and later the rhythmic art of Jaques-Dalcroze ; before *Die Musik und die Inszenierung* there had been Wagner, and before *L'Œuvre d'Art Vivant* there was Dalcroze. Thus it is possible to group Appia's work into three periods : the Wagnerian period, the Dalcroze period and, finally, a period of synthesis which has as its goal the creation of what he will have us call " l'œuvre d'art vivant," the living work of art.

It was the study of the possibilities for a new visual realization of the Wagnerian music-drama which led Appia to recognize the importance played by the arts of time and the arts of space in the realization of this new form. Poetry and music develop in time ; painting, sculpture and architecture in space. So, since the art of the theatre is addressed to our eyes as well as to our ears, how is it possible to reconcile in a harmonious unity these two opposing elements of time and space ; elements which by themselves unfold on apparently different planes ? Is there a term which is common to both ? Can spatial form be a part of successive intervals of time, and can these intervals be expressed in terms of space ? In space, duration is expressed by a succession of forms, that is, by movement. It is movement, mobility, which controls the arts and can cause them to converge in the art of the theatre. All of Appia's speculations have this same point of departure, although the solution of the problem which he proposed in his Wagnerian period differs from that which he finds under the influence of Dalcroze.

In the performance of music-drama, music takes, so to speak, a spatial form. The mise en scène must translate this music into terms of space. The actors in this music-drama can have no liberty of gesture or movement, since all is regulated and prescribed by the rhythm and tempo set down in the score. Nothing must be left to chance ; every movement of the actor is determined by the music. Thus the movements of the actor, each of his steps even, fixed by the music, measuring space as music measures time, give to the tempo of the music form in space and, by consequence, determine all the proportions of the mise en scène.

In order that the music may emanate from the actor, filling the stage ensemble, there must be a material point at which the actor and the stage decoration meet. This point will be the " practicability," that is to say, the plastic character of the setting and groundwork on which the actor moves. Thus the conclusion is reached that *the arrangement and ordering of the stage in all its details is to be found contained in the music*. Wagner himself, hardly conscious of the reforms, from a visual standpoint, implicit in his work, never imagined a decorative technique different from that of his contemporaries. If the actors, on whose shoulders the new action rested, were the object of his special attention, he found it perfectly natural, on the other hand, to place about them and behind them vertical, painted canvas drops —a procedure which, by its nonsense, reduced to nothing all effort towards æsthetic harmony and truth in his work. Thus, though the Wagnerian reform is concerned with the conception, with the essence, of drama, Wagner himself never knew how to reconcile the representative form, that is to say the mise en scène, with the dramatic form which he adopted. The result was a gap so great between his intentions and their visual realization that all his work was disfigured thereby.

In order to restore the works of Wagner in the ambience which they seemed to demand, Appia applied himself to the study, measure by measure, of the works of the master, seeking in the scores themselves the visual form for that drama. In this way his designs for Wagnerian stage decorations, which date from his first period, were born. Here he starts with the living actor and his position, no longer in front of, but in the midst of those volumes and lines particularly determined for him and, at the same time corresponding to space and duration as dictated by the music. Appia's beautiful designs for the operas of Wagner are so well known that we have felt it unnecessary to reproduce the whole series, and have contented ourselves with the two shown in plates 34 and 35. These designs, in which all childish romanticism has been laid aside, reveal a straining towards a classic purity which is characteristic of all of Appia's work. Rather, since a certain romanticism is inherent in the Wagnerian drama, let us say that in these designs romanticism is purged of all that appears ridiculous to us to-day, showing only what it contains of the truly great and eternally human. And, finally, over and above all theory, these designs not only reveal to us a great artist but at the same time disclose a great soul.

We regret that we have not been able to show more, because no one of these designs by itself can give an idea of the different aspects of Appia's settings when seen under different arrangements of lighting. Recall the different phases of light which he has set down in the series of designs for the rock of the " Walküre," or those for the third act of " Tristan." In fact, for Appia, after " plasticity," light is the most important stage factor ; and it is because he realized even before 1899 the importance of the rôle which light was to play in the future of the mise en scène that he must be looked upon as the chief forerunner of the modern theatre. It is in this respect that we see him as, in a way, the father of the most modern reformers, and it is in this field that his early work still maintains its importance for the theatre of to-day.

It must always be kept in mind that Appia's designs are not the arbitrary products of his imagination but the results of a profound study of the work to be produced. Appia himself lays particular stress upon this point. His designs are without figures in most cases, even though, as we know, all his work takes the actor as its starting-point. He says himself that these designs have no significance without the moving body of the actor and that it is just because of the impossibility of showing the actor in movement that he has left out all indications of his presence.

In tying the plastic body of the actor to the plastic elements of the stage, Appia was forcibly and inevitably compelled to reject painting and to deny it any place in the work of collaboration. What then remains for painting, since it must play some part in the creation of this integral work of art? Colour perhaps—but colour, far from being the exclusive property of painting, is even more closely allied with light; in short, it is unthinkable except in terms of light. For colour is dependent on light in two distinct ways; either light seizes on colour and becomes one with it, dispensing it in space, in which case colour shares the existence of the light itself; or light contents itself with the illumination of a coloured surface, and in this latter case colour only takes on life by virtue of the variations in the light which makes it visible. The life of colour is thus dependent both on light and on the object which carries it.

So, in order to introduce colour into the ensemble of elements which constitute the mise en scène, the new artists of the theatre often employ light alone, replacing with it all colour fixed on a canvas, no matter in what form. Thus light becomes the artist's veritable palette, and in later productions, following the development of a modern technique of lighting, we have seen light assume the preponderent place which Appia outlined for it at the beginning of the century. In looking back at his work, we see that even in Appia's earliest studies, and independently of their application to music-drama, two principles are set down for the new art of the stage: the plastic character or "practicability" of the new stage decoration, and the collaboration of light in the creation of the visual spectacle.

Later on, Appia had the opportunity to collaborate with Jaques-Dalcroze at Hellerau, and the impressions which the artist received from his contact with the art of rhythm definitely confirmed what he had more than half realized from the beginning. This experience helped him to extend his theory and to give it that general form expressed in his work *L'Œuvre d'Art Vivant*. Here, again, the starting point of his speculations is movement. While in the case of music-drama the practicability of the stage arrangement sufficed to form the tie between music and plastic form, it is now rhythm, the actor's body itself, the living body, the nude body that is called on to assume the principal rôle in a fusion of the arts.

The living and mobile body of the actor is the representation of movement in space, and the part it must play is thus of capital importance. The actor takes possession of the text with one hand and, holding as in a bundle the arts of space in the other, irresistibly brings his hands together, creating by that movement the integral work of art. It is in this way that the living body, in retaining the secret of the hieratic relations which unite such diverse factors, becomes the creator of a new art.

But the body is not only mobile; it is plastic as well. This plasticity places the body at once in the closest accord with architecture, while painting, by its very mode of existence, makes any such intimate association impossible. Up to this point Appia's conclusions, so far as they concern the form which the setting must assume, do not differ greatly from those of his first period. However, his studious observation of the evolutions of the pupils of Dalcroze seems to have led him to another important conclusion.

The body reclining, seated, or upright, expresses itself in space through the movements of the arms, the torso, and the head ; the walk being excluded since it is concerned solely with the activity of the legs. Thus we have two sets of planes distinct from each other ; planes for walking and planes intended to heighten the value of the body as a whole and in repose. These two sets of planes overlap, and it is only the bodily movements which determine to which category they belong. For example, inclined planes and stairs may be considered as belonging to both sets of planes ; the obstacle they form to free walking, and the expression they give to the body are consequences of their vertical quality.

We now have to do with two principal planes ; the horizontal and the vertical. In the case of the horizontal, it is important to remember that the body rests on a plane, and in so resting must express its weight. Consequently the structure of the ground or whatever represents the horizontal plane must be of such a nature as to throw this expression of weight into relief, always making the weight of the body evident. A failure to maintain the simplicity of this plane diminishes the expressiveness of movement. A bathroom, for example, in which there are hangings, divans and cushions, is in direct contrast and opposed to true expression through the body ; whereas if the same bathroom presents only plane and rigid surfaces, the nude body takes on its real æsthetic value. Again, nude feet ascending a carpeted stairway are just unshod feet, and we ask at once why they are so, whereas the same feet on a stairway without carpet are simply and frankly nude feet and so charged with expression.

Anything which tends to alter the expression of weight, whatever end it serves, weakens bodily expression. The first principle for what Appia henceforth calls " living art," perhaps the sole one from which all the others are automatically derived, is this : all forms other than bodily forms tend to be in opposition to the latter and never become one with them. It is the opposition offered to the body by space which makes it possible for space to share in the life of the body, and, reciprocally,

it is the body's opposition which animates spatial forms.

Let us imagine a square, vertical pillar with its sharply defined right angles. This pillar without base rests on the horizontal blocks which form the floor. It creates an impression of stability, of power to resist. A body approaches the pillar ; from the contrast created between the movement of this body and the tranquil immobility of the pillar a sensation of expressive life is born, which neither the body without the pillar, nor the pillar without the body, would have been able to evoke. Moreover, the sinuous and rounded lines of the body differ essentially from the plane surfaces and angles of the pillar, and this contrast is in itself expressive. Now the body touches the pillar ; at once the opposition becomes more evident. Finally the body leans against the pillar, whose immobility offers it a solid support ; the pillar resists ; it is active. Opposition has thus created life in the inanimate form ; space has become living.

Suppose, however, that the pillar is only solid in appearance, and that at the slightest contact from without, its substance can unite with the form of the body which touches it. The living body now becomes encrusted in the soft substance of the pillar and, as a consequence, simultaneously loses its own life and takes away the life of the pillar. The same experiment holds good for the ground. An elastic ground which allows the foot to sink into it at each step but which, when the foot is released, at once resumes its former shape, will, because of this lack of resistance, always remain a dead thing ; further, it will deaden the play of muscles to such an extent that the body will become a mere unlifelike mechanism, a caricature of life. In contrast, look at a floor of rigid stones awaiting the foot in order to resist it, to throw it back at each new step. This floor, by its rigidity, excites the whole organism to a will to walk. It is in opposing itself to life that the ground, like the pillar, can receive life from the body.

In following this brief résumé, we see that

Appia finds in weight and rigidity the primary conditions for the existence of what he calls living space. From them will spring the choice of lines and the form which the creation will take in space. Something of this is to be seen in the settings which he arranged for the performances at the Dalcroze school; settings in which, like a reflection from classic antiquity, there survive sobriety, purity of line, order and measure, all present in a rhythmic space and interpreted by the living body. This is what the art of Appia, under the influence of the art of Dalcroze, shows to us. We present in plate 38 Appia's setting for " Orphée," as produced at the Dalcroze school. In plates 36 and 37 are two of his designs, called " rhythmic spaces," in which he reveals the full value of the human body through the application of those principles which we have just discussed.

But once this principle has been established, it becomes for Appia the only stage form with value, the sole mode of expression in the theatre which is admissible. Afterwards he attempts to apply it to other problems of the mise en scène, and it is there that we discover his limitations. Thus, for " King Lear," Appia has established some settings in the same manner, examples of which we show in plates 40 and 41. We must admit frankly that for us these beautiful and harmonious arrangements are not in accord with the essence of the tragedy; its superhuman stature and all that it holds of barbaric cruelty. A setting like that of Geddes, which we show elsewhere (pl. 94), certainly better expresses the world of Shakespeare's play. Appia, in his recent rhythmic style, has again taken up the problem of the Wagnerian stage decoration, and we now see him present his rock of the " Walküre " in the form shown in plate 39. There is certainly no stronger contrast to be found than that existing between this setting and the one representing the same subject shown in plate 35. Does this new form stand for progress? We are tempted to say " No." Not that we demand descriptive accessories— what is lacking is the envelope, the psychological atmosphere, the mood; in a word,

the expression. Admitting that the new setting perhaps corresponds to a physical rhythm, it is nevertheless completely removed from the soul of the drama itself. This rhythmic art which now dominates the ideas of Appia may very well be a perfect art, but it appears as a form which cannot without danger be applied to all the other manifestations of art existing side by side with it—and existing with as good a right as the art of rhythm itself.

It is certainly not in this way that Appia understands and envisages the future of the art of the theatre. The Dalcroze experience left so decisive an impression on Appia's mind that he has since been unable to conceive of a perfect art or of a complete stage spectacle under any other form. " Music," he says, " imposes its successive intervals on the movements of the body; this body transmits them to the proportions of space; the inanimate forms oppose the body with their rigidity, and this closes the cycle; beyond that there is nothing." With all our profound respect for this great artist, we believe there are many things beyond that. In particular we believe that every attempt to confine scenic expression to a single rigid and immutable principle diminishes the art of the stage instead of completing it.

Starting with rhythm as a basis, Appia has envisaged an art of the future, the sole art which for him has value, and of this art he speaks in terms which are deeply moving. It is again from music that this living work of art will be born. The new being, we ourselves, will be marked by music. To incorporate sound and rhythm into our organism is the first step toward the living work of art. This new art implies a collaboration; living art is social; it is in an absolute way social art. Not that the fine arts are placed at the disposition of every one, but that every one must lift himself to the level of this new art, an art resulting from the collective discipline of the body. Our modern art, destined for spectators imprisoned within themselves, can never serve as an example nor as a norm. Our touchstone will be our experience of beauty—an experience made in common. Then all of us will wish to live this art and not merely play with it. Our hands will no longer be extended to receive, but to give. Other hands will come to seize ours, filling them with the same living warmth which they give off, and so the immortal pact will be concluded.

This dream in which the speculations of Appia seem to have ended appears to reproduce in a more general way the life at Hellerau. We cannot help being a little sceptical before all these aspirations—and Appia's are not unique—which would like to change earth into a kind of artistic Utopia, rhythmic or otherwise. Although rhythmic community festivals may offer humanity a new source of beauty and happiness, they do not constitute the sole form of art which we can imagine for the future, and they ought not to be the sole form. The forms of art are innumerable, and it is an error to wish to enrich humanity through the medium of any new art-form in eliminating at the same time all others. Instead of following the master on this road to Utopia, we prefer to recognize and appreciate the very real value which his reforms have had for our present-day art in the more modest domain of stage decoration.

CHAPTER V

EDWARD GORDON CRAIG

APPIA is not the only one who has pushed the reform of the theatre to a point where a new conception of the spectacle has been envisaged—a conception destined to replace the current forms of the theatre. The second great reformer is Edward Gordon Craig. Possessed of different gifts from Appia, and approaching the problem of the theatre from a different angle, he arrives at different conclusions. But Craig, like Appia before him, dreams of an art of the theatre of the future and attempts to draw, somewhat vaguely it is true, the larger and more significant lines of such a theatre. Since he has made a few attempts to realize his theories, we can consider his work under two aspects : first, his conception of a theatre of the future ; and secondly, the partial application of his ideas to the existing stage.

The theatre, says Craig, has up to the present confined itself to the representation of plays. It can, and must be, more than this. It must be a *revelation*. For representation the theatre employs traditional materials : the human body, spoken words, and the visible world. In the future the theatre will reveal invisible things ; it will reveal them by means of movement.

" You now will reveal by means of movement the invisible things, those seen through the eye and not with the eye, by the wonderful and divine power of Movement. . . . I like to remember that all things spring from movement, even Music ; and I like to think that it is to be our supreme honour to be the ministers to the supreme force-movement. For you see where the theatre (even the poor, distracted and desolate theatre) is connected with this service. The theatres of all lands, east and west, have developed (if a degenerate development) from movement, the movement of the human form. We know so much, for it is on record : and before the human being assumed the grave responsibility of using his own person as an instrument through which this beauty should pass, there was another and a wiser race, who used other instruments."

The decadence of the theatre commenced, then, according to Craig, with the appearance of the priest or priestess dancer. " I do not hold, that with the renaissance of the dance comes the renaissance of the ancient art of the theatre, for I do not hold that the ideal dancer is the perfect instrument for the expression of all that is most perfect in movement. The ideal dancer, male or female, is able by the strength or grace of the body to express much of the strength and grace which is in human nature, but it cannot express all, nor a thousandth part of that all. For the same truth applies to the dancer and to all those who use their own person as instrument. Alas ! the human body refuses to be an instrument, even to the mind which lodges in that body." The human body refuses to serve as the instrument of the soul, of the feelings or of the intelligence. The body will always have the last word.

We would hardly have expected such severe words from one who has, in the past, so enthusiastically espoused the ideas and the art of that inspiring artist and personality of the last generation—Isadora Duncan. But Craig is not only up in arms against the dancer, but above all against the actor. " Acting is not an art," he says. " It is therefore incorrect to speak of the actor as an artist. For accident is an enemy of the artist. Art is the exact antithesis of pandemonium, and pandemonium is created by the tumbling together of many accidents. Art arrives only by design. Therefore in order to make any work of art it is clear we may only work in those materials with which we can calculate. Man is not one of these materials. . . . Therefore the mind of the actor, we see, is less powerful than his emotion, for emotion is able to win over the mind to assist in the destruction of that which the mind would produce ; and as the mind becomes the slave of emotion it follows that accident upon accident must be continually occurring. So then, we have arrived at this point : that emotion is the cause which first of all creates, and secondly destroys. That, then, which the actor gives us, is not a work of art ; it is a series of accidental confessions."

It is hardly necessary to point out the profound misunderstanding which is at the bottom of such a theory as this. It is willingly or involuntarily a complete failure to understand the art of the actor ; a failure to comprehend the double state—conscious and unconscious at the same time—of the actor during a stage creation. You may rest assured that he who does not understand the actor does not understand the theatre, or at least understands it as something quite different from the rest of us. According to Craig, before plays were performed by human beings, the spectacle in the theatre consisted of combats between animals. Later, man took the place of the animal because of a sort of commercial agreement between the poet and the actor by the terms of which the actor was to recite the verses of the poet. Thus " his body would have to become the slave of his mind ; and that, as I have shown, is what the healthy body utterly refuses to do. Therefore the body of man, for the reason which I have given, is *by nature* utterly useless as a material for an art."

If Craig considers " Divine Movement " as the basis and origin of the theatre, and then later tells us that in the beginning the theatre consisted in combats between animals, it seems that we might with justice and quite logically ask Craig to explain how, and in just what way, an elephant is better fitted to express this " Divine Movement " than man—the human body. But we must not demand too much logic from one who loves to express himself in paradox, and we must at the same time accustom ourselves to the oracular " thus-spake-Zarathustra " manner. For Craig, the actor is perforce a crude and imperfect mimic of Nature. He resembles the ventriloquist. So, says Craig, we should give up the futile attempt to introduce " life " into the play of the actor. " Do away with the real tree, do away with the reality of delivery, do away with the reality of action, and you tend towards doing away with the actor. This is what must come to pass in time, and I like to see the manager supporting the idea already. Do away with the actor, and you do away with the means by which a debased stage-realism is produced and flourishes. No longer would there be a figure to confuse us into connecting actuality and art ; no longer a living figure in which weakness and tremors of the flesh were perceptible."

One would do Craig an injustice in disputing or discussing such an argument as this. His point of view is that of the savage who, never having seen a theatre nor a play acted, believes that the actor killed on the stage has been actually assassinated, and rushes to his assistance.

On the other hand, if we take the actor off the stage, by what are we going to replace him ? By an inanimate being, says Craig, by the " Ueber-marionette." This super-marionette is the descendant of the ancient idols, as the marionette of to-day is the degenerate image of a god—the last reminder of a noble and beautiful art. The super-marionette will depict the body in ecstasy. " Its ideal will not be the flesh-and-blood, but rather the body in trance—it will aim to clothe itself with a death-like beauty while exhaling a living spirit." This will be then the reign of law, and Craig will evoke the calm, the impassibility of Egyptian art, the fêtes of creation in forgotten Asia.

To express or represent movement, then, we must substitute for man an automaton more or less immobile. Craig claims to have made certain experiments in this field in an effort to construct a mechanism capable of expressing rhythm. So far, he says, he has only succeeded in expressing the simplest rhythms. It will be thousands of years before the great movements can be grasped; in that far, dim future this art born of movement will be the final and universal belief.

Let us be just: we see here, pushed to excess and loaded with paradox, a postulate of the art of the theatre, namely, the reign of rhythm on the stage. But in pushing this idea to the absolute we inevitably put outside the theatre all those elements which live of their own life. This reduction of the theatre to a play and interplay of abstract rhythms may be realized some day, although we are not sure that such a state would be altogether a happy one, since in the process we would have to abandon all progress realized through the differentiation of our sensitiveness. We would, in short, have returned to a rigid and hieratic concept almost Chinese; the automatonization of expression.

After all, the Craig theory does give us something complete—a perfection. This cannot be denied. Whether such a consummation is to be desired is debatable, but it is by no means inconceivable. Hence it is curious to note how Craig applies his theories.

In realizing his ideas in the theatre, Craig makes use of the very elements which he rejects in theory. He tends to make the stage altogether rhythmical by introducing rhythm into the stage decoration, the gestures and movements of the actor and into the lighting. This is of unquestionable importance. Fortunately, this paradoxical seer is not only a man who has lived in the theatre, and who therefore understands the stage, but is at bottom an artist as well.

The art of the theatre does not lie, says Craig, in the play of the actors, nor in the stage setting, nor in the dance: it is composed of elements which make up the play of the actor, the drama, the setting and the dance; of gesture, which is the soul of acting; of words, which are the body of the play; of lines and colours, which are the very existence of the stage decoration; and of rhythm, which is the essence of the dance. That is to say that Craig distils from each element of the art of the theatre its abstract essence in order to create with these abstractions his scenic ensemble. Of these elements gesture is the most important. We go to the theatre to see and not to hear, he says. The finished production, the mise en scène, must be a harmonious combination of gesture, word, dance and image. The plays of Shakespeare, by their very nature, are unfit for production on the stage. They gain by being read rather than acted. The fact that they are played proves nothing. The day will come when the theatre will no longer have plays to present and will then be forced to create works fitted for it—works which are incomplete when read, incomplete everywhere but on the stage. This seems to be in a way conceivable. It is certainly consistent with the theory.

However, this new work born in the theatre must be the product of the same brain, the same imagination which is to realize it on the stage. Thus we have the new artist whose duty it will be to regulate the rhythm of the movements of the actors, design the stage decoration and costumes, create the music and even the play itself. He alone will know how to combine these abstract elements of the theatre, line, colour, movement and rhythm.

This producer will combine colours which harmonize with the tone of the play. Then he will choose some object to form the centre of his sketch; a portico, a fountain, a balcony or a bed, and about this he will group the other objects which must be seen. In his sketch he will arrange the entrances of all the characters and will design their gestures as well as their costumes. Only after that will he give out the parts. He holds the actors on the stage, he illuminates them and regulates the play of light. He plans all their movements and directs the delivery of their speeches.

The actor is moved as a part, a fragment of the whole composition, a definite form. He is presented to us in a manner prearranged, passes such and such a point on the stage in a certain light, the head turned at a predetermined angle, all the body in harmony with the drama and uninfluenced by his own ideas.

Admittedly this is a very elevated and very complete conception of scenic unity and one which condemns all naturalism—naturalism of movements as well as naturalism in the stage decoration and costumes. So far as movement is concerned, gesture must no longer be spoken of as either natural or conventional ; gesture can be only either necessary or useless. The necessary gesture will always be the natural gesture in the instant it is described, that is to say, the gesture which symbolizes the situation —the symbolic gesture. In fact, Craig advises the producer to imagine different characters, as for example a savage and crafty man, another courageous, bold and at the same time tender, a third spiteful and ugly. " For example, make a barbaric costume ; and a barbaric costume for a sly man which has nothing about it which can be said to be historical and yet is both sly and barbaric. Now make another design for another barbaric costume, for a man who is bold and tender. Now make a third for one who is bold and vindictive." He must compose for these characters symbolic gestures ; gestures which express guile, others which express daring tenderness, and still others which express vindictive ugliness. The same principle holds good for costume. It is no longer necessary to seek historical truth or accuracy, but rather we must aim at rendering a symbolic truth concerning the character. Hence we must devise costumes which are symbolic and which evoke the character by means of their cut and colour. One for the crafty savage, one for daring and tenderness and a third for hate and ugliness. In the same way the setting will furnish only suggestions, and these through line and colour only. Having fixed on the colour of the setting, we shall determine the general lines and their directions—a suggestive and symbolic line and a symbolic colour.

It is to be noted that Craig himself in his sketches reduces these symbolic lines almost exclusively to the vertical. The organization of a stage rhythm by means of horizontal levels is almost completely foreign to him. For him, the rhythm of the stage decoration resolves itself almost completely into a disposition of verticals. This is probably so because the suggestive force of the vertical is found almost altogether in its proportion to the actor on the stage. Thus, in Craig's designs we see verticals which, in proportion to the actor, attain a height of fifty feet, and which are placed on a stage not more than twenty-five feet in width. Never fear ascending lines, he says. " Do not be afraid to let them go high ; they cannot go high enough ; and remember that on a sheet of paper which is but two inches square you can make a line which seems to tower miles in the air, and you can do the same on your stage, for it is all a matter of proportion and nothing to do with actuality." Proportions such as these are highly interesting, often thrilling in the design, but transferred to the stage and realized there they tend more or less to deform. In addition, Craig almost always places the actor in the same proportion relative to the setting in these constantly recurring applications of the vertical to his creations. He does not vary the relation. The result is that he ends by greatly reducing the expressive force of this proportion on which he lays such stress. Except in certain settings for " Macbeth," Craig has practically deprived himself of the possibility of expressing an atmosphere of oppression, of evil conscience, of murder—demanded by many tragedies—by means of a very low and lowering setting.

In this predilection for the vertical it is difficult not to recognize a certain form of English æstheticism—that taste, that penchant for the exquisite and the precious, which from the time of the Pre-Raphaelites has been continued by Beardsley, S. H. Sime, and others, and is to be seen to-day in Craig. It is a great pity, he says, that the theatre is no longer either exquisite or precious. In place of employing gross materials, such as prose, wooden planks, painted canvas, papier-mâché, powder, and so on, he wishes he might use precious materials like ebony, ivory, gold and silver, exquisite silks in exotic colours, marble and alabaster, and lastly fine minds. Here we see him, through his æstheticism, bringing back into the theatre the same naturalism in the use of materials which a moment before he cast out as opposed to the true idea of the theatre.

It is again from this æstheticism that his prejudice in favour of symbolism proceeds. " For not only is Symbolism at the roots of all art, it is at the roots of all life, it is only by means of symbols that life becomes possible for us ; we employ them all the time. The letters of the alphabet are symbols, used daily by sociable races. The numerals are symbols, and chemistry and mathematics employ them. All the coins of the world are symbols, and business men rely on them. The crown and the sceptre of the kings and the tiara of the popes are symbols. The works of poets and painters, of architects and sculptors are full of symbolism ; Chinese, Egyptian, Greek, Roman, and modern artists since the time of Constantine have understood and valued the symbol. Music only became intelligible through the employment of symbols, and is symbolic in its essence. All forms of salutation and leave-taking are symbolic and employ symbols, and the last act of affection rendered to the dead is to erect a symbol over them."

It is here necessary to dissipate a misunderstanding. We must first dismiss from the discussion what are called conventional signs, marks and tokens, like letters or mathematical, musical, or stenographic signs, which have all been generalized by a tacit or explicit agreement, and which already represent a second step in symbolic evolution. They have come down to us from a distant past and from a first degree of symbolism to which such tangible symbols as the sceptre, the crown, the tiara and the flag belong. Thus in the hieroglyphic period letters were still symbols

of the first degree. Now these tangible signs have been able to become symbols because in the beginning they were realities. Such symbols as the crown, the sceptre, the tiara and the flag represent after all very real functions, and our highest religious symbol, the Cross, has become a symbol because it was a reality —a tragic reality—in the beginning. In the domain of art creation of the work of art corresponds to this symbolization produced by historic evolution. Art only creates through the medium of symbols in utilizing realities which have become symbolic. To attempt to utilize the symbol detached from its substratum, and so reduced to an abstract play of lines and colours, is a misconception in the theatre as it is in the other arts. Art does not look for the symbol ; it presents it.

So, if we accept rhythm as a means whereby we may reinforce scenic expression, we must not allow it to end in an abstract symbolization. Besides, the stage itself refuses to admit such a dematerialization of the setting by opposing to it an element which always remains three-dimensional, real and plastic—namely the actor.

The symbolist setting aims at giving us only the soul of events. It tends to environ the actor with a reflection of the drama in a four-dimensional world. But try as the actor will to stylize, to make rhythmic his gestures and his words, he remains always three-dimensional. He does not act only with his soul, his unconscious mind, or whatever we choose to call it, but with his body as well. No effort to symbolize gesture and movement will be able to attain the degree of abstraction reached by the setting. Under these conditions we see the actor, a real being, a physical being, moving among symbols which belong to another world than his. In opening this gulf between the actor—the three-dimensional being—and his dematerialized environment, the symbolist setting destroys the very scenic unity to which it aspired. And there it falls into the same error as the painted setting does. If on the one hand the painted setting with or without *trompe l'œil*—that is, the two-dimensional setting—failed to attain to the world of the actor, the symbolist setting, on the other hand, overreaches it. And for the creation of complete scenic unity the one is as dangerous as the other.

But, says some one, the symbolist setting only employs elements which are altogether plastic. The curtains and pylons of Craig are as palpable as the ribbons and battens of Pitoëff. It is the way in which they are used which disengages their symbolic value. That may be true. It is none the less true, however, that the use which is made of these same elements often enough renders them valueless.

Let us explain. The letters of the alphabet —leaving their symbolic genesis apart—have a significance which is determined and fixed. But these same letters, when they are employed in an algebraic equation, are instantly denuded of their real signification and become pure algebraic signs. In the same way the plastic elements which make up the ensemble of the symbolic stage decoration are seen to be denuded of their real value—of their plastic value—by the symbolic use made of them, and by consequence become mere dematerialized, abstract algebraic signs. As such they no longer belong to the same world as the actor. Craig felt this dilemma very clearly, and it explains quite simply his resentment against the actor—this irreducible, plastic element; and we see at once how he arrives logically at his primordial concept of the theatre without the actor. Nevertheless, in imposing a rhythmic unity on the entire stage, which includes the actor, he forces the actor into his ensemble.

Certain producers in the modern theatre, profiting by the teaching of Craig, have pushed this symbolization of the setting to its extreme limits. A simple line traced in the void by means of a ribbon, a couple of battens or a block of wood has at times been all that has been offered us in lieu of setting. With these last vestiges of an expressive ambience we were to create a world.

Such an impoverishment of the stage as this can perhaps be explained on the ground that it corresponds to certain æsthetic tendencies of the day, but it seems to us that there is at bottom a reason much more banal and by consequence much stronger. Under present-day conditions the man of the theatre makes much of material considerations, such as cost and facility of execution. From this point of view, the ideal stage decoration is the one which is non-existent. Thus the commercial side of the theatre accepts with joy the technical benefits and the cost reduction which this dematerialization of the setting brings with it. We are modern in being poor; we create the impression of being extreme when in reality we are only saving money.

But the exaggerations which decorative symbolism has engendered must not be laid at Craig's door. With Craig, we remain still within the domain of the " stage setting," within the realm of beautiful things, sometimes perhaps a little too precious and attenuated, but always on a high plane of dignity and purity.

CHAPTER VI

ARCHITECTURAL STAGES AND PERMANENT SETTINGS

THE further we advance in our examination of stage reforms the more the world of the theatre seems to become restricted. In looking back on the Reinhardt productions we recognize that they revealed to us the different possibilities of the mise en scène. With Appia and Craig, we see the elaboration of certain theoretical proposals, while in the case of other reformers dogmas have been announced which, when applied, impose on the stage definite and limited solutions to the exclusion of all others. Now, while such voluntary restriction has at times produced important and interesting results, we cannot help feeling that by it the world of the stage has become definitely narrowed.

If Appia and Craig approach the theatre from the outside with definite æsthetic theories, each is nevertheless too much of an artist not to look for the inspiration of each new mise en scène in the particular character of the drama itself. After all, they create settings which are allied to the feeling of the play, and as a result they are always discovering new solutions which are in conformity with each new piece. It is inconceivable that either Appia or Craig would ever wish to impose a rigid frame on the theatre and then seek to force every play without distinction into it.

On the other hand, we cannot help believing that, in the case of other reformers who attempt to reduce the stage to a few architectural elements, the forcing process becomes inevitable. Like Appia and Craig, those who propose such stage reforms have taken as their premise the idea that the stage in its entirety must be, not a pictorial creation, but a spatial one; but have aimed at securing this spatial quality by establishing on the stage various fixed and immovable architectural elements. Some of these systems are supple enough to allow of variation. Variety is secured through the different positions given these architectural elements, or by combining them with still other elements, such as, curtains, variable plastic units, and even painted pieces. In whatever way the idea is applied, the three-dimensional character of the stage is to be safeguarded by the presence of these same primary architectural elements. Again, there are other, more rigid, systems which bring into being for their purposes a unique architectural skeleton incorporated in the stage itself and altogether immutable.

It is necessary from the outset to distinguish between those systems in which the architectural and permanent elements form a part of a setting more or less mobile, and those in which these elements form a part of the architectural construction of the stage and are definitely incorporated in it. In the first case, to which we give the name " permanent setting," the architectural elements are movable, and consequently the scheme is legitimate. In the second case, the elements are so fixed that only the pick of the wrecker could alter or remove them. Now it often happens that these same elements will be utilized by one reformer as a part of a permanent setting and by another as a means of carrying the construction of the stage itself. In outward appearance the two stages seem to be the same, but the possibilities of practical application are quite different. The permanent setting with its movable elements offers considerable suppleness and fairly extensive possibilities for variation, but when these elements become a part of the actual architectural construction, their rigidity seriously restricts the possibilities of the mise en scène. In part, these reforms are derived from certain proposals by Craig which, when generalized, were made to serve as frame for all sorts of plays, and in part they are a conscious return to certain lost traditions of theatre architecture.

The extreme manifestation of this fixed architectural arrangement is to be found in the so-called modern Shakespearean stage. The proponents of this idea rationalize it as follows : the tradition of the theatre as it developed from antiquity was interrupted by the perspective stage of the Italian theatre which is still dominant to-day. Now, if we wish to free ourselves from the tricks of the stereoscopic scene, with its wings and painted drops and the rest, we must again pick up the tradition at the point where it was interrupted, that is to say, in the theatre of Elizabethan London.

At the risk of being burned alive as dangerous heretics, we venture to say that this conception seems to be based on an erroneous conception of Shakespeare's theatre. That theatre was a survival of the stage of the Middle Ages, having been handed down to Shakespeare and his contemporaries through the medium of the improvised platforms of travelling companies. The stage of the first London theatre was such a platform, temporarily erected in the little arena which served also for bear-baiting and broadsword combats. The stage of the Middle Ages was a simultaneous stage and, even when reduced to its primitive expression, the elements of a simultaneous stage are to be found there. It is these elements of the poor improvised theatres which were incorporated into the Globe and Swan with practically no attempt to change or better them. It seems absurd to try to find in the primitive platform of Shakespeare's theatre a stage means of any particular use to us to-day. Moreover, we know that whenever Shakespeare gave a command performance at Court he used

beautiful settings—at least beautiful for his time—and this fact alone is sufficient proof that the impoverished stage of the Globe was only what it was for lack of a better. Shakespeare and his fellows used it because, in general, they had nothing better and could not get anything better.

All that the theatre of Shakespeare proves to us after all is this : that a great dramatic genius or a gifted actor can always, when put to it, dispense with all external assistance. It seems a little hazardous to attempt to build an æsthetic of the theatre on the basis of that collection of improvised means which made up the English stage of 1600.

There have been, however, many attempts to reconstruct that stage, not only in its spirit but in its technical details as well. As early as 1852 Karl Immermann produced " Twelfth Night " in Düsseldorf on a special stage. This stage was really closer to the plan of the Roman theatre than to that of Shakespeare, and so by that very fact assumed a superior form. The royal entrance, which occupied the centre of the ancient stage, was enlarged sufficiently to permit a small scene in its entirety to be placed behind it and so corresponded in a way to the inner stage of the Elizabethan theatre. As for the other entrances, Immermann's stage, profiting by the arrangement of the antique theatre, or rather, the adapted architectural theatre of the Renaissance, increased their number to six (pl. 42). Such an arrangement as this offers many possibilities for stage movement, and it might even be interesting to attempt something of the same sort to-day, provided always it were done on the understanding that it was for only one play and not towards the end of establishing a stage-form suitable for all plays. Immermann himself never had any such idea, and his stage did not survive the performance of " Twelfth Night."

The Immermann stage was rather closer to the Renaissance stage than to anything else, but the stage established by the Freiherr von Perfall at the Hoftheater in Munich shows a compromise between the Elizabethan and the old illusionist stage of the nineteenth century.

Here the greater portion of the stage floor was occupied by a veritable scene in which the painted setting reigned in all its glory (pl. 43). Later, the installation of this stage was changed, and painted settings were installed even on the fore-stage itself. Such a compromise, which tries to reconcile the spirit of the architectural stage to the antiquated concept of the illusionist theatre, is certainly far from satisfying; but, on the other hand, the pure Shakespearean stage does not itself seem to be any more satisfying. The only stage means which it offers, or can offer, is a simultaneous scene composed of fore-stage, inner-stage and balcony. This is certainly not a stage means that issues from our modern requirements, but is rather an archæological reconstruction exceedingly difficult to reconcile to our present-day demands.

Before describing the attempts at an exact reconstruction of the Shakespeare stage we should first mention the stage devised by Killian and Klein for the Hoftheater in Munich. Here we have a compromise. In plates 44–47 are shown scenes for " Hamlet " and " Julius Cæsar." The stage arrangement consists of a deep inner proscenium pierced at either side by a portal behind which the changes of scene take place. This proscenium, which occupies a depth of ten feet, is permanent, the space within it constituting an unlocalized area which is defined in the course of the play by the pictorial indications placed in the frame of the proscenium. So, while this is not strictly speaking, a Shakespeare stage, it nevertheless belongs to that category.

Two men, Max Krüger in Germany and William Poel in England, have attempted an exact reconstruction of Shakespeare's stage. In Krüger's project the balcony, which cut off the actors to their waists by its balustrade and broke the movement with its two pilasters, was faithfully reproduced following the best documentation available. The stage was divided into two parts by a curtain, giving a fore-stage and an inner-stage. The inner-stage under the balcony was approached by a few steps and could be closed from sight at

will by the drawing of the curtain. The general background remained always the same ; a wall with a door right and left, a balcony and a curtain masking the inner-stage (fig. 1). The fore-stage was an unlocalized area which could be localized at will, either by the actors speaking the indications of place when the curtain of the inner-stage was drawn, or by the lines and some significant properties placed on the inner-stage in cases where the inner-stage was exposed. Thus it is seen that the inner-stage may contain properties which indicate the locale. For instance, the stage direction, " Enter the King in bed," as W. J. Lawrence explains it, means simply that the curtain of the inner-stage was at that point opened, disclosing the King lying in his bed. As soon as this was done, the unlocalized fore-stage became a part of the King's room, and the characters which later enter through the doors right and left were entering the bedchamber of the King (fig. 1). William Poel, who created and carried on for years the Elizabethan Stage Society of London, has experimented with reconstructions along the same general lines, often employing, as in the case of Ben Jonson's " Poetaster," a background of black velvet curtains, against which the figures of the play, dressed always in Elizabethan costume, appear in sharp silhouette. In America, at Harvard University, a reconstruction was made for a performance of " Hamlet " in 1910, and since then various other universities have experimented in the same field. The Maddermarket Theatre at Norwich, England, should also be noted in this connection.

It must be evident that with such a system as this, practically everything in the performance which can interest the eye has been abandoned. It is puritanism become theatre. After such an impoverishment, to look at the gorgeous ostentation of the Catholic Italian theatre of the Bibienas, with its fantastic and overcharged settings, becomes almost a pleasure. With the Shakespearean stage the imagination of the producer is exhausted trying to find different combinations of play on the fore-stage, inner-stage and balcony, used either singly or together. As there are only five possible combinations, the matter is quickly finished. Unfortunately, when the producer has a play of five acts to stage, with only these restricted means at his disposal, the result, the greater part of the time, is on the whole profoundly boring.

Of course, as opportunity occurs, all the variations which are necessary to animate the stage of which we have been speaking. (pl. 48, 49 ; fig. 2). Here the setting is altogether architectural and constructed in cement. It was so architectural, in fact, that the outer wall on the left formed the limit of the visible stage, and consequently no actor could enter from that side. Stage movements thus became seriously restricted, reduced as they were, once for all, to entrances and exits from right and back only. Besides, this stage almost

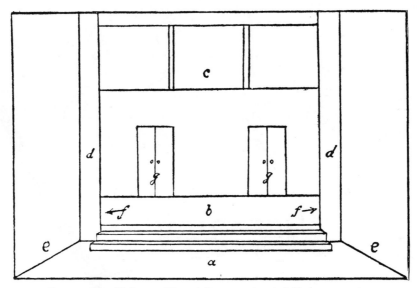

FIG. I.—Max Krüger : Plan of the reconstructed Shakespeare stage.

a. Fore-stage.
b. Back-stage.
c. Balcony.
d. Wings, limiting the back-stage.
e. Curtains, limiting the fore-stage.
f. Entrances to back-stage.
g. Doors in the back wall.

stage can be introduced to supplement this framework—different curtains, change of setting on the inner-stage while the play continues on the fore-stage, and so on. But as soon as all these amplifications have been introduced we find that we have stepped sharply out of the frame of the Shakespearean stage, properly speaking, in order to make use of means of expression which rightly belong to the modern permanent setting.

The stage of the Vieux Colombier, Paris, which Jacques Copeau built after plans by Louis Jouvet, is not far from this Elizabethan invariably showed the same setting for all plays ; always the same colour, always the same form. A few variable properties, such as a stairway, a little curtain for the door, some pots of plants, were expected to create the environment, to change the tavern of the " Paquebot Ténacité " into the palace of the Governor of Lima. In the same way, some panels decorated in the " art-nouveau " style of the nineteen-hundred period had to create the atmosphere for " Twelfth Night " (pl. 49). This is certainly a bastard method of procedure, since it is neither synthetic enough nor realistic enough. After having established a stage construction which made necessary the abandonment of illusion, the attempt was made to introduce realistic elements without sufficient means to harmonize them. With such a stage the environment of the action

to abandon his enterprise was the growing weariness of his public at being always faced with this drab puritanism.

It seems, in fact, that all those who seek an immovable stage architecture refuse to take into consideration the visual side of the theatre

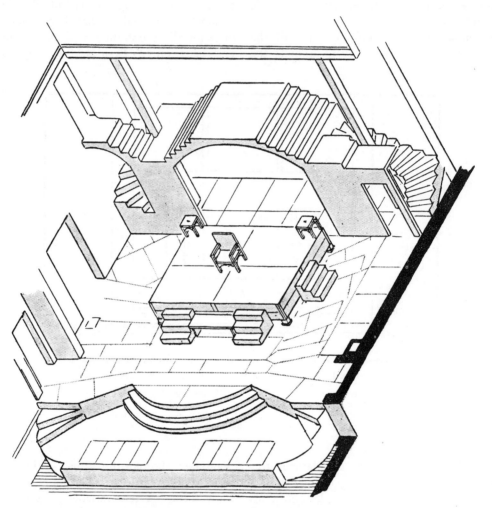

FIG. 2.—Louis Jouvet : Stage of the Théâtre du Vieux Colombier, Paris.

cannot be characterized and, moreover, it is incapable of serving the mise en scène on the psychological side. As for open-air scenes, they must be played before the curtain. Hence, as in the case of the Shakespearean stage, the result of this rigid construction is for the most part an unbearable monotony. It is not improbable that one of the reasons which obliged Copeau

at all. Thus we see that in creating what they call " a single locale for drama," conceived in architectural terms, they move inevitably toward the stage without setting. The advocates of this tendency support their puritanism by two principal arguments. First, the locale of the dramatic action, nude and unchangeable, gives to the actor his full importance, while a too extensive development of the visual spectacle diminishes him. Secondly, it is necessary to appeal to the imagination of the spectator, which, left quietly alone, will itself complete the stage impression.

As we have seen, the elements in production are the word, gesture, movement, colour, music, costume, settings, light. The realization of the play on the stage demands a perfect equilibrium between all these factors, and it is precisely the part of the producer to hold all these elements in balance and not to permit any one of them to leave its place of relative importance. From this point of view, to augment the importance of a single scenic factor, even of the actor, is a doubtful procedure, since it is equivalent to the creation of a new unbalanced state. This " non-existent " stage could be defended if it were possible for it actually to efface itself and become for the actor only an empty platform. It would seem that nothing could be of more advantage to the actor than an empty cube of air. But as soon as we watch these players for three hours knocking their heads, their legs and their whole bodies against the walls of this cube, our attention, which ought to be concentrated on the actor, is, on the contrary, irritated by the continual presence of this ambience called " non-existent." In fact a stage of this kind ends by assuming, solely by its negative qualities, an importance as great as that of the most gaudy and aggressive stage setting.

There remains the appeal to the imagination furnished by this sort of stage. But two sorts of spectators have to be taken into consideration : those who have imagination, and those who have not. The latter will certainly not find their imagination expanding to any extent before the prospect of a grey wall, and as for the spectators with imagination, it is unbelievable that these will be satisfied in the presence of a production which makes no sort of visual appeal. On the contrary, they are continually irritated by a spectacle which itself lacks imagination and, disappointed after a few trials, they desert the theatre where they are forced to witness without distinction the plays of Shakespeare, Merimée and Vildrac framed in the same fixed setting. If the literary theatre of our day gives us plays which are interesting and in part mounted intelligently, but which as spectacle are impoverished and dry, is it to be wondered at that the public runs to see ballet, revue and motion pictures —that is to say, seeks movement, colour, and visual satisfaction ? It was Edward Gordon Craig who said : " We go to the theatre to see and not to hear," and Craig has produced not revues but the plays of Shakespeare. In order to understand a play it is enough to read it in seclusion. What we want of the theatre is a complete realization by all the means at its disposal. We want a world.

Fortunately, other experiments in architectural stages offer results which are much less rigid. For example, the stage which Jouvet again installed for Delacre at the Théâtre du Marais at Brussels is much more supple and contains many more possibilities of variation (pl. 50–52). We also have the fairly tractable system of stage architecture known as tripartite. This consists in the erection of two fixed pillars between the stage proper and the back-stage, thus dividing it into three compartments, each of which can be closed by curtains. Thus, following the requirements of the play, either the front-stage may be used alone, or we may show three different scenes in the three compartments either simultaneously or in succession, or again we may employ the three, both front- and back-stage together, including of course the two pillars as part of the architecture. In this latter case, we may present a great hall, or even open-air scenes, in which the pillars function as the stage frame.

The tripartite stage, like so many other forms, comes to us out of the past. Such an arrangement, even with its front-stage, is to be found in the interesting project of Charles Nicole Cochin (1719-1796) (fig. 3). This is nothing more than a transformation of the stage of Palladio, which, in its turn, was inspired by the classic stage. The modern application of this tripartite idea shows us what a distance separates the permanent setting, supple and applicable to all the exigencies of the mise en scène, from the immovable architectural stage. It was Max Krüger again who in 1912 first proposed, under the name of " Stilbühne," a form of this tripartite stage. With Krüger's " Stilbühne " we are at once in the domain of the permanent setting. In 1914, profiting by this idea, which was put forward but not realized by Krüger, Van de Velde installed a tripartite stage at the Cologne Exhibition. Here again, the pillars shows some of the possibilities of change which can be obtained by the use of such a system. The curtains, painted in the manner of the Bayeux tapestry, together with the pillars, present a hall of the early Middle Ages, the back-stage here of course being closed off. The settings were organized in such a way that the action took place on the front- and back-stages alternately, the setting being changed on the back-stage while the next scene was in progress in front on the fore-stage. Sometimes, as in the scene on the

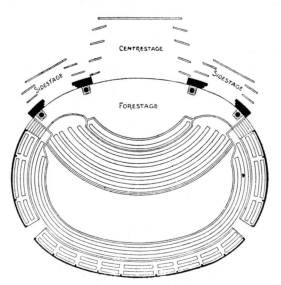

Fig. 3.—Charles Nicole Cochin (1719–1796) : Plan
showing a tripartite stage.

are conceived as a part of the setting. Since this was a theatre in an Exhibition, the architect, conscious of the necessity of creating a stage which would meet the demands of the different producers who would make use of it, suspended his pillars on rails so that they could on occasion be removed, permitting the action to take place on a clear stage. Later still, in 1923, W. R. Fuerst used the same idea in mounting " Tristan et Yseult," by Georges de Bouhélier, at the Odéon in Paris. For this production he established a stage with pillars in the form of a permanent setting, which made possible the rapid changes which the twenty-one scenes of this play necessitated. Figure 4 ship, the whole stage was used, the pillars being masked by the sail of the boat ; and at other times, in order to give variety, a whole setting was placed in front of the pillars, as, for example, the chamber of Yseult. It is clear that with such an installation the fore-stage must be in shadow each time that the scene is played on the back-stage. Used in this way a system of this kind has many real advantages, but it must be understood that it is established only for a single piece whose style is such that this method of treatment is in accord.

The " Ringbühne " which Strnad invented about 1923 may also be considered as a form

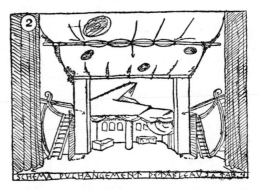
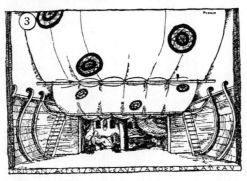

FIG. 4.—Walter René Fuerst : Settings for " Tristan et Yseult " (St. Georges de Bouhélier), Odéon, Paris, 1923, tripartite pillar stage.

    1. First act, scene 3 : back-stage only, side-stages closed.
    2. Shift from sc. 3 to sc. 4.
    3. First act, sc. 4 : Whole stage, pillars hidden behind the veil.
    4. Shift from sc. 4 to sc. 5.
    5. First act, sc. 5 : Fore-stage only, back-stages closed.

of tripartite or even five-compartment stage. In this case it is a question of fixed architectural elements, the columns which support the ceiling of the circular auditorium being continued across the stage proper, dividing it into three or more sections. In Chapter XII this interesting project is examined more fully, but it can be said here that this system is not in danger of monotony, since the circular revolving stage in the form of a ring discloses the various settings behind the three stages in the same way as Reinhardt's revolving stage does (pl. 349, 350).

The tripartite stage established by Auguste Perret for the Exhibition of Decorative Arts in Paris in 1925, coming as it did after so many others might have been excellent, but proved,

grave in view of the fact that this stage, like that of Cologne, was created to be used by the producers of all countries, who had been invited to demonstrate their ideas in the field of modern stage decoration. Hence, instead of giving them a full opportunity to show their individual and personal conceptions, this

FIG. 4.—continued.

6. Fourth act, sc. 1 : Fore-stage, centre-stage, and one side-stage.
7. Third act, sc. 2 : Back-stage only, side-stages closed.
8. Second act, sc. 1 : Fore-stage only, centre-stage and pillars hidden behind back-drop.
9. Fourth act, sc. 3 : Whole stage.

on the contrary, to be the least satisfying of all. Here no technical invention was introduced to counterbalance the rigidity of the fixed architecture, and this rigidity was coupled, moreover, with a very bad visibility, only a little triangle on this sixty-foot stage being visible from all the seats in the house. To make this worse, there was a complete lack of all technical facilities, the height was insufficient, and many other faults were apparent (pl. 54). These errors were the more

stage attempted to force on them the concept of the architect who had brought it into being. In looking at this, it is difficult to understand why the companies of New York, Moscow, and Amsterdam should leave their own well-equipped theatres in order to create a mise en scène in the implacable frame of this rigid system. Why should a producer adopt a new stage arrangement and special conditions which are not in the least applicable to his own ideas, simply for the pleasure of playing for three days on this inappropriate stage ? The result was, of course, a complete failure. Not a single one of the productions announced was given, and the fixed tripartite stage went down in ridicule, serving finally, for lack of anything better, for third-rate dance exhibitions given before bewildered provincials who had by chance strayed into the auditorium. Such an episode should serve as a lesson to all those who wish to impose on the theatre an immutable and consequently anti-theatrical conception.

On the other hand, many men in the modern theatre have sought for variable combinations of architectural elements and have elaborated various systems of permanent settings. The measure of the success of these systems has depended in large part upon the extent of their possibilities of variation. In all of them the appearance and reappearance of the same elements assured a unity in any series of settings for a given play. This is what the old æsthetic called unity in multiplicity. The first experiment in this field was made by Alfred Roller in Vienna, 1905, in his settings for Mozart's " Don Giovanni " (pl. 55, 56). Here, for the first time, the now well-known movable towers or pylons appeared in place of wings. This innovation spread rapidly, and shortly after the pylons were seen in the form of mobile walls on the stage of the Künstler-theater, Munich, then under the direction of Georg Fuchs. This stage of the Künstler-theater and in general the ideas of Fuchs have had considerable influence on the theatre of our time, and in consequence, merit a somewhat detailed study.

According to Fuchs, the theatre should be a feast for the whole audience. People come together in the theatre in order to exalt their inner life ; an exaltation which they achieve through the common medium of art. The means whereby this exaltation is to be reached is to-day, as in the past, to be found in rhythm, since rhythm is the very core and essence of every ritualistic festivity. Thus, to him, dance became the point of departure for the art of the theatre.

The dancer in his exaltation, said Fuchs, accompanied his movements with cries of joy. These cries, at first involuntary, later became conscious and formed the basis of song. Song itself in the beginning was without words. In its turn, the word became little by little a particular and personal creation which is the origin of poetry. Thus, at its very genesis, poetry, and particularly dramatic poetry, is found to be allied to the rhythm of the dance. Therefore, according to Fuchs, there can be no true drama unless the poet conceives his work in rhythm ; a physical rhythm shared by the whole audience.

If one person in this primitive crowd detached himself from the mass, he danced either before, with, or against this same crowd, thus establishing the distinction between the chorus and the actor. The chorus is, in fact, a part of the crowd, which assumes the functions of movement, song, and dance. In face of the crowd appeared at first one actor, then two, and later three, and finally, as a last group, the orchestra detached itself from the chorus.

According to Fuchs, the work of art, the complete stage work, is movement perceived as harmony. This work of art does not exist, however, in advance, but is realized in the spectator in the moment of its creation on the stage. But what produces this inner realization of the work of art ? Necessarily all the means of exaltation to be found in the actor, his environment, the phenomena of acoustics and optics, the word, light, proportion, music. In short, says Fuchs, here is to be found the art of the theatre, consisting essentially in a choice of the means of exaltation.

In consequence, the architecture of the theatre must be conceived in such a way as to produce the closest possible union between the stage and the audience. Boxes and balconies must be done away with. The stage must be organized in such a way as to produce the most perfect transmission of optical and acoustical impressions. And now Fuchs begins to be deliberate and dogmatic, for he states that the only form of stage which will assure this perfect transmission for both the eye and the ear is the " relief stage," or, in other words, an extremely shallow stage on which the actor stands out from his background as a figure in a bas-relief.

In order to justify the relief stage, Fuchs made much of the fact that actors have the habit of playing down by the footlights. He saw in this habit a desire on the part of the actor to enter into closer contact with his audience. He stated that dramatic action itself drew all the culminating points of the realization into one plane. Finally, he announced the following proposition : " The relief stage is the spatial form which is in accordance with drama itself, its innate law and its means of expression."

Now, if we place all the action in one plane, it is apparent that a background parallel to the plane of action becomes indispensable, that is to say, a unified plane before which the relief will appear. Therefore, the stage is disposed as follows : a background, and a plane of action amplified by the proscenium.

The transformation of impressions into dramatic action—a transformation which we believe occurs subconsciously in the spectator —Fuchs found in a particular place, materially and topographically located : the proscenium. This part of the theatre, which, until then, had never been considered as anything more than a line of demarcation between the stage and the audience, Fuchs made into a mystic plane in which the mystery of dramatic action was to be fulfilled.

Consequently, with the stage divided into two parts, Fuchs always, and on principle, presented the actor detached from his background. A certain danger of isolating the actor is likely to result from such a stage concept. After all, if we consider movement as one of the most suggestive elements which the actor has at his disposal, why deprive him of the full exercise of this means ? Why make impossible the advancing movement toward the audience that is from up-stage, down-stage, from the depth of the scene to the footlights, and by consequence the movement of recoil

from down-stage, up-stage to the depth of the scene. The sudden entrance of an actor by a door at centre-back is bound to be more significant and expressive than one made parallel to the frame of the stage. A movement of recoil can depict the fear of a character much better than a recoil described in the same plane. We see, therefore, in this theory of Fuchs', a reduction of stage movement and a consequent impoverishment of the means of expression.

However, if we lay aside prejudice, we shall find in these realizations of the Künstler-theater remarkable elements of simplification. The very shallow stage of this theatre presented an architectural arrangement in three planes : first, the proscenium, which had been given thickness sufficient to permit a doorway or entrance in each lateral member ; secondly, the middle scene, placed a short way up-stage, consisting of two sections of wall joined by a bridge of the same thickness. This arrangement was mobile ; that is to say, the bridge could be raised or lowered and the two walls moved on- or off-stage at will. This movement, of course, always took place in the same plane. When they were brought together the two formed a complete background closing the scene. In passing off-stage, they entered directly into the wings, which had the same width as the stage proper. This was nothing more than an application of the old principle of under-stage wagons or carriages whose rods, bearing a variety of decorations, travelled in slots in the stage floor. The walls were painted in a neutral tone and each was pierced with a portal and a window. These could on demand represent a street, an interior, or even the neutral frame of the actual background. It was, in fact, much like another, inner and plastic, proscenium arch. The double purpose of these walls, serving as they did either as decoration or as frame for another decoration, is without doubt of great advantage. We must remember, however, that similar architectural elements have been employed in many theatres which have in no way subscribed to the theories which Fuchs put forward regarding them.

The back-stage of the theatre was closed by

a back-drop which entered directly into the scene dock, and the floor of the back-stage could be lowered when a landscape was represented, so that the base-line where this back-drop or cyclorama met the stage was concealed. This was the third plane.

It can easily be seen that such a disposition of the stage imposes certain solutions for the scenic problem and excludes certain others. According to Fuchs, the system forces the producer to present only the essentials of the scene and to indicate only the points of greatest importance. In other words, it compelled the producer to see in the large. We recognize at once the advantages offered by such a scheme, but, on the other hand, we cannot overlook the fact that it is at the same time unnecessarily confining.

The continual sight of the same walls on the same plane produces an inevitable *ennui*. If the spectator is interested in the simplified representation of Shylock's house suggested by means of a section of wall, a little stairway, and another low wall silhouetted against the sky, he is bored when he sees these same walls return as the street in " Faust " (pl. 58) or the rampart in " Judith." Besides, the fixed stage decoration placed in a single plane does not allow of any change in the proportions of the scene. We can change the height of the stage by lowering the border but we cannot alter the depth. But since proportion is one of the most expressive of stage means, how can we remedy this immobility ? It can only be done through the medium of light.

And, in fact, the lighting system at the Künstlertheater was studied with the greatest care. The fore-stage and the middle-stage were lighted from above, while the back-stage was illuminated by special light units placed both above and below, those at the base being concealed in a pit constructed for this purpose. Fuchs increased the number of colours used to five. Besides white, yellow, blue, and red, he employed green, thus making possible greater richness and many more gradations.

One of his theories, and this time a theory justified by practice, was that the back-stage should be completely dematerialized by means of the light. The result was that in this theatre, where the back-drop was only a few yards from the spectator, astonishing effects of atmospheric distance have at times been realized. An impression of winter night on the battlements at Elsinore, seen through a cold, foggy atmosphere seemingly heavy with snow, was achieved solely through light (pl. 59).

In many cases the problems of the stage setting were solved with the greatest economy of means ; take, for example, " The Merchant of Venice," where a public place was suggested by a single column raised on two steps and silhouetted against a deep blue sky. By these simple means Venice was evoked.

We must here note one very instructive fact : the relief stage cannot dispense with the illusion of depth. What the dogmatic reformer takes away on the one hand must be restored by the artist through the play of light on the other. Only in those scenes in which the producer was successful in dematerializing the background was an impression produced. We must recognize that the question is to replace real depth by the illusion of depth and distance, and such a procedure is perfectly justifiable from the scenic standpoint without violating the principle of the relief stage.

Unfortunately, the relief stage had recourse to a much more questionable means, namely, painting. The Künstlertheater admitted painting under special conditions, for, according to Fuchs, painting, when admitted as such, was justifiable in the theatre and just as true as the plastic elements employed. It is certainly true so long as it confines itself to planes and does not venture on three dimensions, that is to say, so long as it is frankly decorative painting and does not try to depict by perspective. It is very probable that the Munich painters influenced the imagination of Fuchs to a considerable degree, so we are not surprised to hear him say that this decorative treatment of the painted backgrounds framed by a plastic architectural arrangement produces the feeling of space and depth and distance. Hence we see the stage divided into two distinct parts, one part which is plastic and architectural, where the actor describes his movements, and another part which is painted, before which the actor passes in living relief (pl. 58). But this in a way destroys the scenic unity. Scenic unity can be maintained only in those cases where either the back-drop depicts the open sky, or is a black background representing absolute depth, or lastly a curtain. The church scene in " Faust " (pl. 57) ; the throne room and the Queen's chamber in " Hamlet," were carried out in one of these three ways and, being realized by plastic elements only, produced in each case a perfect impression.

But, after all, interesting effects such as these are independent of the theoretic principle of the relief stage, for elsewhere mobile walls have been brought into play independently of the ideas of Fuchs, as for example, the stage settings of Stern for his " Macbeth " at the Deutsches Theater in Berlin. Here the different interiors and exteriors of the castle were represented by different positions of a triple row of walls which disappeared into the wings, leaving the entire stage clear for open-air scenes. Later, under the influence of certain innovations of Craig, these walls return in the form of mobile pylons forming the basic elements in other and different systems of permanent settings.

One of the most characteristic, and at the same time one of the most practical, realizations of this idea, was the first permanent setting in America, established on the stage of the Arts and Crafts Theatre, Detroit. Plates 62–64, show some of the settings obtainable by this system, which has been copied in one form or another by many of the experimental theatres in America. This permanent setting included the following units : four pylons, constructed of canvas on wooden frames— each of the three covered faces measuring two and one-half by eighteen feet ; two canvas flats—each three by eighteen feet ; two sections of stairs three feet long, and one section eight feet long of uniform eighteen-inch height ; three platforms of the same height respectively, six, eight, and twelve feet long ;

dark-green curtains slightly longer than the pylons, divided into six sections ; two folding screens for masking, covered with the same material as the curtains and as high as the pylons ; and two irregular tree-forms as set pieces. The pylons, flats, and stairs, and such added pieces as the arch and window were painted in broken colour ; the whole arrangement was backed by a plaster sky dome, and lighted by a special lighting system.

Other artists have sought to find a setting capable of many variations through the combination and repetition of elementary forms, such as cubes, blocks, and cylinders. Terence Gray in England has obtained some excellent effects with what he calls a system of hollow boxes (pl. 65–68), and the Austrian, Hans Fritz, has invented a " Würfelbühne " in which all the stage constructions resolve themselves into multiples of a cube (pl. 53). Others still have established on the stage a single architectural element, by preference a wall with one or two openings. Gaston Baty in Paris, has created one of this sort for the stage of the " Chimère," which in its other technical details follows closely the Künstlertheater of Munich. Fig. 5 shows different applications of this Baty wall with double bay, a large and a small opening. It is to be noted that in the case of any device of this kind, the number of changes that can be effected is extremely limited.

Finally, we see certain artists seeking an architectural construction which will be new for each play, but will remain more or less immutable for the duration of that piece. Thus Norman Bel Geddes has produced for " Jehanne d'Arc," not a stage decoration, but a stage structure on which all the scenes of the play are to be acted (pl. 70). Geddes himself says of this : " The setting represents not a scene, but a stage structure to play all scenes upon. On this single setting ten scenes are played, each of a totally different nature— some interiors, some exteriors, and while the dialogue is being spoken the change of the settings is made in full view of the audience. Never for an instant does one see the change in the scenes being made, from a street to a cell, from a cell to a palace, by the use of properties, banners and decorations carried by actors who are part of the scene they are making before you. The rear of the stage is filled with architectural embryos, which are never more than dimly seen in the half-light until they suddenly evolve in such significant forms as the Château of Chinon, the Altar of Rheims

York created for the performance of " As You Like It " a semi-permanent setting in which he used a form of the ancient " telari " to form the pylons for his inner-stage frame (pl. 75, 76).

With such creations as these we have already passed out of the field of the permanent setting properly speaking, and entered that of the architectural setting. To repeat several architectural elements throughout the course

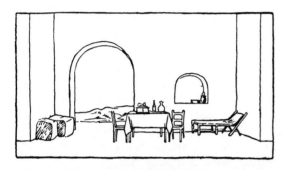

FIG. 5.—Gaston Baty : Various arrangements of a permanent setting.

Cathedral, the ramparts of Compiègne, the streets of Rouen " (pl. 70). For " Lazarus Laughed," by Eugene O'Neill, the same artist has created an architectural setting in two parts, which in its different positions forms the different sets for the play (pl. 69).

We see the same idea behind Strnad's settings for " Hamlet " (pl. 71, 72), and in Norman Macdermott's successful permanent settings for Shaw and Shakespeare (pl. 77, 78). Lee Simonson at the Theatre Guild in New

of the play is of common usage in many modern stage settings, which otherwise present very few or even no appearances of the permanent setting. It is always a question of attempting to give unity to the spectacle by the reappearance of definite motives, without at the same time giving the impression of establishing a principle once for all. We will find this basic idea developed in a number of the stage creations which form the subjects of subsequent chapters.

CHAPTER VII

THE PLASTIC SETTING

WE have seen that the return toward a stage architecture appeared first under two different aspects. On the one hand certain reformers, each proclaiming his own system, established on the stage constructions which were more or less immovable, while on the other hand another group of artists, beginning with Appia and Craig, sought for scenic means which would make it possible to give to each play a new spatial expression. These latter express environment and mood by means which at the same time assure the three-dimensional unity between the actor and the setting. As we follow this evolution we see it pushing toward a plastic synthesis always more and more pronounced, until, finally in the very latest experiments, such as Russian constructivism, its tendency seems to be solely to expand the possibilities of stage movement by means of constructions in volumes. In fact, constructivism goes even further. It often neglects quite intentionally all expression of environment and of mood.

This evolution toward a greater and greater architectonization of the stage ensemble is quite in accordance with the general tendency of the epoch. To-day, in all the arts we see this predominance of pure construction. Architecture abandons its search for style and finds a new expression in those things offered by modern construction itself as well as in the proportion of volumes. Modern decorative art, in so far as it is truly modern, is no longer the art of the decorator, but of the architect. We have even seen easel-painting when seduced by "volume" attempt to introduce architectural principles into the organization of the picture.

Since modern art is eminently constructive and plastic, proposing even for painting the principles of architecture, it is only logical that we should find its final expression in the theatre take form in settings which are architecturally constructive and plastic. It might be said of this new art of the theatre that it springs from our new sensitiveness, from what we might call our modern body-feeling, our " Körpergefühl."

The appearance in our period of the constructor, of the creator of rhythm in space, corresponds to this feeling. We have recaught a feeling for spatial rhythm to the extent that we have recaught a consciousness of physical well-being, a physical well-being produced through the muscular innervations of exercise, that is to say, produced through sport. The architectonization of all the arts which we see to-day corresponds in a way to the physical feeling of this typical man of our period, the sportsman and athlete ; and it is in part due to physical training and athletics in general that we are conscious of, and sensitive to, the play of those rhythmic articulations involved in all architectonic creation. The sensibility for plastic rhythm is based on physical sensations, and in the case of all architectural realizations it is almost as if we felt the rhythm of the movement of arms and legs. When we see the problem of the spatial stage decoration presented to us in this new light, we recognize the fundamental affinities which exist between architecture and the art of the theatre.

This feeling for space appears as an adventure of the body, since it relates man to the space which surrounds him. It is an irradiation passing from the space to the body and from the body to the space : that is to say, it is a tactile feeling. What we call " expression " in a rhythmic creation across space, majesty or gaiety or sadness in architecture, proceeds from a correspondence physically felt between man and space. Consequently, in the presence of a piece of architecture, the proportions of its different parts in relation to the human body give us the measure of its architectonic expression. In the same way the architect, the constructor, in the moment of creating his work is in bodily " rapport " with his creation in space. He stands, so to speak, with his body in this imaginary space ; he feels it on his skin, on his whole body ; he is conscious of it, and he lives in this ambience created by his imagination as the actor lives in the space of the stage.

In short, the actor and the architect resemble each other, as all creators of plastic rhythm do. Does not this " Einfühlung " [1] in space, which is a transmutation into the rhythmic articulations of space, grow out of the art of the actor ? The creator in terms of architecture is transfigured in his column and feels on his shoulders its stresses and strains. Space is the rôle of the architect ; a rôle which he plays, thanks to his particular and personal feeling, his bodyfeeling, his " Körpergefühl." The architect is the actor in space, in the same way as the stage actor is he who gives plastic shape to the word, the moulder and former of the word.

To put it in another way, we can say that the architect proceeds from his body to space as the actor proceeds from the psyche to the gesture. It might be said that the gestures of the builder also exist, and that these mount in space, and there, in separating from him, take on architectural form. The lift of his column, the movement of his vault and its rhythmic return are, after all, a language of gestures ; it is as if the feeling of an arm gently or violently raised could, so to speak, be fixed in material form.

This relation between man and space is, however, more complicated in the case of the

actor. His body is already the material of creation of the stage work. Enclosed in his body, and in the space of the stage, the actor is doubly tied to spatial expression. It is true that in speaking of expression through gesture we are accustomed to consider only the close association existing between the inner life and the body, as if the body by itself alone were already able to give the expression. In fact, all bodily action is through space and in space. In each one of its gestures the body claims space ; seizing it, or pushing it away. Hence expression is dependent on the contrast between movement and immobile space and, by consequence, gesture is only comprehensible to us because it manifests itself to us as a new relation between the body and space.

It is the stage decoration which prescribes this space about the actor. Therefore, the movement of the actors and the rhythm of the spatial setting complement each other ; and it is in this particular point that spatial creation for the stage differs from the work of architecture properly so-called.

The architect creates a relation between the space which he has organized in terms of rhythm, and consequently in terms of movement on the one hand and the immobile body on the other, but the art of the theatre creates a relation between the body in movement and the apparently immobile space surrounding it. When we contemplate a work of architecture, it is our own body which gives us the measure of its proportions, and in so doing, gives us its expression. On the contrary, it is the body of the actor which gives us the measure of the stage ensemble. Certainly, the elements of the stage decoration have their own value, but the height of a vault, the immensity of open sky, the feeling of oppression produced by a low ceiling, only become immensity, oppression and height on the stage by virtue of the relations which the actor establishes with space. Scenic expression is determined by the harmony or contrast of two rhythms— the rhythm of the movement of the actor, and the rhythm of space.

Moreover, the actor must be surrounded by

[1] Untranslatable term of Lipps' Æsthetics.

an appropriate space, because the actor detached from space is isolated in an intolerable solitude. He finds himself reduced to monologue, and the consciousness of his solitude is *for him* tragic. Thus, *for him*, being allied to space means being allied to life. The actor who in a growing passion moves up-stage carries with him the surrounding space ; he holds this space in his arms ; it is his world. For him an empty platform may take the place of space, but the decorative back-drop never. All human contacts and relations which are forced to appear before a plane incapable of being spatially conceived, lose their causality, and the spectacle becomes only a play of marionettes. Acted drama is detached from its world the moment it is detached from space. From this point of view the relief stage and similar modern solutions of the stage problem may seem inadequate, because they separate man from space and present him to us like a star in the void, detached from all the social and human contacts which drama implies. Such a procedure is bewildering because it gives too strong a physical reality to the actor and at the same time forces him to move in an altogether unreal world. This explains our feeling of frustration and uneasiness when we first see men moving in a void ; it is as if we had to accustom our eyes not only to the page we are reading, but to the distant horizon at the same time.

We have pointed out that the organization of the space about the actor is essential to the life of the drama, and if this be true, then the task of creating the stage decoration must fall to the constructor. The creative artist in architecture who himself starts from his body in order to arrive at spatial creation, requires no new effort on the part of his imagination to put himself in the place of the actor. This is true simply because by his work in spatial creation he finds himself in that place. On the contrary, the painter will always see the image of the scene before him as a picture. Only the creator in space can build from the inside out. Certainly he also will be forced

to view the stage ensemble from outside, to objectify it, but this will not be difficult, for by a sort of redoubling he lives inside his creation even as he contemplates it from without.

So, by virtue of this analogy existing between the architectonic creation and the art of the actor, we can understand why for most of the more important modern producers the plastic setting is the only form which by its very essence can conform to the needs of the mise en scène, and at the same time to our modern sensitiveness.

But in adopting this theory we expose ourselves to a disconcerting objection. We have brought all the manifestations of the art of the theatre to a fundamental conception : namely, the plastic unity of the stage. We have attempted to demonstrate that the plastic setting is opposed to the painted setting, in fact, to all settings conceived in two-dimensional planes. We replace the old *trompe l'œil* setting with its false high-lights and shadows by a plastic construction which we consider as a stage truth, a setting which has scenic verity. In place of depicting innumerable details by means of painting, we project one single element which seems characteristic, and we present it completely : thus a single column, plastic, three-dimensional, evokes a church, and in the same way a real curtain replaces the back-drop. And yet in replacing the pictorial representation by spatial elements do we not ourselves deceive the spectator ? The old scenic artist, by means of childishly exaggerated perspective, showed us forests, mountains, immovable seas, and houses whose roofs were on a level with the actor's nose. But in deceiving us, he did not dissimulate. Painting always avowed itself as painting ; it was never disguised scenic reality ; no desire to make us believe the painted tree a real tree. In our new scenic art expression is produced by means of selected elements which impress themselves on the spectator by virtue of the physical reality which we confer on them, and by consequence seem to take on a real existence. Now, by such a procedure, are we not much more guilty of deception than the old school, and in a much more dangerous way ?

The paradox of a synthetic and at the same time a realistic creation seems to give some value to the accusation of " illusionism " brought against the plastic setting at the outset of the movement. At least for the first period, that of stylized realism, the indictment seems to have a certain force. But is it true that the plastic setting rests on deceit, and does the plastic setting necessarily imply naturalism?

It would seem that from the moment a three-dimensional body presents itself frankly for what it is, there can no longer be any question of fraud or deceit. Will a plastic cube be more of a fraud than a painted one ? A pyramid more than a triangle ? The error is not there. Plastic execution does not deceive in itself, but nevertheless by the fact that it suggests the existence of physical forms it seems by the weight of its presence to hold us close to reality and to prevent psychological suggestion and interpretation.

But have we not seen that the plastic setting represents above all the art of spatial rhythm, an art of architectural abstraction ? To mistake the rhythmic language of spatial organization for naturalism is to show oneself insensible to the essence of architecture. To reproach the modern three-dimensional tendency with illusionism is thus to confuse the means with the bad use that has sometimes been made of those means. It would be equally consistent to say that architecture, the abstract art *par excellence*, is naturalistic. On the contrary, it is because of the relationship which exists between the laws of the stage and the laws of architecture that we can push synthesis so far in the creation of the plastic setting.

In fact, the line which the art of the theatre has followed in its evolution from the days of stylized realism, a course in which the synthetic character of the plastic setting was always more and more accentuated, has been itself the best argument against this early misunderstanding. It is perhaps worth while here to illustrate the course of this evolution

through a series of settings for the same play —" King Lear." First we have the celebrated setting for Antoine's production at the Odéon, Paris, 1904, of which we have already spoken (pl. 3, 4). What the merits of such a setting could have been, even from the naturalistic standpoint, it is difficult to understand to-day. Admitting the moral value of Antoine's struggles for the " Théâtre Libre," his productions when viewed to-day seem to have very little in the way of artistic quality to recommend them.

Next, we show Reinhardt's production of " Lear," with settings by Czeschka (pl. 17, 18). When one realizes that only four years separated these productions, the progress seems astonishing. In these settings and costumes, Czeschka, by means of large decorative motifs and a special use of colour, attempted to create the impression of a state of barbarism, but the whole remains still more or less decorative. The settings which Professor Strnad has designed for Reinhardt's new production of " Lear " at the Josefstadt mark a further advance toward the creation of the mood. The impression of grandeur is secured primarily by the height of the setting, which seems to lose itself in the great blackness above, an effect which unfortunately the reproduction cannot give (pl. 197).

This tendency, constantly more and more accentuated toward a psychological expression, the creation of the mood, is excellently illustrated in the " King Lear " designed by Norman Bel Geddes (pl. 94). Geddes himself gives the following commentary on its significance : " The whole of this play is in the mood of pitiless shadow and tempestuous motion, as though the primary forces of nature were in a state of violent convulsion, maliciously tearing things from their proper places. Nearly all of the characters are primitive, cold, hard, stone-like, and so I visualized them and costumed them accordingly. The garments are heavy and seem to hold the body inside of them fast to the earth. The movements of the people are of a nature to carry out this massive statical quality. The scenes

are all dominated by a feeling of age and cold-
ness. They come and fade away in ironical
darkness, replacing one another without pause.
Shapes focus according to their importance.
The common elements used throughout are
huge rocks in one form or another."

Here we are far from the stylized realism
of the Reinhardt period. The suppression of
reality continues, however, and finally Paul
Medenwald produces a" King Lear " at Gera,
with settings by Paul Ott, which are reduced to
some stairs, a few properties, light and movement (pl. 194, 195). " What is important,"
says the director in his commentary, " is
the tension of the movements and their direction. Throughout the performance Lear enters
from up-stage, mounts the stairs, descends in
front and disappears in the depths of the fore-
stage. Regan is placed at the left and Goneril
at the right. They mount the stairs each

toward the other—midway, the line of the
father's movement, separates them. All the
messengers enter from the depth, necessitating on the part of the actors on the stage a
great concentric movement forward toward
the depths of the fore-stage." In Jessner's
arrangements we shall find analogous scenic
means employed, but with less rigidity.

It is to be noted that throughout this
evolution the mise en scène has been seeking
for expression by plastic means, sometimes
finding those means in the stage decoration
properly speaking, sometimes in certain elements only, or lastly, in the movements of the
actors. A more detailed study will assuredly
impose certain restrictions on this general
observation but in its broad lines this is the
road which the theatre of this generation has
followed. It now remains to study it in detail,
taking it up step by step.

CHAPTER VIII

THE EVOLUTION OF THE MODERN SETTING

THE evolution of scenic conceptions which this brief résumé has shown us, corresponds to both the artistic and literary tendencies of the epoch. In the stage decoration of the naturalistic period—even when it takes such charming form as Dobujinsky's set for Turgenieff's " A Month in the Country," produced by Stanislavsky (pl. 7, 8)—we note that the concern to evoke the atmosphere of the play results in a faithful copy of an interior with a plastic rendering of all its details, even to door-frames, ceiling consoles and the rest. Such a procedure generally produces settings which are difficult to support to-day, but when touched by the feeling of a true artist it is undeniable that this laborious reproduction of reality often succeeds in creating the atmosphere of the piece. However, as we move forward, we very soon find literature itself proposing other problems. In Germany we witness the birth of a new drama of style, represented by the works of Hugo von Hofmannsthal, Vollmoeller, Eulenberg and Schmidtbonn, to mention only a few. Many of these plays, which, from the point of view of our feeling to-day, are distinctly romantic, found their ambience in the stylized settings of the first Reinhardt period. The " interplay of souls," as it has been called, which is the essence of the poetic works of a Maeterlinck, were visually interpreted by the gauze hangings with which Ludwig von Hoffmann composed his settings for "Aglavaine et Sélysette " (pl. 15, 16). These settings, which are quite different from those of the naturalistic school, present a poetic envelope for the action —half real and half unreal—and this semi-

real effect is reinforced by the interplay of light and shadow.

At the same time, the architectural setting of which we have just spoken was developing under the influence of Craig and others. In spite of its evolution this type has often preserved something of its primitive aspect. Creations such as those of Rosse for " Casanova," Thompson for " The Firebrand," and Isler for "Arlechino," although of a later date, show us this form much as it was in the beginning (pl. 86–88). But in general this architectural setting moved toward a greater synthesis. Already Gordon Craig had enunciated the principle that an outstanding and characteristic object, a portico, a balcony, a fountain, must be chosen as the centre of the stage setting, and about this crux all the other scenic elements must be grouped. Naturally as the idea of synthesis took possession of the field the secondary and subordinate elements tended to disappear into the background and finally became blotted out. The part for the whole, the scene suggested by a single characteristic element, became one of the chief means of expression employed by the modern mise en scène.

Here, however, it is necessary to make an important distinction. This choice of characteristic elements was in the beginning inseparable from the disposition on the stage of these same elements ; a disposition or manner of setting them which gave them in spite of all simplification more or less the aspect of a complete stage decoration. This is true for most of the settings at the Künstlertheater in Munich. For example, in the setting which

Fritz Erler created for " The Merchant of Venice " a single column placed before a low wall backed by the empty blue of the sky suggested the piazza in Venice. The important point here is that this setting successfully evoked the impression because at bottom it lacked nothing ; a piazza can appear like this from one point of view. The first simplified stage decorations always remained, so to speak, within the limits of verisimilitude (pl. 57, 58).

Synthesis, as one hears it talked of in our own days, is, however, something quite different. To-day we often present the characteristic element removed from every other relation and outside all naturalistic verisimilitude. A setting such as that of Emil Pirchan for " Boris Godounoff " (pl. 90), or that of Hrska for " As You Like It " (pl. 91), suggests a forest to us by means of some trees placed on a platform in the centre of an otherwise empty stage. In his setting for the "Napoleon" by Grabbe, César Klein makes the Paris mob dance about a single great red lantern (pl. 93). To-day we are no more surprised to see a house bathed in full sunlight appear before a black velvet curtain (pl. 223) than we are in Pitoëff's " Saint Joan " to see the steps of a parallel and platform lead up to three Gothic arches isolated in the middle of the stage. Robert Edmond Jones evokes the atmosphere of " Macbeth " by means of a series of deformed arches which raise themselves in the void (pl. 201) ; Jo Mielziner's fixed setting for " Faust," a construction of steps and arches, is isolated before the cyclorama (pl. 95), and so on through many other examples.

In leaving the artist free from all concern for exterior verisimilitude in his setting, this new concept permits him to move toward the realization of greater emotional expression. It is no longer important to suggest an exterior reality, but rather to allow the scene designer full play to express and transmit through the medium of his setting, the emotions which the play awakens in him. In this way this new form of stage decoration becomes definitely involved with expressionism in its literary-dramatic form.

Expressionism in dramatic literature, born in Germany before 1914 and reinforced later by the upheavals produced by the war, has given to the world only a few formless plays, a mass of scenes consisting of impressions and expressions escaped for the most part from the poetic will and animated by such rigid symbolization of human types as those we see in Kaiser's " Gas." These dramas are emaciated constructions—" constructions of glass and iron," in the words of Bernhard Diebold, " in which men in the form of cubist marionettes proclaim mechanically and artificially in telegraphic style their revolutionary speeches." However, by liberating the stage in a sort of frenzy from all established laws of drama, and by taking up again the loose dramatic technique of Büchner and Grabbe and making it à la mode, the expressionists forced the visual presentation to conform to its theories, to forget all its preoccupation with the true and to present only more or less abstract forms. Now we see the settings characterized by twisted and deformed lines and towering, tumble-down or cubist masses ; all attempts to express a soul state. It has to be admitted that some of these expressions were at times arresting, and we agree with Diebold that the visual images realized in the presentation of expressionist drama have been much more interesting and much more important for the history of the theatre of this epoch than the actual expressionist plays themselves.

In the following chapter we analyse the elements employed by this school of psychological expression, but here we go no further than a description of the outward aspect of its representative settings. In the majority of cases the most striking exterior characteristic of this synthetic stage decoration is the fact that at bottom it is an incomplete setting, consisting of isolated elements on an otherwise empty stage. Any attempt to complete the stage picture would in fact be a movement toward reality, which is no longer wanted and is no longer a desirable end. This fear of reality was so strong that we have seen even interiors presented by indications only. Sometimes, as in Robert E. Jones' setting for " Beyond," it is a window or a door adroitly placed which evokes the entire interior (pl. 96, 97). Sometimes, as Lee Simonson has done in his extremely interesting and ingenious series of settings for Werfel's " Bocksgesang," in order to reinforce the characteristic atmosphere, the ceiling and some sections of wall are removed and these incomplete interiors are placed in the middle of a landscape formed by the cyclorama which surrounds them (pl. 100, 101). Or again, we are allowed to see a construction at one side, as in the case of Hofman's setting for " Une Affaire de Famille " (pl. 99). But the usual solution in this manner is the screen, and we shall find that screen settings occupy an important place in modern stage decoration. Plates 106 and 107 show Emil Pirchan's screens for Wedekind's " Marquis von Keith " and for " Boris Godounoff." Jean Hugo has set Ben Jonson's " The Silent Woman " with screens (pl. iv). Babić at Zagreb uses two gold screens placed in different positions for the setting for " Twelfth Night." Lee Simonson uses them for " Back to Methuselah " and for " The Faithful " (pl. 108), here following the indications of the author himself. W. R. Fuerst created for " Le Mariage de Figaro " a screen, both sides of which could be utilized. By giving its leaves different positions all five settings for the play were produced (pl. 110, 111). And finally this means conquered tragedy in Craig's screen settings for " Hamlet " and in Terence Gray's luminous screens shown in plates 114–115.

Again, more or less realistic settings are made " modern " by presenting them incompletely. Hermann Krehan, for example, places his setting for Kaiser's " Jüdische Wittwe " before a black curtain, leaving an architectural construction in the centre through an opening in which the sky is seen (pl. 89), though it is clear that without the black curtain it would make an ordinary setting. But the most typical example of such an adaptation is to be seen in the setting for Gorky's "Lower Depths," as produced at the Volksbühne in Berlin (pl. 104). Here it was a question of modernizing a play which had been known for years as the very incarnation of naturalism. How was it to be done ? Nothing more simple. A perfectly naturalistic setting was arranged on the stage ; then the ceiling was removed and on the back-drop the title of the play was written in luminous letters ; the trick was done. To say the least, this seems a very superficial utilization of the modern means of expression.

Again, the modern incomplete setting is often combined with certain fixed elements. In this case it is not a question of a fixed architecture for all plays, but of the employment of a number of invariable elements for the duration of one play. Some platforms and stairs make possible the arrangement of special movements and groupings, but being more or less unchangeable for the time of the play, they are altered and given variety by the addition of variable elements.

Later we shall see what an important aid to the producer platforms and stairs can be ; how they facilitate and expand stage movement and hence make for an enlarged scenic expression.

The greater the evolution of the mise en scène toward synthesis the more important it became to have different levels on which to unfold the action. These levels were achieved by means of platforms, inclined runways and stairs, all of which sustained and developed the movement of the actors. We now arrive almost at once at what was called scenic dynamism. It can be said here that of all the plastic elements which have appeared, it is the organization of the practicability of the stage, the organization of the stage in terms of levels, inclines and stairs which is most likely to survive in the modern stage decoration ; even as Appia prophetically declared.

This organization of the different levels is, as we have just said, sometimes combined with other elements, and again it is sometimes seen with practically no decorative illustration. For example, we see Jessner in his setting for

" Richard III " abandon almost altogether the use of any decorative element. This setting consisted of a platform raised below a wall pierced by a portal with sometimes a great stairway leading up to the platform ; this disposition sufficed for the action of the entire play (pl. 123). There is Strnad's " Hamlet " in Vienna with again an arrangement of two platforms and some plastic pillars (pl. 71, 72). Pitoëff creates for " Macbeth " a very interesting arrangement of steps and platforms (pl. 117). The " Richard III " of Babić at Zagreb has a platform in three inclined levels (pl. 119). In plate 217 we see the beautiful surfaces of Heckroth's stage construction at Münster for " Alexander Balus " and the blocks and planes of the same artist for " Theodora " (pl. 120–121). Here we note the possibilities for the grouping of masses inherent in such a conception of the stage decoration. Often we meet with platforms in three levels as in " L'Homme et son Désir " of the Swedish Ballet (pl. 122). Finally, Emil Pirchan in Jessner's production of " Empörung des Lucius " of Bluth presents a stage construction which by its inclined planes and its aspects in general is already very close to the creations of the constructivists (pl. 124). Traugott Müller uses a similar method to suggest the ship in " Segel am Horizont " (pl. 125).

Sometimes the great expressionist producer, Jessner, adds some plastic elements or some portions of painted settings to his organization of different levels. His production of "Othello" shows two platforms with steps superimposed one above the other (pl. 126–129). He uses only indications of settings, but they are always plastic. A balcony, two sections of an enormous double door, a bed, give all the necessary ambience. In his "Macbeth," designed by Walter Reiman, the same platform recurs in all the scenes (pl. 130, 131). Here the very expressive settings are more complete.

We now arrive at a new stage. It is now the stairway, the platform, the different planes for the action which are charged with maintaining the plastic character of the stage. The other elements, of which a highly developed synthesis no longer demands a verisimilitude, can henceforth be represented by flat painting. In fact, by abandoning all exterior verisimilitude, expressionism has often enough come back to painting for a part of its scenic expression, and further on we shall see a complete, expressionist, painted setting develop side by side with a plastic one. As for the plastic setting itself, we see the spatial organization of the stage-block combined with painted elements. These take the form of little painted set-pieces, a species of embryonic decoration, or units which suffice to place the action. Thus the platform in three levels which Ludwig Sievert arranged for " Penthesilea " has been combined with settings in two dimensions (pl. 118) in the same way as a similar construction by Pitoëff for " Le Juif du Pape " (pl. 216). Harry Täuber in Vienna mounts " When We Dead Awaken " with platforms cut to form angles which repeat in a way the rhythm of the landscape executed in flat-painted wings and set-pieces (pl. 134, 135). For the production of " Faust " at the Odéon, Paris, W. R. Fuerst established a platform in two levels and then altered its aspect by the settings in two dimensions placed on it (pl. 223). This is evidently a principle which is attended with a certain risk, but often the question of economy is more important than the question of æsthetics. The talent of the scene designer and the intensity of his vision must save the ensemble. It must be remembered that great as are the possibilities for scenic expression inherent in all such procedures, there is, nevertheless, in all of them a tendency to impoverish the stage spectacle.

Often it would be preferable to do away with all compromise, and in place of allowing the substitution of elements, which are only makeshifts, to show us the stage construction in all its nudity. In a setting like that of Heckroth for " Theodora " (pl. 120, 121) we have already seen what great beauty lies in an arrangement of blocks. In the same way Reinhold Ockel in " Bauernzorn " groups his actors on different levels and thus achieves an arresting effect solely through the opposition of these different levels aided by the lighting (pl. 137). Claude Bragdon shows in " Cyrano " an arrangement consisting of silhouettes before an illuminated cyclorama placed on an almost bare stage (pl. 136), and finally Berg in a mise en scène at the Intima Teatern, Stockholm, offers us only a simple groundwork placed on an otherwise empty stage (pl. 139).

It is evident that the plastic mise en scène cannot be stripped beyond this point. But if the aim is to achieve an abstraction of all concrete reality, another means is often employed which, while conserving its plastic character, at the same time remains sufficiently abstract to make possible a variety of interpretations. This means is found in draperies or curtains, and we are not surprised to find that they have acquired a place of considerable importance in modern production.

These curtains first appeared decorated, particularly in England, with designs in the style of nineteen hundred. To this class belong the curtain settings of Wilkinson, Rutherston and Rosse, shown in plates 140–143. Later, the curtain idea was adopted by the vaudeville stage and the musical revue, and in recent years we have seen it triumphant in silver and gold in the " Follies " and its prototypes in all the capitals of the world. In general the legitimate stage has preferred simpler curtains. We find them at the beginning of the movement in settings such as those of von Hoffmann for " Aglavaine et Sélysette " (pl. 16). Their use quickly became generalized, and to-day there is hardly a " modern " theatre, no matter how poor, which does not possess a stock. We see them sometimes in dark blue or black, serving as a neutral background for the setting proper, and sometimes in a determined colour, forming a part of the stage decoration, or even the entire setting. Many pleasing solutions have been obtained in this way, as for example, Vlastislav Hofman's arrangements for " The Bacchantes " and " Columbus," produced at the National Theatre, Prague (pl. 144, 145). Again, there

are the two Molière productions of Josef Čapek, " Le Misanthrope " (pl. 146) and " Le Bourgeois Gentilhomme " (pl. 147). Robert E. Jones suggests the great fountain in " Pelléas et Mélisande " by means of gauze draperies arranged over skeleton frames (pl. 204). In short, it would require pages to illustrate the different applications of this decorative element.

In the modern theatre the use of curtains increased to a point where it became almost an abuse. Above all, the custom of playing certain scenes on the apron before the front curtain seems to have no justification. For while a curtain on the stage proper can signify most anything, according to the intention of the producer, the same cannot be said for the front curtain of the stage. This drapery, which the spectators have seen used simply as a means for closing the proscenium opening, has become for that reason unfitted to serve as a decorative means ; the imagination is unable suddenly to accept it in another way. It might be possible to play in front of this curtain whenever the character of the scene is such that the action may be said to require nothing to complete it ; when it is, so to speak, played in " the void " ; when the background has no function whatever to perform. But in many cases the immediate presence of the curtain gives it a character much too real to admit of any such negation. It is forced on the attention for what it is in actuality—the front curtain of the stage. The result is that it is no longer sufficiently " non-existent " to create that " non-existent " ambience which the producer is seeking through this means. On the contrary, the spectator is only too conscious of the fact that it is nothing more than a makeshift, a way out, that is to say, a means of concealing the stage during a change of setting.

If, on the one hand, we see decorative synthesis followed by combinations made up of platforms or different levels, coupled with suggestive elements, we shall see on the other what we call the complete stage setting seeking expression by adopting the tendencies of contemporary art. Oblique lines and cubist masses make their entrance on the stage. At first, it is not cubism properly speaking, but a conception which approaches cubism. A creation such as Vesnine's interesting setting for " L'Annonce faite à Marie " at the Kamerny Theatre, Moscow (pl. 150) is less cubist than that by the same artist for " Phèdre " (pl. 151), or that of Heckroth for " Salome " at Münster (pl. 148). But the movement progresses, and finally in Jorgulesco's designs for " Macbeth," produced in Boston (pl. 361), we feel as much as in Vesnine's " Phèdre " the force which cubist forms can express. More dogmatic and less expressive, Oskar Schlemmer creates for Grabbe's " Don Juan und Faust " pure stereometric forms without concerning himself about the discordance between the naturalistic costumes of the actors and the setting in which they move (pl. 154). And finally the Italian futurists, in their advanced theatres, carry this stereometric scene to its ultimate expression (pl. 156, 157). Unfortunately, while the ideas of a Prampolini are often interesting as projects, realization, such as his " Pantomima Futurista," presented in Paris, reveals a dilettantism which accords very badly with the grandiloquent utterances with which futurists in general have regaled the world.

The majority of these settings make clear the influence which modern mechanism in general has on the thought of the artists concerned. Many of them are haunted by the beauty of the machine, and if it were not outside our field, much might be said of the results of that obsession on modern art in general. It is astonishing how much lack of understanding exists. We see artists influenced out of measure by the work of the engineer and, as they often have no knowledge concerning the technical laws which control machinery, we see them bring into being strange assemblages of forms which outwardly resemble a machine of some sort, but a machine which does not go ; in short, a parody of the machine. The machine of the mechanical engineer is beautiful because its forms correspond to a law of economy of force, an inner law not visible but manifest in the strength of its form, but the machine of the artist is usually only ridiculous and silly, because it corresponds to nothing. If we hear Gino Severini speak of " Mechanism in Art " or Fernand Léger of the "Æsthetic of the Machine," we can certainly share their admiration for the machine, but it will be for the true machine. We refuse to discover any beauty in the infantile machines which Depero proposes for the theatre, such as his " machina scenografica," which carries the recommendation " rumoreggiante in movimento."

Since a quite new form of dramatic literature was inspired by the machine, a language of forms had to be found to represent mechanism on the stage. There are in fact a number of dramatic authors who have come under this influence in the same way as the painters ; but, while the painters have drawn from this inspiration only an exterior formalism, the playwrights have found new themes. These themes are largely sociological, whether they have considered the evolution of mechanism as a new slavery for man and have described a revolt of the working class against this tyranny, or whether they have seen in it, on the contrary, the liberation of man through the conquest of the forces of Nature. Such plays as Kaiser's " Gas," Čapek's " R.U.R." and Toller's " Maschinenstürmer " have been played all over the world. Everywhere they have compelled the artists in the theatre to find new scenic solutions for this new mechanism.

In looking at the results, the best solutions seem to be those which most closely approach the true machine. Thus, the setting which Fritz Kiesler has created for "R.U.R." (pl. 158, 159) is an extremely seductive and imaginative transposition of the elements of the machine. It is a setting which acts, which plays a part and lives with a plausible electro-mechanical life of its own. Mahnke's settings for " Anarchie auf Silian " (pl. 160) and Täuber's for " Gas " (pl. 161), are examples of successful arrangements of the same kind, though deprived of the life which Kiesler gives to his.

But very soon the machine setting becomes independent of the machine play, and we see a strange flowering of ballets, pantomimes and other productions in the machine theatre. Thus Picabia has created a setting for " Relâche " composed entirely of reflectors (pl. 155) with which he produced a series of changing light effects. The settings of Robert E. Jones, designed for the ballet, " Skyscrapers," in New York, are associated in a way, but they do not belong in the category of machine settings, being rather a decorative expression of a machine theme without themselves being machine. But what is there to say of those futurist ballets such as " L'Anikam de l'an 2000," by Casavola, of " The Psychology of Machines," a mechanical ballet of Silvio Mix, or of Depero's " Balletto della Locomotiva," in which the dancers represent parts of a locomotive, while the setting shows a dissected railway system ? It is difficult to believe that these things can ever get beyond clever spoofs ; although sometimes, as in those which we reproduce (pl. 157, 162, 163), rather charming and amusing ones.

With the advent of constructivism the plastic organization of the stage presents itself in a new aspect. It might be said to be the end of another branch which sprang from the same preoccupation with technical construction, but (whether the results be good or bad) the point of departure of this constructivist conception is at least a point of view essentially of the theatre. Constructivism proposed to develop an element inherent in the theatre itself : that is to say, scenic dynamism.

Already Tairoff and what he calls, for want of a better name, " Neo-Realism," show analogous tendencies. According to Tairoff : " Everything must serve the actor. The actor must serve himself. He must clothe himself with the spirit of his concept or idea as with a mask, and each object and agent must clothe itself with the spirit of its particular art expression. The voice of the actor must sound like music, his movements must give rhythm to the play, his technique must be the external form of the internal. The stage that serves these expressions must have different rhythmic levels and the scenery height, width, depth and moving surfaces." [1] This sounds cryptic but, in fact, Tairoff (in developing the rhythmic elements in stage movement) has achieved an extraordinary scenic life. He has given a dizzy movement to an old operetta like " Giroflé-Girofla " (pl. 166), and a remarkable dynamism to " Phèdre," which attained a great tragic style and at the same time a style altogether new and modern. From the theatrical point of view, Tairoff, with his concern for scenic life, belongs among the great producers of the Reinhardt type ; but from the æsthetic standpoint he is much more in accord with modern feeling. In developing a new scenic dynamism, based on an almost scientific study of rhythmic movement, and hence on a rhythmic stylization of movement and bodily expression, he approaches the researches of a Meyerhold.

If, in the work of a Meyerhold or an Eisenstein, there were only a seeking for a new style to be applied to the action and the movement of the players in general, one could accept their realizations without reserve. But it is not only that—these researches themselves are based on another conception, a conception more or less deceptive. In fact, for Meyerhold, the actor is nothing more than a worker on the level with the industrial worker. With the assistance of studies in " bio-mechanics," the actor learns to be conscious of himself and of his movements as if he were a perfected machine. This is the " robot " of Čapek become actor. If this actor-robot had been conceived in the spirit of Craig's " Uebermarionette " in order to escape the imperfections, which, according to Craig, are inherent in the actor, one could understand it. But both Meyerhold and Eisenstein envisage the actor from quite another point of view. For them it is simply a question of bio-mechanism, of the greatest economy of effort, of the application of Taylorism to the stage (fig. 6). It is this flat, mean rationalism which spoils their

[1] Huntly Carter, *The New Spirit in the European Theatre*, London, 1925.

conception of the stage action as it spoils their conception of the setting.

Constructivism in the theatre aims at giving the maximum of intensity to the stage movements by establishing different planes for the action ; these planes being created by platforms of such a height and depth that the movements of the human body can be fully developed. It is evident that all realizations along these lines correspond perfectly to the third end or purpose of the stage decoration, that of the establishment of a plastic unity between the actor and the scenic ensemble. But we often find constructivism far from

pression in compensation it gives to the actor his full importance. For it remains for the actor alone on this scaffold to reconstruct by his own efforts the atmosphere of the drama. But glance for a moment at the form in which constructivism presents his acting.

Inclined planes, slopes pitched to an angle of forty-five degrees, stairs, ladders in a vertical position, platforms at dizzy heights—these are the elements which constructivism offers to the evolutions of the actor. Besides, the actors of Meyerhold have to submit to an education similar to that given to acrobats. In his school of the theatre there are courses in " The

FIG. 6.—Taylorized Gesture in the Russian Theatre.

According to Huntly Carter a spirit which he calls Taylorism—American Taylorism—animates the modern Russian theatre and manifests itself in a new style. The aim of this system is to produce the greatest efficiency in the worker even though reducing him to the status of an energy-saving automaton.

(*By courtesy of* Mr Huntly Carter.)

all seeking for characterization in terms of the setting, far from all expression of mood or of atmosphere. We are not surprised to hear a representative of this tendency say, with disdain, " I care nothing at all about mood " ; and settings like those by Rabino-vitch for " Lysistrata " (pl. 169) or for " Don Carlos " (pl. 168), especially the former, with all its highly spiritual interpretation of the Greece of antiquity—are rejected by the pure constructivists as being too naturalistic. They wish to discredit, in fact, all experiment in the field of decorative expressionism by the term " illusionism." Every setting which aims at reflecting the atmosphere of the play is compromised in advance by the epithet of " illusionist."

If constructivism eliminates dramatic ex-

Technology of the living Body " and in " Bio-mechanics." Here they learn to run, to climb, even to jump a train. All the movements are standardized. This education—valuable certainly if utilized in the service of a great art—prepares the actors of Meyerhold solely for Communist propaganda. It is felt in the choice of plays. But even if the actor-acrobat finds himself at home on his high scaffold, playing a rôle of social passion, it is difficult to imagine a classic drama or a psychological play presented in the same way. Also, quite logically, Meyerhold condemns the psychologic theatre for " its lack of equilibrium to the detriment of the body." To concern oneself with psychology on the stage is, according to him, to " search an ash-heap without value."

Certainly it happens sometimes that a producer can bring a stage construction of this kind to the service of a play with which it accords, and for which it is in keeping. Thus Tairoff with his constructivist setting for Chesterton's " The Man Who Was Thursday," with its elevators and its little interiors, established on little platforms (pl. 175), produced an impression of seething life. Karlheinz Martin has utilized a constructivist scaffold for Wedekind's " Franziska " (pl. 176). But, in general, it is the physical gesture, which is most at home on the constructivist stage with its platforms and varied levels. It is a mixed form of spectacle in which admiration for the prowess of the acrobats is confused with interest in the action. Also, many constructivist settings recall the stage arrangements of certain acrobatic acts in the music-hall and in vaudeville.

Here another factor enters into play : the modern passion for the circus and the music-hall. It is very much the fashion just now (if one wishes to be the very last word) to find in spectacles of this kind a form superior to the theatre, and that not only in Russia, but in the rest of Europe and America as well. There is boundless admiration for the clown, who, solely by his acting and a few properties which he carries with him, produces all the atmosphere he requires. In Russia, it is, above all, Eisenstein who, in his " Proletkult-theater " was inspired by circus performances. His actors are workmen acrobats who " perform biting satires on Russia and the outer world on the trapeze or slack-wire, by dancing upside down, by kicking off each other's hats, standing on each other's faces and making funny grimaces."[1] Is it necessary to insist on the dethronement of intelligence which such spectacles as these reveal ? (pl. 182.)

By pretending to be concerned solely with the development of the possibilities of stage movement, the constructivist setting has an air of false modesty. This stage decoration effaces itself before the actor much less, in

[1] Huntly Carter, *op. cit.*

fact, than the fixed architectural setting. It attracts the eye by its unusual and novel appearance, and turns the attention from the acting, which it modestly wishes to serve. Its construction is in harmony perhaps with the evolutions of the actor, but by the fact that, in many cases, there is no connection between this construction and the play itself, this setting takes on a life of its own entirely outside the dramatic action. There is one element, above all, which seems dangerous in this sense ; the studied visibility of all the constructive elements. Other stage settings employ platforms as well, but they are covered or hidden by flats or other parts of the set. Here, however, nothing must be hidden, all is in the nude. If these assemblages of open woodwork resembling bridge-construction give us an æsthetic pleasure analogous to that which we receive from the beauty of machines, it must be said that this spectacle, beautiful as it may be in itself, has little connection with the drama, at least with the drama which we know. Evidently a new " commedia dell'arte " would fit very well into this frame.

It is interesting to look into the reasons why Russian constructivism holds so strongly to the visibility of the constructive elements employed in these settings. In condemning all stage illusion, it proposes to present solely " that which is." In a world as unreal as that of the stage, where everything—action, acting, and gesture—takes place in unreality and only becomes real through the medium of a series of tacitly accepted conventions, in a world where nothing presents " that which is " and cannot present it, constructivism wishes to present a quite limited reality, a constructive reality adapted to the movements of the actor. Thus, constructivism under its abstract aspect and under the seductive forms which the Russian imagination knows how, sometimes, to give it, hides the same frankly rationalistic idea that we saw dominating its conception of acting.

Consequently, we are not astonished to hear Russian stage directors, when they employ mechanical objects of everyday use, give as a

FIG. 7.—Diagram of Movements for a Course in Physical Education.

The Russians are attempting to train for citizenship through compulsory physical education. This is manifested in the workers' theatre in a course in "Bio-mechanics." The Director of the physical training school is Eisenstein, inventor of the circus stage.

(*By courtesy of* Mr Huntly Carter.)

reason, that these objects are familiar to the workmen who make use of them in their work. Hence the constructivist settings can be composed of ladders, gangways, reaping-machines, as in Meyerhold's " Earth Turning "—a jazz will be produced by motor-horns, typewriters, pieces of metal, not at all because of the scenic qualities of these elements, but solely because they are there comprehensible to the workman. It is by this rationalistic and rather simple spirit that the constructivist principle unites with Meyerhold's preoccupation with social problems. For him the art of the theatre has no right to exist unless it serves society ; no right at all if it does not itself engender some social events in that society. The actor must become " an instrument, a bill-poster for social passions." For the masses, he says, nothing is of any value except that which unites them collectively. It is in a spirit of social utilitarianism that he envisages his art, and it is this same sense of practical reality which Russian constructivism reveals throughout. Despite this rationalistic spirit, constructivism has given the stage an abstract form such as it has never seen before, and it is in this drive toward the abstract that the real novelty of constructivism resides. This abstract aspect has seduced many men of the theatre in all countries. In Germany and in America, and even in little Belgium, constructivism has found its disciples. The travelling Flemish theatre " Het Vlaamsche Volkstoneel " carries constructivist settings with it through all the little towns of Belgium (pl. 179). Scenic elements have been borrowed from Russian constructivism without the spirit which gave them birth always being borrowed at the same time. It is possible that this constructivist tendency might evolve a quite new form of theatre, but it is also possible that it will end, on the contrary, by tiring us out quite quickly, just as in the end we are wearied by every tendency in the theatre which lacks inner emotion. Already there are indications of a return, and we have seen the same Karlheinz Martin who mounted Wedekind on constructivist scaffolds re-

turn to what is called to-day " Neue Sachlichkeit."

But the most striking indication of such a return has been given by Meyerhold himself. In his recent productions the great Russian producer seems in fact to have completely abandoned constructivism. Let us look at his mise en scène for " The Inspector General " (pl. 183) or even his work of 1924-25 shown in plates 184, 185 ; here we look in vain for any trace of what we know as constructivism. If he remains true to his principles in his direction of the action and in his use of projections (pl. 184) the same cannot be said for the exterior aspect of the stage, which is distinctly reminiscent of the scenes shown in plates 138-139 ; that is to say, an empty stage. He goes even further, for his stage is not only empty ; it is also perfectly flat, completely lacking in levels for the action, and stripped of all platforms, ladders, "practicables " and the rest. It appears, then, that production is possible without these means. Here in Meyerhold we see how ephemeral even the most revolutionary dogmas can be.

Although the form of constructivism has to a large extent disappeared, the spirit of realism which gave birth to it seems to survive still in that new tendency called in Germany " Die Neue Sachlichkeit " ; the very last word in production. The term itself cannot be translated ; " Neo-Realism " is not synonymous with it, and besides, the term " Neo-Realism " has been used by Tairoff to designate his own personal tendency in production ; a tendency which must not be confused with the " Neue Sachlichkeit."

In Germany the term " Neue Sachlichkeit " has had a great success. In every field of the arts it is à la mode. The latest school of painting is " Neue Sachlichkeit " ; the theatre has followed, and now there is hardly a manifestation of everyday life which has not been tagged with the same title. In Karl Sternheim's bombastic comedy, " Die Schule von Uznach," in which a group of young women make full use of their erotic charms in the name of " Neue Sachlichkeit," we see it enter the field of dramatic literature.

Although the term is found everywhere, it is by no means easy to define. When applied to the stage it seems to indicate a tendency to employ the means of expression at the disposal of the mise en scène, not in any illustrative sense, but simply when and where those means are needed. The practical demands of the action justify their use without further explanation. If you need an elevation, a platform, put it on the stage, and don't be concerned about its significance for the scene. If you need a stairway on which to group your people, put it there and don't worry over the fact that the action is supposed to pass in the Sahara. It is evident that any such broad interpretation of the word is bound to cover experiments which are widely separated and quite different in character. For example, we have seen Karlheinz Martin, in the name of " Neue Sachlichkeit " use a painted stage decoration of very much the old style (pl. 281). Evidently, since the producer " needed " a painted set, the " Neue Sachlichkeit " can justify it.

In this way—if we have understood the broad and enigmatic term—the " Neue Sachlichkeit " may be either all or nothing. And yet it seems that behind this tendency there exists the same respect for the practical, the same rationalistic spirit which we found constituting the basis for constructivism. The " Neue Sachlichkeit," like constructivism, would reduce the mise en scène to " what exists " ; would also disregard all and every need for expression in order to satisfy only the immediate necessities of the realization. " Don't get lost in the fog," it says, " be ' sachlich '." It is probable that if this counsel be followed in a frankly rationalistic way, the arts will very soon be empty and devoid of significance.

Fortunately, the danger of this happening does not seem very great. To-day, artistic tendencies pass with the swiftness of new styles in hats, and the " Neue Sachlichkeit " after a brief life will descend into the tomb to join its comrades, Naturalism, Expressionism, and Constructivism. There is, however, this difference : all the other reforms have bequeathed us something which can be set down as an acquisition, a definite asset, something durable which has survived them. But with the " Neue Sachlichkeit " it is difficult to see as yet what it can leave to enrich the store acquired from former experiments ; the stock of modern means which we have here attempted to group and classify.

CHAPTER IX

THE MODERN MEANS OF EXPRESSION

WE have seen that nearly all modern stage decoration, under all the forms that we have passed in review, tends toward a more complete organization of that cube which is the stage ; toward a three-dimensional setting, which, by its very three-dimensional quality, assures a plastic unity between the actor and the ambience. It now remains for us to see what elements are employed to represent the environment and to create the mood.

In so far as environment is concerned, we no longer demand of the setting that fidelity to detail which was so dear to the older schools. The art of the theatre, like all the arts, is searching for character and expression. To-day, we represent a forest by some tree-trunks, the shore of an ocean by a plane placed before an empty sky, and, in the same way, when we wish to characterize a historic environment, we choose only certain essential elements. It is no longer a question of digging about in documents nor of substituting for the old mosaic setting composed of hundreds of details, a new collection of details of the same kind. We try, rather, to bring out those fundamental conceptions which have given birth to the language of forms. We ask ourselves in what way the visual concept of an epoch is made manifest, and this characteristic concept we interpret according to our sensitiveness.

In every epoch we find a characteristic organization of proportions. Thus, without entering into any of the details of architecture, we can render the Greek world by the single means of harmonious proportions ; the balance of horizontals and verticals. Even if we should heap upon a stage construction all the details of classic architecture, we could not succeed in evoking the ancient world as we can through the use of these simple rhythms. In order to render the Middle Ages it is not necessary to present all the details of Gothic architecture, but only that which characterizes it—verticalism (pl. 190, 202, 203). A very pronounced vertical rhythm, perhaps merely an ogival doorway, suffices. If we are called on to suggest the Versailles of Louis XIV, we do not try to present a perspective of gardens. We make two sections of hedge and between them we place a stairway much broader than it is high, since French art of that period always sought an effect of representative breadth. To suggest the Egypt of " Cæsar and Cleopatra," Jorgulesco employs two pylons in different combinations (pl. 212 – 213). Proportion is the means of expression *par excellence*, but we find it all too often neglected in modern stage decoration. On the one hand, the designer who is not an architect commits the gravest errors in proportions, while, on the other hand, in all fixed systems to which so many producers and designers are devoted, the proportions are unchangeable.

Each epoch, moreover, brings with it new relations between what might be called empty and occupied spaces, or better, between walls and the openings in those walls. For example, the character of defensive warfare in the Middle Ages is expressed by plain walls which are only occasionally pierced by openings in the form of *meurtrières*, while, on the contrary, antiquity at once dissolves this plain wall into columns ; hence a series of beautiful cylinders before a clear sky evokes for us all the spirit of Greece.

67

It is also by proportion that we express whatever an epoch has of sombre or of gay, of freedom or constraint (pl. 215); by proportion and finally by colour. Barbarous, but refined colour, coupled with ornamentation in large and decisive *motifs*, is characteristic of ancient Asia. Does not the sensuality of woven or velvet tapestries in harmonious colours suggest the Renaissance, just as sobriety in colours and ornaments suggests the classic world ?

Consequently, proportion, the organization of the occupied and unoccupied spaces, and colour are the means by which we present the characteristics of an historic environment. It must be remembered, however, that the reduction of expression to these three elements is of no value unless the setting is realized plastically ; for, if such a simplification of the setting as this be applied to the painted stage decoration, the results will be nil. The pictorial setting is always charged with details that we can tend to suppress in the spatial setting. This does not mean that we must push the suppression to the point where we fail to complete the impression, but that the use of details will depend on the style of the production.

Certainly, the freer we are the less we shall concern ourselves with any attempt to express the higher truth of the drama by the creation of environment. On the contrary, we shall often place psychological truth above all verisimilitude, and the stage elements which we have at our disposal for the production of environment must at the same time co-operate in the creation of the mood. The more this evolution advances towards suggestion, and at the same time toward the creation of mood, the more it tends to eliminate direct reality and to focus on the inner truth of the dramatic spectacle. The expression of this inner truth has been the concern of the foremost stage decorators and producers up to the present time—that is, up to the advent of constructivism ; and, as visual concepts evolved, all the means of modern art have been drawn into the service of this expression.

It is still proportion which determines the spatial rhythm, and to which psychological expression corresponds. Differences in height ; the dimensions of the stage, whether narrow or wide, deep or shallow ; the barrenness of a wall ; the aspect of a great curtain ; all are means to reflect the psychology of the drama, to create the mood. Open-air scenes are likewise arranged in accordance with spatial rhythm ; the verticalism of trees ; the proportion between earth and sky, a silhouette placed in opposition to the blue, all become in this way equally factors in expression. When in 1903 Alfred Roller composed his setting for the second act of " Tristan und Isolde " at the Vienna Opera it was considered a revolution (pl. 186). In this realization there was no longer a garden in the romantic taste, no castle loaded with *motifs* in romanesque style, and no full moon, so dear to all frequenters of the opera : there was nothing but the verticalism of a bare wall before a starry sky and, in the shadow, two stone benches on which the play of the two lovers took place. The down-stage plane of this setting, with its painted foliage wings and border, is not, it must be admitted, to our taste, but otherwise this stage decoration marks a decisive step toward the realization of a new psychological expression, toward the creation of mood.

In Martersteig's production of " Gyges und sein Ring," which dates from the beginning of the movement, we have another example of expressive verticalism (pl. 188). Later it is used by Gordon Craig in the creation of some of his most beautiful designs. So through all the evolution of the stage setting we constantly encounter this element of expression even down to Strnad's extremely expressive set for " Danton," with its enormous guillotine (pl. 192), Gutzeit's setting for " Faust " (pl. 193), Jones (pl. 196), Wildermann (pl. 187), Strnad's settings for " Lear " (pl. 197), Ott's designs shown in plates 194–195, and yet again in Feuerstein's expressive settings for Marlowe's " Edward II " (pl. 202–203).

Under the influence of expressionism verticalism began to be deformed (pl. 201–3). The simple vertical no longer sufficed. The feelings of this disturbed and super-excited period no longer responded to it, and, as a consequence, we see these once pure lines become oblique and concentric, sometimes throwing themselves towards the bottom of the scene, sometimes spreading themselves on high as if to implore heaven, or coming together above as if to shut out the light and hold the play in an atmosphere of death and despair. Yet creations of surpassing expressiveness have been achieved in this way. Ludwig Sievert, the Frankfurt scene designer, has utilized these means in many of his arresting designs (pl..205, 206, 207). This is how he explains his setting for Brecht's " Trommeln in der Nacht " (pl. 206) : " A bowl crashing in ruins. The walls remain throughout the play symbols of chaos and revolution. An atmosphere charged with tenseness and energy. One cannot imagine a beginning and one cannot see an end. The eye is drawn upward and loses itself in the height. The rooms melt into the beyond and are lost insensibly in houses, roofs and landscapes. In other scenes madness of a night during the revolution—dancing in a bar, a flamboyant vision of reds and yellows, and always above the whole the moon like a bloodshot eye. Real events in a real world stylized into the lyric unreality of the ballad and the dream."

In Kokoschka's " Mörder, Hoffnung der Frauen " (pl. 207) and in Strindberg's " Grosse Landstrasse " we see Sievert make use of analogous means—great masses with oblique lines. And then we see him twist these lines to create the baroque environment for " Don Juan " (pl. 205). Everywhere the use of expressive line and proportion became general. In " Malédiction " (pl. 209) at the Maly Teatr, Warsaw, we see lines employed to accentuate the movement of the crowd towards one point on the stage, and at Paris, " L'Homme et ses Fantômes," by Lenormand, is mounted in a frame of curtains whose different forms accentuate the expression of the setting, providing at the same time a technical installation for change of scene (pl. 208). The proportion of masses also became an element of expression, as witness the designs of Jorgulesco for the Boston production of " Cæsar and Cleopatra " (pl. 212, 213) or the settings that Buchholz created for Hagemann at Wiesbaden (pl. 214, 215).

This search for expression has been pushed to a point where the producer now wishes to detach the elements of expression from all material support in order to utilize them as pure abstractions. This derives from Craig and his ideas of symbolism. For example, in Lenormand's " Mangeur de Rêves," Pitoëff tried to present an ambience which was completely abstract. To this end he established in the middle of the stage a unique symbol in the form of a single ribbon in colour, stretched in a determined direction, and this with a few battens constituted the setting.

Now it must be evident that this symbol— a line of colour traced in the void—cannot incorporate itself with the actor or with his movements and gestures. No matter how ingeniously this symbol is chosen, it always remains an abstraction in juxtaposition to the drama itself. We perceive it only as we perceive an illustration for the text of a book. Such a stage setting leaves acting in a void, and attempts to illustrate it on another plane of apperception. But, as we have tried to show, the setting must not illustrate ; it must be, in a way, the drama itself. With such abstract creations as this, in order that the actor may be in the same plane with the setting, he should logically be dematerialized, only his " disembodied " mind being permitted to subsist.

Another danger in the use of such symbols as these is that the symbols will be created by the producer following the associations of line and colour which the character of the scenes in the play evokes solely in him. Why should the producer be privileged to impose on all the audience this personal, abstract association ? We know something of the scholarly experiments which have attempted to prove that fixed associations exist between sound and colour. We also know that the results have been negative. To one person "A" calls forth an impression of sky-blue, while the same sound to another evokes green : " C " presents itself to one as deep violet and to the next as citron-yellow, and these associations vary in the same person, depending on his physical state at the time the experiment is made. If such simple abstractions as these are in no sense general and in no sense common property, how can we hope to find, in the case of a situation so psychologically complex as that presented by the stage, a purely abstract association which will have value for a whole audience ? These symbols thus do not correspond to any intrinsic need that must be satisfied through them. On the contrary, they are proposed and put forward in a manner which is absolutely arbitrary. It is all very well to say : " That is the way," but it must always be remembered that " That " could very easily be something quite different.

This seems to be the double danger presented by a movement toward complete abstraction : the arbitrary selection of the symbol on the one side, and, on the other, the destruction of the scenic unity, and by consequence the isolation of the actor in a world to which he can never belong.

With the abstract, symbolist stage decoration we leave the field of the plastic setting, but we return to it again with those stage means which have assumed so much importance in our own day—the use of platforms, the organization of different levels for the action, and stairs.

Once again, it was Max Reinhardt who first employed these means. His revolving stage offered the fullest possibilities in this direction. The construction of settings on this device with its facilities for quick change, made the use of different levels and stairways a simple matter. Moreover, the limitations imposed by this revolving stage actually necessitated differences of level when an extended series of scenes had to be created. We saw in Reinhardt's first productions how greatly the stairway increased the rhythmic possibilities of the action. On the one hand,

it made possible the effective use of masses, of novel groupings and crowd movement, and, on the other, it reinforced the lone actor and heightened his effectiveness by the position it gave him in relation to the space surrounding him. Watch a man, alone and isolated, slowly descending a great stairway. In that movement there is sadness and a sense of his loneliness that no other stage means can give to him. At the point in " Richard II " where Richard relinquishes the crown, his descent into the courtyard sums up the tragedy of the whole scene. Therefore, in the setting for this episode, the stairway will be placed on the axis of the stage, with the result that the fullest stress is laid on this tragic descent. Look at a figure placed at the top of a stairway, or on a raised platform in opposition to other masses on the level, as in the " Napoleon " produced by Jessner, with settings by César Klein ; if the variety of movements, of ascents and descents be noted, the importance as a means of expression of such an inanimate object as a stairway at once becomes apparent. Throughout the evolution of the setting we have seen, following the stairway, such new substitutes as the platform, different levels for the action, and the inclined plane assume a constantly growing importance ; and, in theatres lately constructed, a number of technical inventions have been installed which give to the producer practically unlimited possibilities for the creation of these different levels. As we approach the present we see that, little by little, this scenic means sheds all its superfluous accessories until, finally, in the hands of Jessner or in such a production as Medenwald's " Lear," we find the action supported solely by a few rostra in combination with light as a factor of expression. As the stage drops decorative accessories it employs more supple means of expression— means which are capable of greater variation than the stage decoration itself. In fact, proportion, spatial rhythm, " practicability," are all immutable for each setting, even though the movement of the actors is varied and the scene itself undergoes a change. So, in order to adapt ourselves to the events of the drama, we now have recourse to light and to colour.

The modern theatre does not always take into account the psychology of colour, although, in general, we are far from the jumble which we inherited from the Italian theatre. It is only opera and operetta which still furnish us with amusing examples. The modern theatre, however, too often replaces the naïveté of the colours of opera with a no less strange naïveté of poster colours. These strong, but banal and inharmonious, poster colours are not confined to certain ballets only, but are to be found even in the serious experiments of the most advanced theatres. It is not that strong colour is not often an excellent scenic means, but it is necessary that the colours be used with care and the gamut chosen in accordance with the expression to be obtained ; for, if applied in an absolute manner, they easily fall into the commonplace and the grotesque. For example, it is an error to believe that the gay is necessarily the motley. We can present gaiety and at the same time preserve harmony.

Colour permits us to modify the expression. We can change the mood of a scene by introducing into the same setting a new colour element—for example, a curtain, a sail, some banners. We can also modify the character of a setting by changing its colour through light. Finally, colour gives us the expressive elements of the costume ; the spot of colour provided by the costume of a new actor entering on the stage will give to an ensemble made up of a number of figures a new psychological accent.

We must ask ourselves what colours are best suited to express the character of a play : this is the procedure of Craig, adopted by Stern as well. It consists in choosing a gamut of colours which, in general, accord with the piece, and then repeating them with all their nuances in both the costumes and stage decorations. The palette must be chosen with sufficient range to permit of variations, for we must be able to realize not only harmony but contrast as well. If harmony is a means of expression, contrast is another, and the contrasts must not be produced by chance. These contrasts—for example, a spot of colour in a neutral ensemble, or a light spot in a dark ensemble—must be conceived as means of expression. In fact all the means inherent in colour are permissible provided that scenic expression results.

The means which best meets the exigencies of each new scene, and which is most completely adapted to express the psychologic event, is, after all, light. Here also, evolution has brought consequences of some importance. The old theatre presented us with actors dressed in velvet and lace and spangled embroidery, and with them employed a perspective in its blue-painted back-drops to represent distance—whilst the yellow footlights illuminated the fraud. Perfected technique in the field of stage lighting was first used to create romantic effects. This is the epoch in which the theatre in a very orgy of mechanical devices realized apparitions, disparitions, palaces which collapsed, rainbows bridging heaven and earth for the gods, ascensions in glory, and astounding red and blue lightings ; and these tricks still survive on certain stages and in many revues. By these devices the art of the theatre was reduced to a sort of séance of Maskelyne and Devant magic.

Finally, naturalism began to assert its influence, and with the advent of this new school stage lighting became more natural. Naturalism subordinated it to the requirements of the play and insisted that lighting must represent nature in as true a manner as the acting. Consequently, we see a constantly growing desire for gradations in the lighting which should more closely approximate natural light, and the final goal reached by naturalism in this question of lighting was the invention of Fortuny, realized in some form or another on a number of German stages.

Certainly it is sometimes necessary to render the nuances of natural light as faithfully as possible, and this becomes comparatively easy as soon as we have a sky dome at our disposal.

But we go farther to-day. It is no longer sufficient for modern means to give us an illumination, full of nuances and appropriate to the environment of the action ; it must in addition reflect scenically the psychological event.

To-day we employ both direct and diffused light. Diffused light, regulated by dimmers, creates the psychological event through nuances ; the nuances of clear or obscure, as well as the nuances of colour. Direct light produces contrasts, and so presents the dramatic event through the play of light and shadow. We know the evocative force of torch-light and the phantasmagoria of misery that can be created by a single candle casting the enlarged shadow of a man on a blank wall, and we know what inexhaustible resources lie in projectors of all kinds with their direct light and resulting sharp-cast shadows. It should be obvious that, in order to create these effects of direct lighting, we must have plastic settings, for only the plastic setting which can cast its own shadow, which lives in the light and by the light, will make it possible for us to develop the whole gamut of psychologic expression and to realize every mood.

It is a mistake, however, to replace diffused light entirely, no matter how produced, by direct light with its cast shadows. This would be to deprive the stage of the means of expression inherent in diffused light, in order to substitute a lighting which is adapted to quite different ends, instead of utilizing each of these two means of lighting—the direct and the diffused—in its proper domain (pl. 216–223). The use of light as a means of expression has undergone an evolution analogous to that described by the setting. First we have natural light reproduced as faithfully as possible ; then psychological expression within the limits of a natural verisimilitude ; and, lastly, psychological expression removed from all contact with reality.

In Jessner's productions above all, we see light following the psychological windings of the drama independent of all natural demands.

The stage suddenly becomes sombre in order to explain the soul state of the character who is speaking, and lights up again on the entrance of a " good " character. The lighting is handled in a quite arbitrary manner and is subordinate only to the drama itself. For Jessner, colour must assume an analogous function. It serves in his hands to explain visually characters and events, but in a way which at times seems a little too obvious and a little too simple. Thus, in " Richard III," Gloucester speaks his opening monologue before a curtain, dressed in black, and at the end of the play Richmond delivers his exordium before the same curtain, dressed in white. Such an expression of the " good " and the " bad " certainly seems to be lacking in subtlety, and we naturally ask ourselves if expressionism, by moving in this way toward a stiff and excessively precise realization, accompanied as it is with a special manipulation of colour, light and even stage movements, as in Medenwald's " Lear," does not finally end in a simplification lacking all finesse and, consequently, deprived of expression.

To the elements which can evoke the psychological atmosphere and create the mood it is important to add another factor, which is addressed to the ear, namely, sound or noise. Schiller was conscious of this dramatic force of noise when he wrote the scene of Wallenstein's death. In this play a single witness of the events remains on the empty stage while the sound of footsteps is heard fading away down an interminable corridor, then the closing of a door, then only a great silence. In the same way we can imagine the effect that would be produced in Lady Macbeth's sleep-walking scene by the sound of footsteps heard at midnight on the flagstones of a hall in the deserted castle, or the sinister presentiment which could be given to the spectator by the noise of the falling irons as the castle gate closes behind the arriving Duncan. There are infinite resources, thus far insufficiently exploited, in sound, in the noise produced by inanimate things, which, when properly employed, become in a way themselves actors in the drama. The elements which produce these sounds, the flagstones which resound, the closing gates, and so on, are often presented by the setting itself.

Thus, to sum up, we see that the producer and scene designer, in order to create a spectacle which is in every way complete, must utilize all the means which the modern stage has at its disposal—line, proportion, mass, different levels, colour, light and sound.

CHAPTER X

THE PICTURE STAGE AND THE PAINTED SETTING

IN certain quarters, the spatial decoration still encounters a marked resistance. Its adversaries assert that the theatre being nothing more than the result of tacitly accepted conventions, the pictorial convention is completely in harmony with the unreality of all things that pertain to the theatre. Moreover, they assure us that, with the progress realized in this field, the painted stage decoration now fully satisfies the demands of modern sensitiveness.

In taking up this subject, we have to deal with an evolution in the theatre different from that which we have followed up to the present; an evolution which takes place entirely outside the modern theatre movement, properly speaking. It consists largely in the application to the stage of those principles which dominate easel-painting, for all the currents of contemporary painting have passed across the stage, from decorative painting to neo-impressionism, on to expressionism, and from there to cubism. We have seen the Russian Ballet, for example, which came to us first dressed in all the ornamental phantasy of a Bakst, present its most recent creations before the back-drops of a Picasso.

The adversaries of the painted stage decoration tell us that between Bakst and Picasso as decorators there is, at bottom, little difference, and that this difference is only concerned with the exterior form and not with the essence itself of the scenic spectacle. This seems to be true, for, in fact, the changes in style to which the painted stage decoration has been forced to submit during the last twenty years, do not seem to have added any new element to scenic organization as we understand it.

From the beginning, all the painters who concerned themselves with stage decoration fell into the error of confusing the stylization of decorative planes with the rhythmic life of the stage, and so, when they transferred to the theatre the methods of a new school, they still remained within the limits of the decorative panel. In the beginning, we see the same stylization of flat surfaces which was applied about 1900 to the poster, the book, and, in general, to all decorative design; a stylization which consisted, primarily, in the exclusion of perspective. As far as the stage was concerned, this could, in a way, be considered as representing a certain progress, since it abandoned the *trompe l'œil* perspective of the old stage setting. We have seen Georg Fuchs, for the backgrounds of his relief stage, accept painting for the stage in this sense. To-day, even, a stage decoration such as that of Aubrey Hammond (pl. 227), altogether charming in itself if we disregard the principles of the theatre, springs from the same decorative spirit. The same is true of the successful designs of Pillartz and von Wecus, shown in plates 228–229.

There is a fundamental difference between this kind of stylization and that which conquered the theatre in the settings of Bakst (pl. 230, 231). His inexhaustible and purely decorative imagination has been able to force acceptance for the dangerous principle on which his settings were based, namely, that of *trompe l'œil*. Bakst, with a conviction which he expressed many times, often used a perspective which many thought had been for ever abolished by the stylized stage decoration. Recall the unbelievable stairway painted on the back-drop of " Thamar," or the stairways in Cretan style which occupied almost all of his setting for D'Annunzio's " Phedra." If these deceits, by means of perspective, were accepted, it is precisely because their decorative treatment conferred on them a conscious and sought-for unreality. Accepted they were, but it was still, undeniably, a little astonishing to see Ida Rubenstein enter the scene on the stage level instead of using the painted stairway of the back-drop which was hanging behind her.

Bakst's contribution to the theatre consists, not in his general conceptions, but in his feeling for colour and the use which he tried to make of colour as an element of expression. Here his influence was considerable.

In the case of a sensuality as complex as that of Bakst, it is difficult to separate the part which springs from a tendency towards expression and the part which derives from certain ethnic qualities, from his half-Russian, half-Oriental pictorial instinct. And following Bakst, we have seen other decorative painters in the theatre, whose works were chiefly attractive on account of these same ethnical characteristics, as, for example, those of Benois (pl. 232) and Lissim (pl. 233). In the case of Lissim, we find a mixture of imagination characteristically Russian, and a decorative stylization in the direction of the preceding school. There are many others whose works are attractive largely because of their decorative Russian theme as well as on account of the distinctive Russian spirit in which they are treated (pl. 236–7). The charming settings of Schoukhaeff, full of a capricious imagination, derive from a very specific Russian romanticism (pl. 234, 235). Similarly, the grand manner of the decorative contortions of such settings as those of Drabik (pl. 239) or Sliwinski (pl. 238) seem a revelation of the Polish soul, just as the bizarre unrest of the overcharged settings of Vlastislav Hofman (pl. 240, 241, 243, 270–272), of Feuerstein (pl. 244, 245), and of Hrska (pl. 246) may spring from some Czech source of which we are ignorant. In Latvia we have the settings of Liberts' creations (pl. 248–249) with a quite special ethnical character, and interesting because of certain qualities which are outside our considerations of the theatre in general.

It often happens, in the case of such settings as these, that we see charming creations conceived with refined taste, and full of beautiful colour, but we can appreciate them only so long as we do not consider them as stage decorations intended for the theatre. From the point of view of the theatre, they will only offer us either decorative panels, enlarged out of all measure, or mere immense posters. All goes very well with them on an empty stage, but, from the moment the actor appears, bringing with him the plasticity of the human body, the scenic irrelevancy of a realization in two dimensions becomes startlingly apparent. To organize the space of the stage about the actor, to create a unity between that actor and a flat decoration conceived in two dimensions, is a task which the painter has rarely been able to achieve.

It should be clear to us by now that the stage is never presented to us as a picture, but as an organization of the space surrounding the actor. In order that the stage should appear to us as a picture, we would have first to pass all the actors through a wringer and then place them well flattened out in the same plane with the stage decoration. This is to reduce the theory to an absurdity. Admitting that the theatre is founded on conventions, the pictorial convention can never find a place there, for the theatre rests on conventions of a quite different order.

Painting has employed all sorts of artifices in an attempt to force the actor to enter into the scenic ensemble, most of them without success. Obviously, the simplest means is not to show the actor at all. Thus in the " Chœurs de la Grande Russie," produced by the Chauve-Souris, we have seen a picture perfectly successful as a picture, thanks to the suppression of the actor, who was hidden behind the decoration. This suppression of the actor is a radical means for guaranteeing the pictorial unity of the spectacle, but there are others more refined.

In order to blend the actor into the decorative ensemble, certain painters (as, for example, Bakst in his earlier creations for the Ballets Russes) have had recourse to an artifice which still springs from painting. Following the richness of their fantastic imagination, they spread over both the stage decoration and the costumes such an abundance of colours and ornaments that they succeeded in weaving a sort of spider's web over the entire stage, including the actor, and in this net the actor was caught. It might be said, with justice, that the costumes of Bakst were snares for the actor. Through them he took possession of the actor, walled him in with an iridescent assemblage of colours and arabesques, and thus tied him to his painted stage decoration. Unity in this case is achieved through the bewilderment of the spectator.

But this procedure, often fatiguing for the eye, does not utilize at all the effects which may be produced by contrasts between the richness of the costumes and the simplicity of the decorative background. On the other hand, it is disavowed from the moment the actor makes his appearance on the stage and comes in contact with the flat decoration. Thus in "L'Après-Midi d'un Faune," the sight of Nijinsky, reclining on a rock executed as a set piece, at once made the ridiculousness of the painted setting apparent, and this in a ballet conceived as a frieze, from which the third dimension was supposed to have been excluded.

Jean Hugo, in his production of " Roméo et Juliette," has found an extremely ingenious means for creating a harmony between the painted setting and the actors. In these settings, small pieces in front of a black curtain were executed in red outlines on a black ground, in such a way that the set pieces lost themselves in the black of the curtains. The costumes were carried out in the same way ; a single decorative element outlined the body on a black ground, the calf of the leg, the chest and so on, and those parts alone were visible, the rest of the costume, and with it, the actor, being lost in the background. By this artifice, the actor became, in a way, an arabesque

moving before the arabesques of the stage decoration (pl. 256, 257).

In analogous cases, there is often an attempt to transform the physical reality of the actor by the use of masks and by a deformation through the costume. Certain realizations in this manner have been very successful, as in the productions of " Les Mariés de la Tour Eiffel " by Hugo, and " La Création du Monde " by Léger, where this deformation has produced excellent results. Above all, in Léger's ballet spectacle, where the gamut of colour was in perfect harmony with the music, the actor appeared simply as a moving decorative object performing his evolutions in a setting which was equally mobile. Even here, however, it would have been preferable to have had more real volume in the mobile parts of the setting (pl. 261). Later on, in the Chapter on Costume, we shall see the great possibilities inherent in the use of the mask, whether concerned with a stage setting in two or in three dimensions.

The third dimension, banished from the stage by decorative painting, seems to return again with the entry of cubism. And here again it is important not to be deceived. The cubist painter does not " feel " space any more than the decorative painter does. His spatial impressions immediately find themselves side-tracked in the direction of his pictorial conceptions. Thus, cubism has done nothing more than reconduct the painter, by the observation of volumes and the example of architecture, to the laws of painting. And here is the astonishing point : the application of cubism to the three-dimensional arts can end up in an altogether false constructivity by presenting, in plastic terms and with plastic means, volumes which are conceived pictorially.

Certainly, the painting of the younger men in the theatre satisfies our feelings and taste much more than the former decorative painting, but, after all, it only satisfies our sensitiveness and feeling for painting and not our theatrical receptivity, our feeling for the theatre. The greater part of their creations reinforce the contrast between the living body and the stage setting. The convention of the perspective of the old stage setting is replaced by a new conception of perspective. The pictorial representation of volumes, abolished by decorative painting, again triumphs on the stage. And thus one would be tempted to say that the more modern painted stage decorations, while satisfying our pictorial feeling, have pushed the theatre back toward a less modern conception closely allied to the ancient setting with its tricked perspective and its false highlights and shadows.

Cubism can certainly claim to have some rights in the theatre when it comes with plastic means. This is the case with the "Kamerny Theatre" of Moscow. Painting, employing the contrasts of warms and colds, here only serves to underline the form which is plastically conceived and executed. The production of "Phèdre" by Vesnine, thanks to the perfect harmony of its extraordinarily atmospheric scenic ensemble, its costumes and its rhythms of gesture and movement, constituted one of the most perfect and finished stage works that we have seen (pl. 151).

Settings such as those for "Dr Caligari," on the contrary, interesting so long as they are seen without actors, contain a fundamental error. We are not insisting on the discordance between the stylization of the settings and the too great reality of the characters in the drama. The fact of seeing living beings pass and move about, without any convention of stylization, in an atmosphere of quite another order, creates a lack of unity that is difficult to support. And this, moreover, was a film. Of course, one might say in the case of a film that the photographed characters are no longer three-dimensional beings, but only moving images in two dimensions. In fact, the photographic process seems to succeed in carrying out a *tour de force* impossible on the stage—that of flattening the actor and placing him on the same plane as the setting, that is, the plane of the screen. It is, probably, because of this distortion that certain German producers have felt themselves justified in making use of painting, in underlining the pictorial character of the setting by cross-hatching, shadows and so on. But photography, at the same time that it causes the actors to move in one plane, presents an optical illusion, for by means of photographic perspective it shows even more depth of stage than we see in reality. Thus the application of painting to the moving-picture becomes doubly disagreeable.

A tendency in modern painting to which we would be inclined to make less opposition is expressionism. We have already seen how strong scenic expression can be when obtained through the means at the disposal of expressionism. Expressionism applied to the setting seems to have a sort of elementary strength like a volcanic eruption, and that eruption in its passion overthrows all established rules, including the rule of a three-dimensional organization of the stage. Just as playwriting of the expressionist school, with its scenes jostling and elbowing one another breaks with all recognized order in dramatic composition, so expressionism on the stage and in the setting destroys all ties, and in its urge toward the maximum of visual expression never pauses to ask if the means that it employs is pictorial or plastic. Any means for it is worth while, provided it is expressive, whether it be a line, a complete construction, a painting, or a wooden lath. And by this abandon it succeeds in convincing us and making us forget any reservations in principle which we may cherish. We have seen the expressive force of the decorations of Sievert, and a similar forcefulness is to be found in the designs of César Klein (pl. 252, 253), Reigbert (pl. 254, 255), of Feuerstein (pl. 244, 245) and of Hofman (pl. 240, 241).

In expressionist painting in the theatre, the elements of reality are liberated from their real and natural order. Is Venice to be expressed ; what must be represented ? The Rialto ? The Doge's Palace ? Very well : place one on top of the other if in that way expression can be obtained (pl. 252). Do as you like, but above all express, and above all, be inspired. It is by this inspiration and this inner force that expressionism becomes convincing, because we recognize in it a high goal for the art of the theatre. Sometimes it will present too much, sometimes it will make mistakes, but, if we are arrested by such a setting as that for " Trommeln in der Nacht," what difference does it make whether the lines which evoke our emotional response are painted on the back-drop or not ? After all, we are the children of our time and cannot easily resist its impress, so that if occasionally our

the light and witty type to which they belong. Viewed in this way, there are two cases in which the painted stage decoration seems almost legitimate : that of the *décor blague*, or ironic setting, and that of the *décor pastiche*, or setting in imitation or travesty of a period.

The *décor blague* does not dream of presenting anything more than an ironic illustration removed as far as possible from all verisimilitude. This was the case in " Ubu-Roi."

The *décor pastiche*, in taking on something of the aspect of an ancient style, characterizes

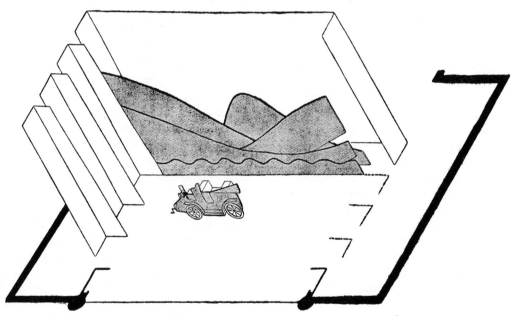

Fig. 8.—Louis Jouvet : " Knock " (Romains).　Comédie des Champs Élysées, Paris.

visual receptivity and the resulting response make us seem to negate our rigid principles it is (perhaps) not so bad a thing after all. Would it not be unjust and a little foolish to refuse to accept such a charming fantasy as that of the " Mariés de la Tour Eiffel," with its stage composition so full of wit and verve (pl. 259), on the grounds of adherence to a principle of some sort ? Or that sprightly production of " Roméo," far removed as it is from Shakespeare ? (Pl. 256, 257.) Or any other witty and errant production, for that matter ? For many spectacles of this kind our indulgence is secured in advance because of

by means which evidently cannot pretend to be called spatial organization.

Who would wish to apply rules to that charmingly ironic, and at the same time expressive, decoration of Professor Stierbecke, with its chairs painted on the wall of the room ; or to that little theatre which Babić constructed in the middle of the stage (pl. 264) ; or to Jouvet when, in a witty and amusing setting, he made the mountains rock in order to produce the impression of a moving landscape behind the automobile of Dr Knock (fig. 8) ; or to this same Jouvet's articulated palm trees arranged to follow the psychological evolution of " Le Trouhadec saisi par la Débauche ? " In order to create the little embryonic settings in which the wandering actors of the " Taming of the Shrew " play their comedy, it is certainly legitimate and appropriate to imitate the style of the old wood engravings of the sixteenth century (pl. 267). Is it not equally permissible, in order to catch something of the spirit of Molière, to play one of his pieces in a setting which, frankly, is in the style of his time and yet not a direct imitation or reconstruction ? (Pl. 266.) How can the settings of the " Chauve-Souris," like those for " L'Enlèvement du Serail " (pl. 268) and " La Traviata " (pl. 235), be judged seriously according to any set of rules ?

Certainly this is not the summit of tragic art, but, when this genre appears as the result of the imagination of a gifted artist, it can reach a very high level. And perhaps one would be inclined to show less disagreement with the painted setting when applied to ballet, dance and revue. One might even establish a scale of " genres " for the theatre, running from drama to opera and from there to the ballet and the revue, and say that, following this scale, plastic realization is more or less indispensable. We have often been conscious of the fact that in the case of dance and ballet creations, painting and the painted setting are less strikingly out of accord than in the case of drama or opera—that is to say, the discordance obtrudes itself less upon our consciousness.

Is it because of the lack of words in these forms, the replacing of the word by pure physical expression, that the action is carried over on to another plane, removed in a way from all reality, with the result that we are less conscious of the changing of the plane of apperception in relation to the setting ? The spectator, carried toward a purely visual, and by consequence more pictorial, perception, no longer takes account of the difference between the bodies and the planes—a difference which nevertheless still exists. Is it perhaps that the dance, in monopolizing in such a sovereign manner the stage rhythm for itself, fills the stage so completely with its own rhythmic life that we no longer notice the lack of rhythm in the surroundings ? Or is it simply that we have accepted the painted setting through habit, the spatial setting never having been attempted in this field.

Whatever it is, we believe that even for the dance the spatial setting is superior to the painted setting. Moreover, a stage decoration for the dance, corresponding to a rhythmic concept, could be the most perfect complement of the rhythmic art itself. This new setting for the dance could well be the same sort that Adolphe Appia wished to create for the music-drama and eurhythmics.

At Hellerau, Appia had the opportunity of creating some settings in this spirit. But the professional ballet seems to have waited until the year of grace 1927 in order to realize this progress. The Swedish Ballet presented " L'Homme et son Désir " on a stage in three levels (pl. 122), but it was only in " La Chatte " and " Pas d'Acier " (pl. 164-165) of the Russian Ballet of 1927 that we saw a first real attempt to give a plastic organization to the stage. Even this was not practicable, and, such as it was, neither the choreographer nor the dancers seemed to know how to make use of it. Hence this application of principle ends in the paradox that, after having invented a setting which conforms to the necessities of the dance, a dancer must now be invented who knows how to utilize it.

We have seen, particularly since the period of expressionism, many modern scene designers returning to pictorial expression, and we have noted at the same time the reappearance of certain scenic elements that we had considered finally abolished. This return toward painting is definitely allied to a rather unexpected recurrence of the old method of composing the stage setting ; wings, borders and set pieces, not to mention back-drops. It must be remembered, in looking at the illustrations, that such outworn procedures as these are used consciously and with malice aforethought. We are, therefore, justified in speaking of a return to older stage forms offered to us, it is true, in the dress of the most recent manifestations in painting.

From this point of view look at a stage decoration as modern as that by Vlastislav Hofman of Prague, for Fibich's " Hedy " (pl. 270). After all, do these twisted forms, expressed in a quite new manner, represent anything more than the wings which played so prominent a part in the good old stage settings of our grandfathers ? The Czech artists employ them to the point of obsession. In his setting for Claudel's " Échange " (pl. 272), Hofman shows cut drops in the form of a semicircle, and set-pieces. In the setting by Wenig for " La vida es sueño " (pl. 273), there are four. The setting by Josef Čapek for Ghéon's " Pain " (pl. 274) discloses a painted backdrop behind a series of borders and wings, and the same principle dominates the charming composition by Hermann Krehan for Raimund's " Bauer als Millionär " (pl. 275). Paul Thiersch, in Breslau arranges almost all his settings in the same way (pl. 276, 277). Rêné Moulaert, in Brussels, has created an interesting and imaginative setting for Shakespeare's " Tempest," by placing the setting proper on a revolving platform and topping it with cut borders which describe analogous curves. The list might be extended indefinitely.

Such an atavistic tendency sometimes takes quite unexpected forms, and this is particularly true when it is a question of presenting an interior. We have reviewed the experiments of the modern theatre in the field of the " incomplete " setting. After all, these incomplete interiors existed long before the advent of the so-called modern art of the theatre, even before the theatre had achieved the maturity of a closed interior or box set. We can all recall having seen in some theatre, perhaps in the country, interiors made up of wings sliding in grooves between which doors and windows had been placed. This grotesque survival of the baroque theatre dates from a period in the past which had not yet dreamed of the box set and was

not in the least concerned with the æsthetics of the fourth-wall convention. Look for a moment at the setting by Vlastislav Hofman for Rolland's " Jeu de l'Amour et de la Mort " (pl. 271), and you will see the walls broken up into wings, between which the doors and windows have been placed just as we used to see them in our country theatre. Now, apparently, we must accept seriously what in those old days appeared to us not a little ridiculous. This is in Vlastislav Hofman's setting, very, very modern—and very, very old theatre.

Sometimes even the " Neue Sachlichkeit," that *dernier cri* tendency, makes use of a pictorial imagery in its settings which carries us back to the last century. Karlheinz Martin, the producer who mounted Wedekind's "Franziska " on constructivist platforms, last winter produced Rehfisch's " Razzia " in settings which concede nothing to the pictorial illustrations of the theatre of 1890. The only difference is that this lineal descendant is introduced to us under a new and very grandiose name—" Neue Sachlichkeit " (pl. 281). All of this gives us a very good impression of the confusion to be found in the present-day art of the theatre ; after having run the entire gamut of synthetic expressions, we set out to find by one means or another a new sensation, and we try to make ourselves believe that we have found it in a species of new realism which employs the most antiquated means of expression.

We are again justified in looking upon the ever-growing use of projections, of cinematographic projections even, as a return, under a new form, to the old theatre. The two means, the projection of the stage setting or decoration, as well as the cinematographic projection, evidently have nothing to do with the organization of the space about the actor. Very often they are directly opposed to such an organization. Above all, take the case of the film projected on to the back-drop of the scene. In the majority of cases it is extremely difficult, if not impossible, to achieve a unity between the background with its moving projection and the stage proper, not to mention the actor who, in his living presence, finds himself directly opposed to the phantoms being projected behind his back. In those cases where the ghostly character of the projection seems justified, as in the interesting realization of " Gewitter über Gothland " by Traugott Müller (pl. 358), we accept these images of the cinema without great difficulty. But, on the other hand, a solution such as that of Piscator of Berlin for the production of Paquet's " Sturmflut " does not seem to offer the necessary scenic unity (Pl. 280).

The question of projected stage decorations will be taken up in chapter XIII, but let us say at once that the fluid, non-existent character of the projected stage decoration determines its use for fantastic and fairy plays, that is to say, plays which are of the same matter, of the same world as the setting. The difficulty is that we are not content to confine its use to the plays for which it is adapted. Our tendency is to generalize and to apply it to plays with which it has nothing in common.

What are we to conclude from all this ? It seems that there is but one conclusion to be drawn, namely, that our modern unrest has opened a breach in the principle of scenic unity itself. Weary of all the results achieved, restlessly seeking new stimuli, we forget everything, even the ultimate end of the art of the stage, in order to begin once more our search for variety and novelty.

It can be said, however, that these experiments sometimes achieve a scenic " expressiveness " which the architectural setting, for example, can never easily equal. We have seen in many cases, as in the case of Adolphe Appia himself, to what extent the " expressiveness " of an art may be impoverished by being forced to submit to the severity of a principle, no matter how right and legitimate that principle may be. It is undoubtedly true that many a new creation, false from the point of view of scenic unity, does nevertheless offer us an " expression " both significant and arresting. We are tempted to believe that with our new art of the theatre we are, in fact, faced with a dilemma ; either we must push forward toward a maximum of expression at the sacrifice of scenic unity, or we must strive above all to maintain this scenic unity, even at the cost of expression. Only the tact of the artist can secure a satisfactory solution. In the meantime, the existence of this dilemma is evidence of the confusion so prevalent in our current art of the theatre.

CHAPTER XI

COSTUMES AND MASKS

IT is evident that the same principles which govern the creation of the stage decoration must also be applied to the costume. An " historic costume " must never be a literal copy of an illustration found in a document of the period. Here, as in the case of the setting, the copy must be replaced by an interpretation—an interpretation of the general characteristics.

Histories of costume, like Racinet's and Hottenroth's for example, apparently aim at being as little characteristic as possible. They are made up of an ensemble of details, the most insignificant appearing side by side with the most essential. Documentation, therefore, must proceed in other directions. Museums of costume and the paintings, engravings and sculpture of the period are the best sources. After a study of the period in this way, the best artists lay aside the documents and even try to forget them. Only in such a way can we create costumes which, by their general characteristics, their cut, their outline evoke the epoch for which they were designed.

In the creation of costumes, the artist should never be afraid of exaggeration. Just as the best portraits are usually on the edge of caricature, so in the creation of the historic costume it is often necessary to deform in order to characterize. Moreover in the case of costumes, the special optical conditions of the theatre must be considered ; for, with the spectator seated in the dark at some distance from the actor, who is moving in a large lighted space, the character of a costume is easily lost. As a result, the costume must be reinforced by whatever artifices are at the artist's disposal.

To the characterization through the outline or silhouette, that is to say, through proportion, colour must enter in to add its psychological element. Beyond this, the expressiveness of the costume depends largely on the material employed in its composition. We laugh to-day at the costumes we see in Opera, with their velvets and silks brocaded in gold and dust, because for us they seem only appropriate for a carnival. The modern theatre often replaces the former naïve colours with poster colours, and, for the too brilliant materials of the costume, substitutes cotton cloth. Poster colours and cotton cloth—thus the whole affair is arranged. The scenic ensemble which results is more like an improvised students masquerade, or a costume-dance in a boarding-house, than anything else in the world. As some may suspect, it is usually the ultra-modern productions which evoke this impression.

If a world continually dressed in silk and velvet seems to us absurd, it must be said at once that all humanity dressed in cotton cloth is equally so. In the past, man dressed for the most part in leather and wool, and these two materials are never ridiculous on the stage. It is, however, never the actual quality of the material which must be sought in the costume, but rather the scenic impression which the material evokes. If the impression can be produced with cotton cloth, well and good ; but cotton cloth must not be used when it represents only cotton cloth, and nothing more.

With such a premise a whole science of materials for use in the modern theatre might be created.

The breakdown of class distinction in modern times has carried with it a tendency which has moved more and more toward a uniformity of dress, in short, to a regimentation in the matter of clothes. We can no longer tell something of a man's occupation and position in society by the cut of his clothes, the form and tilt of his hat and the colours he employs. We often forget that formerly things were otherwise, and in the case of period plays to-day we often neglect to differentiate our figures. Each costume presents a problem which must be solved and no general solution is adequate.

There is a dissonance of another kind which can break the unity between the costumes and the stage decoration. If, for example, in a setting conceived in large volumes we set in motion costumes conceived in little details and swarming with ornaments, a separation between the costume and the stage decoration is immediately produced. Plastic unity and unity of colour must be dominated by a unity in the whole decorative conception, to the end that the costumes and settings may spring from the same principle of stylization. Only then will they possess the same general character and manifest the same style as the mise en scène.

Moreover, this style must not remain on paper but must be realized in the actual execution of the costume. If the design be intended for the stage, then it is unfulfilled until it is realized. How often have we seen charming costume designs so completely transformed in their realization that the actualized costume bore only the faintest resemblance to the artist's design—a barely perceptible reflection of his intent! How does this phenomenon, so characteristic of the costumes conceived by the painter, come about? It is because in his projects the painter fails to take into account the exigencies of the living body of the actor. Instead of conceiving his costume from the point of view of movement, and especially of the evolutions of the body which the costume must undergo, the painter builds up his costume in the same way that he builds up a picture. He arranges beautiful lines and composes delightful colour harmonies

—and is afterwards surprised to find nothing of all this in the costume actually worn by the actor. It is, after all, an important matter. The more the costume is stylized, that is to say anti-naturalistic, the more necessary it becomes for the artist to take into consideration the deformation which his stylization will undergo when combined with the movement of the living body. We have seen cubist costumes, interesting in the model, whose cubism in the execution was reduced to a kind of meaningless ornamentation, no longer conforming to the stylist conception it was supposed to represent. We show a very characteristic example of this in plates 300–303, Larionoff's costumes for "Chout." If the artist's design be compared with the costume as realized, the discrepancy between the plastic cubism intended in the designs and the purely ornamental and almost non-existent cubism of the realization can be readily seen. In the same way, it is with difficulty that we can imagine a way of executing the costumes of Mme. Gontcharova which would still preserve the angular stylization of the designs (pl. 304, 305).

The more one considers the matter, the clearer it becomes that, for the creation of a real costume, there is but one point of departure. That starting point is the living body of the actor. Stylization of the costume in any direction and to any degree will be possible the moment it is based on the possibilities offered by the movements of the body. Jean Hugo's interesting costumes for "Roméo et Juliette" are an excellent example (pl. 298, 299). Stylized effects are here based on the accentuation of the graceful outlines of the leg and torso. And, in this regard, national costume, with its embroideries accentuating certain parts of the body, can furnish valuable lessons. In the case of Hugo's costumes the stylization was in harmony with the stylized movements of the actors. In other productions Hugo has achieved some clever and astonishing deformations, as, for example, those seen in the delightful costumes for "Les Mariés de la Tour Eiffel" for which we show (pl. 318–323) both the designs and the realizations. Here are deformations faithfully rendered, precisely because the deformation itself takes perfect account of the body to which it must adapt itself.

Thus every sort of fantasy is permitted to the artist who knows how to obey the laws laid down by the living body. With this reservation, we can look with pleasure on models of costumes such as those shown in our illustrations, where we see reflected the most varied tendencies. First of all, we have the decorative stylization of the beginning of the century, and it is still a decorative stylization which we

" Bauhaus " in Dessau, the actor was transformed into what might be called an animated and articulated doll. The creations of the Bauhaus artists are interesting so long as they deal with purely architectural creations and at times even in the field of stage decoration. Not content with this, they have attempted, with what seems an astonishing lack of discernment, to submit the costume to laws which are in no sense applicable to it. Thus, for Oskar Schlemmer, the transformation of the body by the costume of the theatre can be conceived under four forms only.

Either the laws of the surrounding cubical

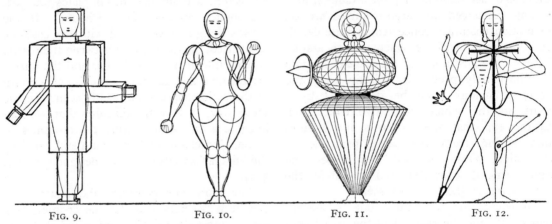

FIG. 9.   FIG. 10.   FIG. 11.   FIG. 12.

FIGS. 9-12.—Oskar Schlemmer : Schemes for costumes. Bauhaus, Dessau.

see in the costumes by Bilinsky (pl. 282-283). Then we have the graceful impressionism of Karl Walser (pl. 286, 287) or the caricaturist manner of Aubrey Hammond (pl. 288-289). With Bakst, it is the exuberant fantasy of ornamentation and colour which overruns the stage (pl. 290, 291) and this occurs again and again in his modern disciples (pl. 292-293). Cubism, as seen in the costumes of Vesnine for " Phèdre " (pl. 151) and even mechanism (pl. 310-313) make their entrance on the stage. If constructivism is lacking it is perhaps because it is so extremely difficult to conceive costumes in terms of skeleton construction.

There is, however, a tendency which aims to present in the costume what is practically the equivalent of constructivism on the stage. With the attempt to realize this idea at the

space may be applied to the bodily forms, in which case the head, torso and limbs are transformed into cubical forms. The result of this is moving architecture (fig. 9); or the bodily forms are exaggerated in the direction of their mechanical functions, in which case we have egg-shaped heads, torsos in the form of vases and ball-bearing articulations, etc. The result of this is the articulated doll (fig. 10); or, again, the costume represents the laws of bodily movement in space. Here the result is a technical organism (fig. 11); or, finally, the forms of the human body are symbolized, e.g., the cross which the spinal column forms with the shoulders, multiplication of forms, heads, arms, etc., resulting in dematerialization (fig. 12).

The error in these conclusions is only too

apparent. With Schlemmer's experiments, how far we are from the comprehension of an Appia, who has demonstrated to us how the actor's body comes to life on the stage precisely because of the contrast which his living form offers to the architectural laws surrounding him! At the Bauhaus, a complete failure to understand the necessities of the body is camouflaged by a mass of altogether ridiculous pseudo-scientific language. An example of the infantile results of these theories concerning the costume can be seen in the "Triadisches Ballett" (pl. 317). Here, the contrast between the costumes and the poor members of the body imprisoned in them is almost unbearable. The pseudo-scientific character given to this experiment in Dessau is again evidence for the contention that the " intellectualization " of the arts, signifies a general lowering of the intellectual level.

Another much more interesting tendency, allied to the stylization of the costume, is the re-introduction of the masked actor into the mise en scène. The part played by the mask in the history of the theatre is too extensive and too far outside the scope of this book for us to deal with it here. The classic theatre of Greece was almost synonymous with " mask " and, on the stage of Western Europe, its use continued down through the commedia dell'arte almost to our own day. For certain forms of oriental drama its use is an unbroken tradition reaching from a remote period to the present day. The resurgence of the mask, in our own generation, has had many advocates, some of whom have made a practical application of it in special plays. Among these, Gordon Craig has been perhaps the most important, and for those interested in the subject his books and the pages of *The Mask* contain a wealth of information on the subject coupled with arguments for its adoption. In America, the mask was first used by Robert E. Jones in the production of Mackaye's " Caliban." Since then, we have seen the masks of Geddes (pl. 333), Rosse, Benda (pl. 330) and others, and, within the

last few years, a play by O'Neill which envisaged its use for certain characters.

We may stylize the movement of the actor and give rhythm to his gestures and his walk, but yet we are forced to consider his face—this mobile, over-direct, and untransformed visage which still remains in opposition to a complete stylization. It is in the actor's face that those involuntary psychological " accidents " of which Craig speaks so frequently and so unexpectedly, happen. This does not mean that, in making use of the mask, we have taken a step toward the " super-marionette "; it means that we have called to our service an aid of the highest value in preserving the unity of style which must exist between acting and gesture.

In fact, we find many modern masks which have an expressive force which the human face could never equal and which, at the same time, have a truly grand style. In this category belong the admirable masks which the Dutch sculptor Hildo Krop has created for Yeats' play " The Only Jealousy of Emer " (pl. 324-327).

Many of our modern masks are inspired by the examples found in primitive Negro, Indian and Mexican art. Even with the masks of Hildo Krop, the reproach might be made that the artist was too strongly under the influence of Javanese art—an influence, however, easily understandable in the case of a Dutch sculptor. Benda's masks, so often reproduced in America, are, with the exception of his demon masks, for the most part almost direct copies of nature and, by consequence, lacking in expressiveness. It is evident that in the mask we have a branch of the modern art of the theatre which is still in its beginnings, but it is conceivable that the use of the mask, once it is well understood, could raise the scenic spectacle to such an ideal plane that, in contrast, the naturalism of the grimacing actor would appear shocking and unbearable.

Often the mask is the only means whereby the artist can realize a critical intent or a concept which demands caricature. In this category we have the masks of Jean Hugo which give such a charming caricature of the French " petite bourgeoisie " (pl. 318-323). Finally, as we have pointed out in the preceding chapter, we can, through the medium of the mask, link the actor with his environment and so, by this means, assist in the creation of scenic unity.

Though the mask is still in its beginnings, it is quite possible that its future development holds important consequences for the art of the theatre, it being always understood that its use must not be generalized, and that it must not be attempted in productions in which it has no place.

CHAPTER XII

TECHNICAL DEVICES

UP to a certain point in the evolution of the modern theatre, that is to say, during the period when the execution of the stage setting in plastic terms was considered indispensable, the modern mise en scène demanded a technical installation altogether different from that of the traditional stage. During the first phase of the history of the modern theatre it might be said that there existed an inter-dependence between artistic and technical progress in the theatre. If modern conceptions of the mise en scène have necessitated certain technical means, it is equally true that it has only been possible to realize certain artistic conceptions because this or that technical innovation had been introduced into the stage organization. During all this period we note a reciprocity between artistic and technical progress. Certain inventions, as for example, the concrete and plaster cyclorama and sky dome, represent artistic progress in themselves.

It must be admitted that to-day many of these magnificent installations are no longer utilized, and consequently Macgowan seems to be not altogether wrong when he speaks of "the twilight of the machines." However, the reasons why these technical means are no longer used are not solely artistic ones; generally they are economic ones. The simplification seen to-day in the modern continental theatre is often based on money considerations rather than on artistic ones. To fill the great spaces of the revolving stage with entire settings or to utilize the hydraulic stages invented to support similar constructions costs an amount of money which theatres after the war have rarely had at their disposal.

The embryonic settings which to-day serve to suggest the ambience are clearly cheaper and do not demand a too complicated technical installation.

However, even among the elements which make up these extremely simplified stage decorations, there are some which necessitate the assistance of modern technical means. Parallels and platforms and stairs would certainly never have occupied a position of such importance in the modern mise en scène if the stage on which they were employed had lacked the technical means necessary to bring them on stage and raise them into position. It is precisely the most modern stage decorations, reduced as they are to an arrangement of different levels for the action, which cannot be utilized unless the stage has a technical installation for their proper manipulation. Settings of this type are often constructed on sliding, sinking or revolving stages, and so, curiously enough, we see these installations which were invented to carry the completest settings in their entirety now serving the constructivist and the Jessner mise en scène, as formerly they served productions of the Reinhardt type. Looked at in this way those who condemn modern technique in the theatre and by their disdain would have us credit them with an extreme modernism, are altogether in the wrong. Those who have had occasion to realize modern settings, no matter how simple, on a stage entirely lacking in modern equipment, will agree that this lack of technical means not only often creates insoluble problems, but even more often imposes on the artist a bastard solution which falsifies his artistic intent.

The difference between the equipment of a modern stage and one of twenty years ago is as great as between the mechanism employed in a Drury Lane pantomime and the stage of the Globe theatre. The rapid shifting of plastic settings by means of the revolving, sliding, or sinking stage, the fixed plaster cyclorama and sky dome, the level stage floor, the deep inset proscenium, projected light, and so on, have become indispensable elements for spectacles of a certain kind. The use of modern stage devices is, however, much less widespread than one would at first be led to believe. In Germany, where before the war many new inventions were first brought into being, we find stages installed with all the modern devices, but even there the number of theatres so equipped is not too great. Even in the most advanced countries it is impossible to speak of a technique which has actually and radically supplanted the old.

Moreover, modern technique has not yet become standardized, while the old theatre technique has at least the advantage of being the same all over the world. This technique does not differ greatly from that to be found in the theatre of Louis XIV. Hence for the last two hundred years the theatre has had a certain generalized type of stage equipment, so that to-day the same traditional technical installation is to be found in Naples, London, Budapest and New York. All that varies is the size; the principle remains everywhere the same.

Modern experimentation, on the contrary, has produced stages which differ widely one from another. The result of this divergence is that it is often difficult, if not impossible, to remove a production conceived for one of these stages to the stage of another theatre conceived in a different manner. Stage settings designed for the revolving stage of the Deutsches Theater must be modified if they are to be used on, let us say, the stage of the Schauspielhaus in Dresden, while a setting conceived for the latter cannot easily be made to fit the framework of the Künstlertheater in Munich. The reason for this is that the engineers and architects who have experimented in this field have followed each his own direction and have consequently arrived at solutions of the technical problem which are dissimilar. As a result, several types of modern stage have been created, each of which is suited to certain needs; but it would be extremely difficult to say which represents a complete and definitive solution. Granting that it has achieved some remarkable results, modern stage technique is nevertheless still in the experimental stage. To reach the necessary standardizations, a number of tranquil years of experimentation were necessary; but as a matter of fact, this technical evolution was interrupted by the war; and after the war economic conditions delayed its resumption. To claim that the failure to undertake once more this line of development was due to a change in artistic conceptions seems to us erroneous. It might better be said that the artistic conceptions themselves are a reflection of the economic state.

That which distinguishes the standard traditional stage of our grandfathers, and often makes it unuseable for us to-day, is the fact that the entire installation was conceived for the shifting of flat settings, while the modern stage has concerned itself above all with the solution of the problem of shifting scenic elements conceived in volumes. Of course it is evident that all modern technical devices are not designed to serve this end. In some respects this technical experimentation has bettered the old system, certain innovations being designed to improve the system in current use, while in others these experiments have brought about truly radical changes in stage technique. If, for example, we look at the stage for the new Theatre at Weimar, constructed by Littmann, we will note a number of improvements; but we shall not be able to speak of a really modern stage.

The most important improvements consist in the substitution of iron for wood in the construction of the stage, an adaptable proscenium, a fixed cyclorama and the electrical control. An enumeration of the installation in this theatre will give a very good idea of the make-up and equipment of a stage of this type.

The theatre at Weimar includes the following : an adjustable proscenium, which may be varied in such a way as to make possible the use of the same stage for drama, intimate comedy and music-drama ; in this last case an ingenious arrangement of a sinking orchestra is brought into play. The stage proper has eighty-five equipments in metal, four for front curtains, seven for border lights, and seventy-four for stage decorations. There is a fixed cyclorama, a mobile cyclorama or " Wandelpanorama " on four drums, and three " Flugwerke " or machines for flying the actors. The stage floor has three sinking parts or sections thirty-three feet by four feet, which carry in addition four small traps and two transportable ones. It has a large sinking platform which descends seven feet below the stage and rises seven feet above stage level. There is a lift for platforms and practicables in general, and another for furniture and properties and for back-drops two more, each fifty-five feet long, which lead directly into the paint room ; and finally, a special lift for the chief engineer. Twelve different electric motors control the movements of these various equipments, one for the front curtains, another for the large trap, two for the adjustable proscenium and so on. The installation is perfected to such a point that even in the dressing rooms there are electric-heaters for curling irons and pans of grease-paint. And yet, with all the conveniences apparent in an installation of this sort, it cannot be said that it represents the type of new stage as it is to be found in certain other German theatres.

Among the reforms which move toward the creation of new types of stage, two different tendencies can be seen ; one strives to find new forms for the stage which correspond to this or that system of theatre æsthetics, while the other, independent of all æsthetic dogma, creates new technical means which are capable of serving all forms of the modern mise en

scène. We have already treated the first of these tendencies in our study of the different forms of the architectural stage. Such installations as that found in the Künstlertheater in Munich belong to this group and have been taken up in their place. It remains to describe the innovations which tend toward the organization of a new technique of the theatre independently of stage æsthetics. As said, these are in part the result of an effort to resolve the difficulties which attach to the placement and removal of stage constructions in volumes during the performance, whether a plastic setting in its entirety or only different platforms or planes of action. The handling of construction of this kind by hand, even with the best of stage hands, necessitates interminable intermissions and is almost always noisy. In order to raise them into place or bring them on stage it has been necessary to find a means of shifting them together with their bases, which are generally portions of the stage floor itself. Consequently the problem has been to displace the stage floor, or some portion of it, and to replace it by another section similar to the preceding one, on which a new setting has been prepared in advance. It is evident that here we have a new problem and one which the traditional stage never had occasion to solve.

It is impossible to imagine more than three directions in which the stage floor can move : up and down (vertical movement) ; from one side to the other and from front to back or vice versa (movement in the horizontal plane) ; and lastly, a circular movement by which the different sectors of a circle are rotated in succession past the proscenium opening. In addition there can, of course, be combinations of these movements. All experimentation has moved in one or the other of these directions.

Since the traditional theatres almost always have space below the stage and in the flies, it was only natural that the first experiments were concerned with the employment of a *vertical* movement. Even before the birth of the modern art of the theatre the existence of an empty and utilizable space above the heads and under the feet of the actors invited certain builders and constructors to experiment with elevator stages and sinking platforms and sections of the stage floor. These men stand to-day as the forerunners of the modern stage engineers. One of the first modern theatres in this sense is the Opera House in Budapest. Constructed between 1875–80, it possesses a stage floor composed of three sections, each equipped with a hydraulic raising and lowering device. Here also there is a circular cyclorama, probably the first in the history of the theatre. The hydraulic mechanism moves slowly, it is true—it takes about three minutes to raise a given section into place—but with all its slowness it is yet forty years in advance of most other theatres on the continent. Almost at the same time, in 1879, Steele Mackaye, father of Percy Mackaye, built an elevator stage at Madison Square Garden, New York, and during the same period a similar system was proposed but never carried out by an Italian engineer for the stage of the Châtelet in Paris. In this project, as in the one set forth by Mackaye, the upper section forms a ceiling sufficiently high above the lower section, so that when the lower or second section is raised to the stage level to take the place of the other, the first or upper section passes into the flies. In this way the setting for the lower or second section must be arranged below the stage, whilst the setting on the first or upper section must be changed in the flies. The difficulty is at once apparent. How is a setting which has been used on the lower section, and has consequently been struck in the space below stage, to be returned on the upper section if required? If no elevator exists by which scenery may be raised from below stage into the flies it is difficult to imagine any group of stage hands complacent enough to be willing to carry it that distance. It was this difficulty which prevented the realization of the project when proposed for the Châtelet.

Thus, with these forerunners we see established, two systems of vertical movement, actualized in the elevator stage and the sinking stage. It is the second which has received most attention from modern technicians. As for the first, apart from the difficulties just mentioned, it seems impossible to combine it adequately with the cyclorama, which in some form has become indispensable for the representation of open-air scenes. In the case of this device it is apparent that an unimpeded view of the full depth and height of the stage is only possible when the first section is in place, flush with the stage floor. The second or lower section is entirely covered with a ceiling formed by the first or upper section, thus necessitating the use of sky borders or some other antiquated masking device. The alternative would be to use this second section for interiors only, but in view of the varied demands of the modern mise en scène, this is a very serious restriction. These requirements could only be met in the case where the stage was sufficiently high to allow a distance of from forty to fifty feet between the two levels. At the time of the construction of Madison Square Garden and the Châtelet these arguments had not become pressing or practical, since sky borders and ceilings were in general use, but to-day their force is much greater.

The most recent experiments in stage mechanics, however, seem to indicate that the problem of the elevator stage has not been abandoned. Professor Adolf Linnebach, one of the best-known technicians in this specialized field, has quite recently adopted the system for the stages of the new Hamburg Opera House and the theatre of Chemnitz. We show the Hamburg stage in plates 341 and 344, and that of Chemnitz in plate 342 and fig. 13. It has been said that the new Théâtre Molière in Paris is to have a similar installation.

The Hamburg Opera has two stage levels superimposed at a distance of thirty feet. The stage is divided into six zones, the first three of which, moved separately or together, carry the two stage floors, that is to say, the elevator stage proper; while the second half of the stage, comprising zones four, five, and six, has no second floor. On the other hand, the back stage section (marked " H " in plate 344) is equipped with two levels in order that a second stage setting may be raised to stage level and then rolled down stage into position, the stage floor in this case forming a large movable wagon. The mobile stage floor of zones four, five, and six serves for the arrangement of different levels in the distant portions of open-air scenes. Plate 344 shows

the system in its present state, enlarged and made supple by the ingenious innovations of Linnebach, offers great possibilities. Thus in the production of " Das Rheingold " in Hamburg, the open-air scenes of Acts II and IV were set up on the upper level, while the bed of the Rhine of Act I as well as Nifelheim were successively constructed on the lower

FIG. 13.—Adolf Linnebach : Cross-section showing elevator stage, Schauspielhaus, Chemnitz.

the six zones at different levels and the upper level of the back stage section as a seventh. The mobile wagons are to be seen on stage floor six and on the back stage section.

In Chemnitz we have a complete stage composed of two floors, as shown in plate 342 and Fig. 13. Following these experiments a similar equipment is to be installed on the new stage of the Berlin Opera, and also in the National Theatre in Munich. Needless to say,

floor. It is understood, of course, that such perfected installations as these are equipped with a large elevator for the shifting of scenery. In spite of its many improvements the fact remains that we are faced with the old difficulty when we come to set up an open-air scene on the lower level, unless, of course, we are content to use the old wings and borders.

On the other hand, the system of sinking stages has proved completely adaptable to the needs of modern production. Its use has in fact grown especially since combinations of this vertical system with horizontal movement have been found. The Burgtheater in Vienna, which was built shortly after the first experiment, has an installation similar to that found in the latest theatres. Here the stage is divided into two sinking sections, each the full width of the stage and forming at the same time a

taken the place of the second. Here we see the first application of the idea of combining vertical and horizontal movement, and this installation of the Burgtheater is still in use to-day. It is true that the sections only descend about eleven feet below stage, which makes it impossible to construct entire settings on them, but all platforms and raised planes of action which do not exceed ten feet in height

FIG. 14.—Adolf Linnebach : Cross-section showing combined elevator and revolving stage.

wagon. Thus the back or up-stage platform, when raised to stage level, can roll forward and take the place of the first, which in the meantime has descended below stage. Changes are simply made. The second setting, arranged below stage on the second section, rises while the first descends and then rolls forward or down-stage into place. While the scene is being played the previous setting is struck below stage and a new set prepared for the next change, the first section now having

can nevertheless be prepared in advance. The Dresden Opera House stage is constructed according to the same principle. Finally, an analogous stage was installed in the Théâtre des Champs Elysées in Paris, with a height below stage of twenty feet—an installation, by the way, which has practically never been used. Later we shall see the application of this system in its completest form in the Neues Schauspielhaus in Dresden.

The *horizontal* movement of the sections

of the stage floor can be effected either up- and down-stage, or laterally from right to left, or vice versa. This horizontal movement of the stage floor was designed to replace the little wagons which in the beginning were used to bring on-stage the plastic settings ; wagons which for the most part were of modest size and necessitated the breaking up of the setting into several units which could be easily handled in this way. These stage wagons (Bühnenwagen) were introduced by Linnebach for the production of " Faust " made by Hagemann at Mannheim. Brandt replaced this system of wagons by a sliding stage. It is apparent that the sliding stage can be installed only in theatres where the actual width of the stage floor is three times that of the working portion directly behind the proscenium arch ; in other words, the space at the right and left of the working stage proper must measure at least as much and even a little more than the portion limited by the proscenium opening. The mobile stage floor, which is two-thirds of the whole, or twice the width of the portion seen through the proscenium, always presents one-half of itself to the spectator while the change of setting is taking place on the other half, masked from view in the wings. This change takes place, of course, on right and left of stage alternately. In the majority of cases it is lack of space which makes impossible the installation of such a system. Moreover it has the disadvantage that the noise inevitably attendant on the shifting of the old setting and the placing of the new can not completely be done away with as with the sinking stage, where all the shifting takes place beneath the stage floor. Again, with the sliding stage the action of the play must continue while the new scene is being set in the wings, so that, besides the unavoidable noise, all entrances and exits on that side are practically impossible.

An up-and down-stage movement is impossible with this device unless combined with some other, for the simple reason that the section which is on stage has no place to go unless into the auditorium. Consequently, it is necessary to lower it or roll it to one side.

The " Schiebebühne " or sliding stage does not offer the possibilities to be found in the stages operating vertically, except when in combination with the latter. Moreover, the sinking stage has resolved in the completest way a problem of the modern stage which for the other must remain an impossibility : the complete removal of the technical labour of scene-shifting from the stage during the performance of the play. The most interesting combination of the two movements, vertical and horizontal, has been realized in the marvellous equipment of the Schauspielhaus in Dresden, constructed in 1914. Here we have an installation which represents in all its details the completest expression of modern theatre technique. Descriptions of this stage are so numerous that we shall limit ourselves to a brief commentary on the illustrations reproduced (fig. 15, 16, and pl. 343).

As every one knows, in this theatre all the horizontal movements of the stage wagons takes place below stage. The stage floor itself is divided into three sixty feet by twenty feet sections which descend and are raised again by means of hydraulic lifts such as we have seen in the Opera at Budapest and in the other similar stages already described. Consequently in changing the different sections a horizontal movement is maintained, and since this all takes place below stage, there is a complete separation between the place where the technical labour is carried out and the place where the play is acted. It is possible to utilize all the space below stage both right and left for these horizontal movements without encumbering the stage proper. The sinking stage floor, either in one, two or three sections, or as a whole, descends to a distance of thirty-six feet below stage level, and consequently even the largest and most elaborate constructions can be put in place in their entirety below stage. Moreover, since each section can rise to a distance of six feet above stage level they can themselves be used without other constructions as platforms and different levels for the action. These sections can be fixed in any position. The section which rises up-stage is rolled down to the front, while the down-stage section descends or the down-stage section rises and the other descends. Thus we have a triple movement ; rising and sinking, then below stage from right to left or vice versa and on stage level from up-stage, down-stage or the reverse.

for more intimate open-air scenes there is a small mobile panorama which can be unrolled inside the larger one. The gridiron and flies, needless to say, contain all the necessary equipment for handling drops and flat scenery. Elevators exist for scenery—the scenery elevator measures fifty feet by ten, and the scenery wagon, once arrived at the stage entrance,

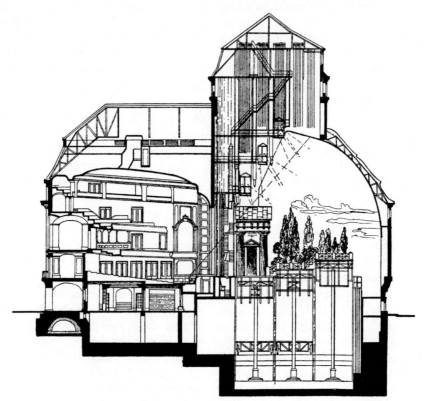

FIG. 15.—Adolf Linnebach : Cross-sections showing stage of the Schauspielhaus, Dresden. (Back to front.)

The hydraulic lifts operate at a speed of three feet per second ; it thus requires about twelve seconds to raise a section or sections to their greatest height. To complete those settings which surpass the width of the mobile platforms, there is at each side a strip or section thirteen feet wide which can be lowered three feet in order to leave a place for small wagons, whose floor then comes flush with the level of the stage. A sky dome or cupola horizon one hundred feet wide, sixty-five feet deep and sixty-five feet high, surrounds the stage, and

can be carried entire by this means to the scene dock below stage—the great sinking platform is provided with traps and so on. In order to give an idea of the ingenuity and the technical perfection of this installation, let us mention that the great platform wagons, once arrived at stage level completely charged, leave their supporting plungers and roll on rails across an empty space sixty feet wide. It reminds one more of a shipyard or a locomotive works with their great travelling cranes than of a theatre and in action this theatre gives one the impression of a factory rather than of a stage. Adolf Mahnke, the Art Director of the theatre, in a little design which we reproduce (pl.343) has pictured this impression. He here shows us not without a certain irony the immense labour proceeding on every level in order to arrange a setting for two poor, insignificant actors who are struggling on the stage.

platforms or sections can wait their turn below stage to be raised into position, is a rare exception. In the case of the revolving stage the number of settings which can be prepared in advance is much greater. Naturally, this depends on the diameter of the revolving platform, and where this diameter does not exceed forty feet it is impossible to place more than

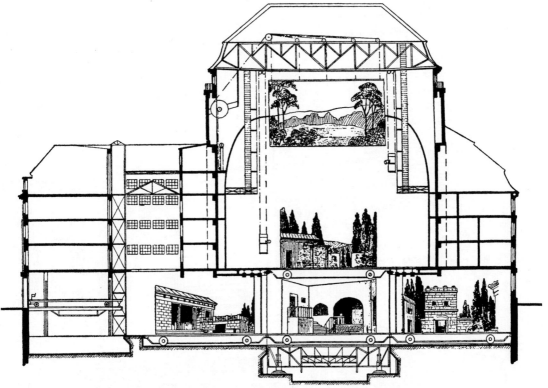

FIG. 16.—Adolf Linnebach: Cross-section showing stage of the Schauspielhaus, Dresden.
(Side to side.)

Horizontal movement in a straight line must be combined with a sinking stage in order to be fully effective, but the same is not true for circular movement. Although, as we shall see further on, this movement gains by a similar combination, it is quite sufficient in itself as represented by the revolving stage.

In the first place, with the wagon platforms and sinking stages, no matter how large, it is generally impossible to prepare more than two or at most three settings in advance. The Dresden Schauspielhaus, where several

two or three. But with the dimensions of the revolving stage in current use—from fifty to sixty-five feet—it is easily possible to construct from five to seven settings. With the exception of a few unimportant changes and additions practically all the settings for a play can be prepared in advance, even in the case of large and fairly complicated spectacles. For a production as packed as that of Reinhardt's "Faust," half the settings can be in readiness from the outset, and a single intermission is sufficient for the change necessary to set the other half of the piece. The result is that the labour of shifting scenery during the

take place in an instant, sometimes without lowering the curtain and at other times in

From "Modern Opera Houses and Theatres."

FIG. 17.—Karl Lautenschläger: First revolving stage in Europe, Residenztheater, Munich, 1896.

performance is reduced to a minimum and often completely done away with. With this device set in advance, the changes of scene

full light, with the actors passing directly from one scene into another. In this way, by utilizing to the fullest the technical possibilities of the device one can at the same time make it serve as an element in the creation of the work of art.

The adversaries of this equipment would have us believe that in order to utilize the revolving stage in this way all settings must be constructed on sectors of the circle, and all be presented in conical or wedge-shaped forms. This of course is altogether erroneous. If we look at the ground plans of the revolving stage for the productions made at the Deutsches Theater in Berlin (fig. 18–21) we shall not

artist can no longer create his stage decorations freely but must always be bound by this interdependence of construction. Certainly, to place on the turntable a number of different scenes, each inch of space must be utilized. It is, in fact, a problem for the architect. The scenes are combined in such a way that the back of one setting becomes the face of the next and in some cases one setting passes over another or between two others. But are these restrictions disadvantages after all? Have we not seen the architect not only take advantage of

FIG. 18—"Henry IV." (Shakespeare).

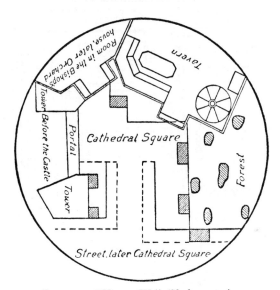

FIG. 19.—"Henry IV." (Shakespeare).

FIGS. 18-21.—Ernst Stern : Ground plans for revolving stage, Deutsches Theater, Berlin.

find a single play for which the settings were arranged in sectors. On the contrary, the revolving stage makes it possible to utilize all the various depths of scene ; the stage being disclosed as far as the cyclorama in one case, and extremely shallow in another. These settings may be rectangular or of any desired form. Often we see through one setting into another and in this way combinations are produced which are interesting and full of imagination ; it being understood always that the settings must be in mutual accord (pl. 346).

It has been said that this necessity to combine scenes in a large production constitutes a serious restriction, and that with the revolving stage the

but even be inspired by the problem presented by an irregular piece of ground, and so attain results more interesting, varied and unforeseen than if he had been perfectly free ? The possibilities in the way of combinations on the revolving stage are almost as inexhaustible as in a game of chess and the spectator in addition gets the benefit of great variety instead of being always faced with the same elements interminably repeated. We are even tempted to say that the obligations imposed on the artist by the revolving stage are a real advantage to him. With a stage such as that of the Schauspielhaus of Dresden at his disposal he is too free. For the man who can really think in three dimensions, the very obstacles of the revolving stage become stimuli for his imagination at the same time that they act as a discipline. The revolving stage, because of the way in which combinations of scene must be effected, prescribes discipline similar to that which many modern artists impose on themselves when they create a fixed stage architecture. Of course, with the revolving stage, the open-air scenes and the combination

separated by a narrow valley spanned at a certain point by a bridge of cyclopean stones. In the valley were two cypress trees and a spring in the rock. This was all, but these few elements when presented from different angles created a great variety of stage pictures and groupings ; constantly changing vistas as the two enemy camps performed their evolutions, with the two hills forming vantage points on which figures could be grouped in

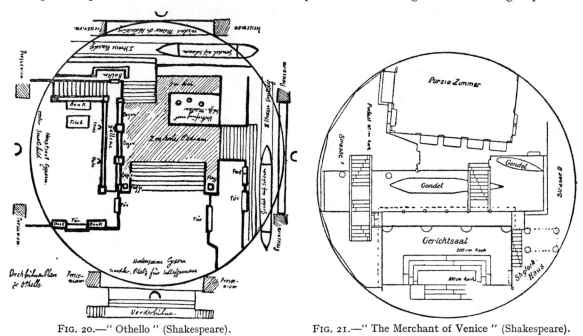

FIG. 20.—" Othello " (Shakespeare).   FIG. 21.—" The Merchant of Venice " (Shakespeare).

FIGS. 18-21.—Ernst Stern : Ground plans for revolving stage, Deutsches Theater, Berlin.

of open-air scenes with others always present difficulty. Here criticism is to a certain extent justified. It is evident that the presentation of open-air scenes is extremely easy so long as all the scenes of the play are set in the open, as for example in Kleist's " Penthesilea," in which all the scenes represent different parts of the Trojan plain. In this piece some scenes were played by a spring in a little cypress wood, while others showed the warriors either on the march or running or climbing a little hill. In Stern's realization of the settings for this play two practical hills were established on the revolving platform, each with a different form and appearance and

silhouettes against the sky. No stage-means other than the revolving stage could have solved the problem so simply and so perfectly. We reproduce an analogous disposition by Stern for " The Tempest " (in plate 345).

In the majority of cases, however, it is a question of combining open-air scenes with other settings such as interiors and here the real difficulties begin. To strike all the stage constructions in preparation for an open-air scene would take too long ; consequently, scenes must be combined. This is possible in two ways. The first consists in showing the open-air scenes between two other settings. This is the way Stern usually proceeds with his gardens, whose straight hedges form the back of the settings at right and left. For example, between the interiors of " Don Carlos " which we show in plates 22 and 23, there is a free space giving a view of the cyclorama at the extreme depth of the stage, the walls forming the backs of the two interiors at right and left being treated on the reverse side to represent the two hedges which border the sides of the garden. The alcove of the king's chamber is to be found in the garden itself. This same method of construction is to be seen in " Twelfth Night " and other plays. The other method consists in placing the exterior scenes on top of the interiors ; thus the corridor of the hall in " Die Räuber " (pl. 13) is constructed under the hill on which the brigands are camped, while in " Faust " (pl. 21) the landscape rises to a height of sixteen feet, and all the space from a height of twelve feet is used for other settings. Stern's designs (fig. 22) show the construction of the stage designed for a similar treatment.

The inconveniences which are evident in such combinations as these have led technicians to look for means of improving the revolving stage. They have turned naturally to experiments analogous to those which ended in the creation of a combined sliding and sinking stage ; that is to say, revolving stages have been invented of such nature that the circular platform can be lowered in sectors into the space below stage. In this case these sectors are almost the exact counterpart of the rectangular sections of the sinking stage floor of the Dresden theatre. It is clear, however, that such a shifting of sectors as this implies a construction in sectors, and consequently imposes a fairly binding obligation on the artist employing it. Recently Max Hasait has invented a stage which calls for a second revolving platform carrying a new series of scenes, which is to be raised to stage level after the first has been lowered below stage. This construction necessitates a space below stage, but only below stage, sufficiently large to accommodate two emplacements. This space may be at the two sides, or one at the side and

one at the back, but each must be large enough to carry a revolving platform in its entirety.

On the other hand Linnebach invented a scheme (fig. 14) in which he applied to the revolving stage the principle of two levels, one superimposed on the other. This revolving stage in two levels was designed for the Schauspielhaus in Frankfurt, but the war prevented the execution of the plan ; so that up to the present there is no revolving stage which is perfectly adapted to handle the changes from open-air to interior scenes and vice versa. But in the design here reproduced it can be seen that even with a revolving stage in two levels the scene designer is compelled to arrange his interiors on the lower level and to reserve the upper floor for open-air scenes only.

It is often asked why so much money and ingenuity should be wasted on developing a system which no longer has an excuse for existence ? The revolving stage was born to meet the demand of realism and died with it. For the stage decorations of to-day it is no longer needed. Those who argue in this way fall into a very serious error. It is quite on a par with all that so-called modern disdain for theatre technique of which we have spoken before. It is only necessary to look at the interesting stage settings designed by Sturm for the revolving stage at the Düsseldorf Schauspielhaus to be convinced to the contrary. Is it possible to imagine a more modern stage construction than the one he has designed for " Paulus unter den Juden " (fig. 23), " Kaiser und Galiläer " (pl. 347) and " Manfred " (pl. 348) ? The whole scene is simply an arrangement of different planes and levels for the action. Is it not apparent that a quite new rhythm of movement is of necessity developed because of this circular disposition of the stage, and that these settings do not merely make use of the revolving stage, but would never have been created without it ?

The most striking argument in favour of the revolving stage lies in a piece of news which will probably astonish the adversaries of this device. At the Schauspielhaus in Dresden, of whose unique and marvellous technical perfection we have already spoken, a great

suffced. The point is that if in this highly equipped theatre it was decided to complete

FIG. 22.—Ernst Stern : Series of sketches showing setting of revolving stage.

revolving stage has recently been constructed on the platforms of the sinking stage. It is unnecessary to say that from the technical standpoint the existing installation more than

the installation with a demountable revolving stage, it was solely because this stage-means, with its varied combinations of settings, one within another, offered artistic possibilities which could not be replaced by the rectangular platforms of the sinking stage.

On the technical side the new installation shows some extremely interesting details. Up to the present the revolving platforms have always been pivoted on a central axis, perfect operation being secured by an under-

lower the platform as much as the height of the little motor in order to bring the revolving platform to the level of the stage.

Circular movement as we see it in the revolving stage is always carried out about either a real or an imaginary axis, situated at the centre of the stage. However, another

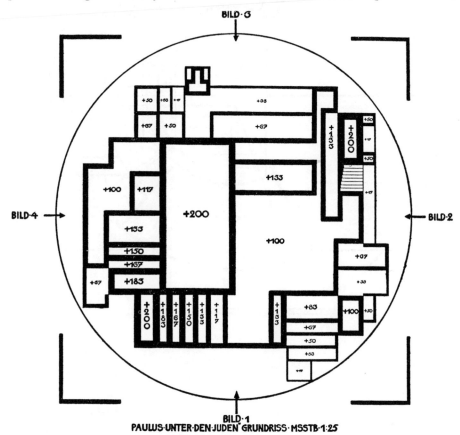

FIG. 23.—Eduard Sturm : "Paulus unter den Juden" (Werfel). Schauspielhaus, Düsseldorf. Plan for revolving stage.

stage construction whose supporting wheels travelled in a circular iron rail. The revolving platform in Dresden has no under-stage construction and no rail. The sectors, which are constructed of wood, each carry two wheels operating directly on the stage floor and propelled by a small motor fixed to the under side of the platform itself and travelling with it, while the eccentric disposition of the installation secures a circular movement without additional aid. It is only necessary to

circular movement has been conceived which has for its central axis a point situated in the auditorium. Here we are faced with a species of sliding stage which instead of moving in a straight line right and left, moves about the auditorium or a portion of it. This plan is called the "ring stage." Adolf Linnebach has constructed the new theatre in Teplitz with a stage equipped in this way (fig. 24). At the right and left of the auditorium there is a circular stage space designed to receive

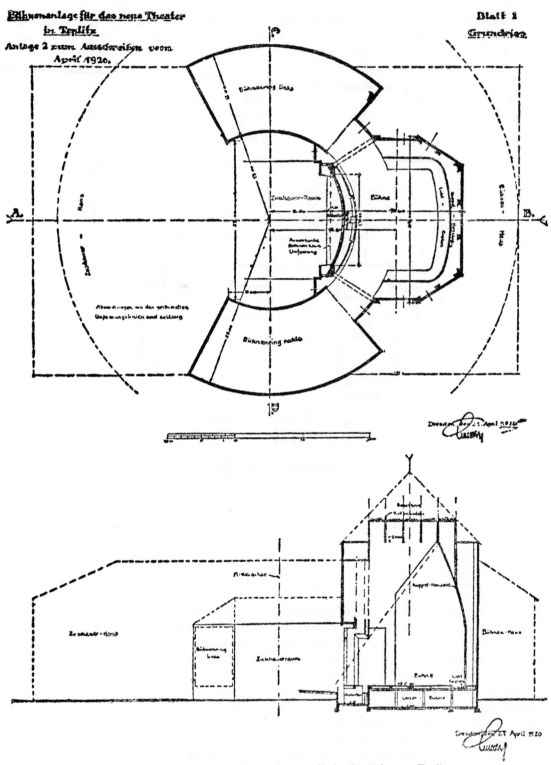

FIG. 24.—Adolf Linnebach : Plans of stage of the Stadttheater, Teplitz.

the sliding stage. In comparison with the usual sliding stage, this system has the advantage that it requires much less width tained within it. He has completed his plan by designing the auditorium in the form of an amphitheatre entered from above by means

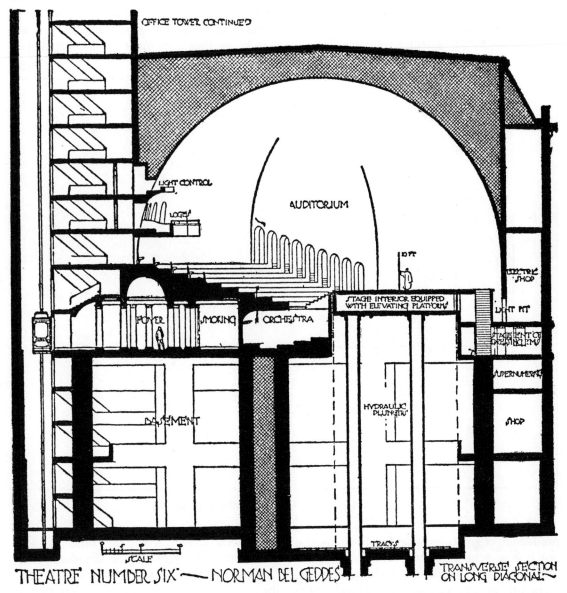

FIG. 25.—Norman Bel Geddes: Cross-section of a theatre with triangular stage placed in one corner.

than is necessitated by the three parts of the Schiebebühne. Strnad of Vienna in his project has pushed this idea to a point where the sliding stage becomes a complete ring encircling the entire auditorium, which is contained within it. of openings placed above the ring of the stage. In this case the stage has from three to five openings, the pillars which support the roof of the auditorium being carried across the front of the stage proper, forming these compartments, which may be used singly or all together as in the case of the tripartite stage with fixed architecture. When all the openings are disclosed, an immense stage is discovered in front of which the two or four pillars stand as a support for the stage frame (pl. 349–350). Such a stage has certain advantages for the

Chapter XIV. There we study all stage forms which are outside the purely technical limitations of the present chapter.

All the devices which we have just reviewed employ a cyclorama or cupola horizon or sky dome. This is in such general use that it seems hardly necessary to insist on its advantages.

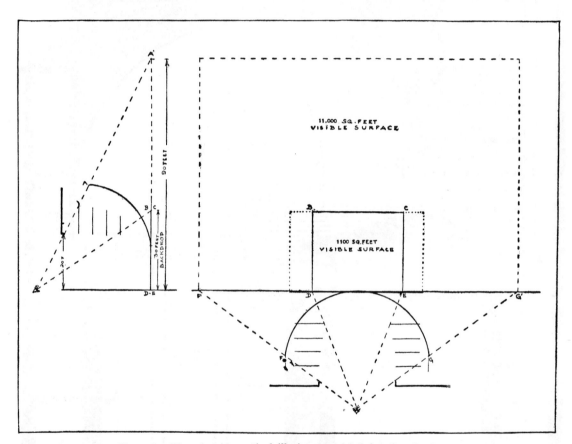

FIG. 26.—Plan showing optical illusion presented by the sky dome.

production of great spectacles involving masses, but it is in general impractical because of the difficulty of obtaining access to the auditorium. Here we have an auditorium completely surrounded by a stage filled with inflammable material and exposed to currents of air, and with no possibility of adequately separating the auditorium from the stage or of minimizing the very obvious fire risks. In a way this project is closely related to the experiments in new forms of theatre which we take up in

It is well known that, like other modern inventions, the cyclorama or sky dome owes its existence to naturalism, which dominated the theatre at the beginning of modern technical experimentation. With such an installation it was possible to present open-air scenes in which the sky produced the impression of stretching to infinity, and besides did away with the necessity, which was always present in the old theatre, of employing sky and foliage borders and wood wings to mask the flies and wings. But outside all illusionist effects, the cyclorama has maintained its usefulness as a simple limitation or boundary of the stage space. We have seen Jessner, for example, present certain stage syntheses before an unlighted cyclorama, thus producing an arresting impression of empty space. Here we have additional proof that such technical innovations as these are not only at the service of a particular tendency in production but that they adapt themselves readily to almost any artistic solution of contemporary stage problems.

The technical details of the sky dome have been described so often that we feel it unnecessary to repeat them here. It may be of interest, however, to examine for a moment the plan here reproduced, which attempts to show the scientific reasons why the sky dome enlarges the visual field (Fig. 26). Briefly, the explanation is as follows : since it is impossible for the spectator to localize exactly the emplacement of the curved surface before him, the eye automatically transposes into the surface at its depth the visible limits of the cyclorama or sky dome. We see that in following the dotted line it represents for the eye a surface exactly ten times greater in width and height than the background whose place the sky dome seems to occupy.

These technical means employed by the modern stage are in the greater number of instances combined with new arrangements of the fore-stage. As these latter are associated with experiments which tend toward the establishment of new relations between the stage and auditorium, they belong more properly to the later chapter dealing with new forms of the theatre.

CHAPTER XIII

STAGE LIGHTING

IT is that branch of the technique of the theatre which has to do with the illumination of the stage that has in our day assumed the greatest importance. The greater the advance has been in the direction of a suppression of decorative elements in the stage setting, the greater has been the dependence on light for the expression of the atmosphere of the drama and in general for the realization of the visual ideas of the mise en scène.

As with the evolution of the technique of stage mechanics, the first experiments in stage lighting took the form of improvements of systems in current use, and it is only within the last twelve or fifteen years that entirely new means of illumination, adapted to meet the needs of the modern stage, have been developed. The invention of the high wattage incandescent lamp and its subsequent adoption for stage use made possible an illumination radically different from that of the traditional stage lighting. It is only after the introduction of this new system that we observe a parallelism, a reciprocal relationship, between technical and artistic progress similar to that which we noted in the case of mechanical technique during the first phase of the modern development. Thus it can be said that, while the evolution of the mechanics of the stage corresponds to the development of the plastic stage decoration, the corresponding movement in the field of stage lighting belongs to the epoch of the modern, synthetic stage setting.

In general, the traditional light installation consisted of a series of border lights, the footlights and some portable bunch lights, to which, if needed for certain effects, arc spotlights were added. This system reaches back into the past and is definitely associated with the old disposition of the flat stage decoration which formed a series of streets or *allées* in which light elements, likewise inevitably ranged in parallel series, were placed. This was always the case, whether the illuminating units were oil lamps, gas or incandescent bulbs. It was solely the power and the quality of the light which changed, the system and the emplacement remaining the same throughout the centuries. The first installation employing electricity used natural glass bulbs, and colour effects were obtained by the use of coloured screens or filters, usually made of glass. Improvement consisted in replacing this single-colour system with another of several colours, in which such elements as light borders and footlights each carried three or four series of lamps, the bulbs in each series being dipped to secure the required colour. This facilitated the search for effects of colour mixture and brilliancy through the control of independent groups of lamps, and this in turn was followed by experiments destined to perfect the means for controlling brilliancy, such as dimmers, shutters, and so on. As was the case with many other stage innovations, experimentation towards improvements in stage illumination was in the beginning seeking to create by these means the maximum of naturalistic effects. Even to-day the prospectus of the Allgemeine Elektrizitäts Gesellschaft, the great German firm manufacturing stage lighting equipment, sums up the objectives of stage lighting as follows : " Stage illumination must render as faithfully as possible all the tones and moods of nature in order to perfect the stage picture and the illusion. It must also

assure complete safety and easy manipulation."
To the A. E. G. the psychological and purely
expressive qualities obtainable through lighting
are apparently of no importance. It cannot
be denied, however, that this search for
naturalistic effects resulted in a very real
progress during this first period.

At the outset it was noted that there existed
in nature two different means of illumination :
first, direct sunlight, which falls on the earth
in parallel rays, and secondly the diffused
light reflected from the dome of the atmosphere
and the objects on the earth. Direct light
illuminates only those objects on which it falls
directly. In an interior, for example, it
illuminates only if it fills the whole space or
falls on a light surface, in which case the
direct light is reflected and changed into
diffused light. If a direct light ray is allowed
to pass through a hole into a room draped in
black it will not illuminate the room at all.
If a mirror be introduced into the room and
placed in such a way as to interrupt the passage
of the light ray, the ray will be reflected in
another direction but the room will still not
be illuminated. But, if the mirror be replaced
by a light, dull surface, immediately the ray is
transformed from direct into diffused light,
and the room is illuminated.

It was this observation which later led
Mario Fortuny to the invention of his system
of indirect lighting. During the early period a
diffused light was sought by means of direct
illumination spread over the entire stage as
evenly as possible. For this border lights,
foots and portable bunch lights were used,
while direct light was produced by lens arc
projectors in some form.

The question of the control of the colour and
of intensity of the light remained to be solved.
A control-system was demanded which would
assure a perfectly smooth passage from full
light to " black-out " without jumping or
flickering. As for colour, it was at once
apparent that the light from incandescent
bulbs was always yellow in comparison with
sunlight and that when this light was used on
the stage to represent sunlight there remained

nothing with which to express a warmer or
more yellow light. After several years of
struggle to obtain natural colour effects by the
use of a three-colour system consisting of
white (or what represented white), red and
blue, it was finally found necessary to introduce
yellow as a fourth colour. This is the four-
colour system as it is in use on many stages
all over the world. In some cases the addition
of green as a fifth colour has been of added
value. The Künstlertheater of Munich has
produced some remarkable light effects by
the use of such a five-colour system. In the
case of projectors, the colour variations were
obtained by means of coloured glass or gelatine
screens and a diminution in intensity by
screens of smoked glass.

One of the most important improvements in
the old system which has occurred in recent
years, concerns the construction of the border
lights. It must be remembered that, before
the introduction of the high wattage lamp,
the border lights constructed in the form of a
metal trough carried three or four series of
small forty to sixty watt bulbs, which were
first dipped in a mixture composed of some
volatile liquid, colloid and a dye stuff corre-
ponding to the colour desired, usually red
or blue. It was soon noted that this colour
screen which covered the bulb when it was
dipped in the dye mixture tended to deteriorate
rapidly in face of the heat developed by the
incandescent filament and the general heat
caused by the adjacent bulbs. To maintain a
pure colour, especially in the case of blue,
which deteriorates with the greatest rapidity,
it was necessary at frequent intervals to
remove the old coating and to redip the bulb
in a fresh mixture. As a matter of fact, the
bulbs were usually redipped without first
removing the old coating, with the result that,
after a certain time, the amount of light
obtainable from the series of coloured bulbs
in a border light had become so diminished
as to be almost negligible. Many experiments
were made in an effort to perfect a coloured
dip which would resist the heat and so prevent
the consequent deterioration in the colour, but

without marked success. The next step, then, was to construct a border light in compartments and to place over the opening of each compartment a glass colour screen into which the colour had been introduced in the pot, and so was unaffected by the heat. The lamp was left in its natural state, and for any given circuit a new set of colour screens could be introduced at will. This assured pure colours and at the same time a greater flexibility. All modern border lights are constructed in this way. We reproduce an example (pl. 351, fig. 8).

Moreover, this installation had to create not only a light spread over the entire stage but also, when required, an illumination different in quantity and quality for each part. Thus, besides illuminating it as a whole, it must be possible to throw on to any part of the stage a light of any desired colour and intensity.

It is well known that gradations in the intensity of electric light are produced by introducing into the conducting line resistance materials which obstruct the passage of the current. The early dimmers consisted of resistance wire and were fitted with a lever which passed over a series of metal contacts arranged on the sector of a circle. The circuit was closed when the lever touched a contact point, and as it passed over the series, each successive contact introduced more resistance into the circuit. In this primitive affair the passage from one contact point to another interrupted the circuit and caused the light to jump. Later developments produced a sliding type of dimmer which is in use in many Continental theatres. Here the bar forming the contacts slides over the resistances and is attached by an iron wire to a lever which when turned, raises or lowers the bar. In America the circular type of plate dimmer which is in general use has been perfected by the Ward Leonard, Cutler Hammer and General Electric Companies to a point which now assures a control as smooth and as graduated as the sliding type so generally used in Germany (pl. 354). The addition of electric controls for the dimmer banks and the placing

of all dimmers and switchboard contacts in a fireproof room removed from the stage (as with the remarkable Majors remote control switchboard) are all added improvements now in current use. A system of light control, in order to approach perfection, should be able to regulate all colour units either singly, or in groups, or as a whole. This means, of course, that the resistance units must correspond in number to the number of colour units. Generally the control levers for a given colour series are placed on the same axis, so that by means of an interlocking device the various units composing the series may be dimmed, either in groups or as a whole ; and a graduated scale makes it possible to determine in figures the exact amount of light being thrown from the unit under control. The Majors pre-selective remote control system provides for a pre-selected arrangement of all the light units so that following a " blackout " the closing of the main circuit is sufficient to produce the new arrangement or set-up without manipulation of switches or dimmer controls.

In general, the installations of fifteen years ago were designed for the traditional stage, no matter how perfect they appeared to be. When the old scheme of setting the stage with flat scenery in parallel planes was abandoned, and the plastic setting with the cyclorama or sky dome background was introduced, the old light equipment could no longer meet the requirements. At the same time, the development of projectors and spotlights of various types carrying incandescent lamps produced a revolution in the field of stage illumination. With the substitution of the high-powered incandescent lamp for the arc came the control from the switchboard of spotlights, floods and other units carrying lamps, ranging from three hundred to three thousand watts, just as formerly the border lights had been controlled. The result was that the old border lights themselves were replaced by high-powered lamps. In some theatres we saw the border light transformed into a steel light bridge capable of carrying any number of spot and flood lights and one or two electricians as well. New ideas in stage decoration necessitated a separation and a specialization of those elements of illumination which up to that time had served merely for general stage lighting. Henceforth the light equipment was divided into two separate and different groups, following the construction of the units and the purpose they were to serve. A first group must assure the proper illumination of the actual playing space of the stage and a second must light the vertical surfaces of the setting. This latter group was in practice divided into two parts, one of which illuminated the stage decoration proper and the other the cyclorama or sky dome.

The invention of the sky dome was followed by a series of experiments similar to those which led Mario Fortuny to the establishment of his system of indirect lighting, commonly known as the Fortuny system. To-day that system belongs to history. Fortuny's dome was tried for years in a little private theatre belonging to the Comtesse de Berne in Paris, but we doubt if the system is now in use in any theatre, at least in the form proposed by its inventor. He deserves, however, the credit for the separation of the light installation into the two groups which to-day constitute the principle elements in stage illumination. Fortuny's scheme employed high-powered arcs which projected the light on to screens composed of silk bands of different colours, the light being reflected from these bands back on to the stage. The dome itself provided a second reflecting surface. This double reflection caused such a loss of intensity that it was impossible to secure sufficient light without a prohibitive expenditure of current. After several attempts to combine indirect with direct lighting, notably at the Berlin Volksbühne and Künstlertheater, Munich, in 1913, the technicians returned to a general use of direct lighting, employing for this purpose the new high wattage gas-filled lamps. On the modern stage to-day very little use is made of indirect lighting, the same effects being secured by means of diffused light.

To light the sky dome of the Deutsches Theater, Reinhardt used a kind of great lantern, composed of several light units and suspended almost in the centre of the stage ; a sort of great pharos from which light radiated in all directions. Such a scheme of central lighting is no longer in use. To-day the light units are grouped in batteries parallel to the stage frame. By carefully regulating their emplacement and by turning the floods which must light the sides of the cyclorama next to the proscenium, it is possible to produce a uniform illumination for the entire sky dome. In many cases the dome is lighted also from below, which facilitates the simulation of the light changes from dawn to daylight and from twilight to night.

The light units in use with this new system are of different forms. One type, cylindrical in form and carrying a thousand watt lamp, is swivelled so that it can be turned in any direction ; it is fitted with a single colour only and is controlled by a dimmer at the switchboard (pl. 351, fig. 1). Another type is equipped with three-thousand watt lamps and is fitted with colour screens operated by an iron wire transmission (pl. 351, fig. 2). Here the intensity is not controlled by a dimmer placed either on the lamp or at the switchboard, but by a shutter placed on the hood and also operated by wire transmission. A light unit of this type will cover approximately one thousand to fourteen hundred square feet of the surface of the dome. The frequent simultaneous use of these two widely different types, the employment of a large number of light units of the same colour grouped independently, and the use of other units carrying different colours but lacking in delicate control, are indications which seem to show that modern lighting technique is still hesitant and has not yet succeeded in achieving definite results.

Recently, the question of the relative merits of the high-powered incandescent lamp and the arc, which we thought had been definitely settled upon, has again come under discussion. Strangely enough, the latest novelty in stage lighting is actually an installation for the lighting of the sky dome equipped with arc lights. This new equipment was constructed by Max Schwabe in 1926 and was utilized by Max Hasait at the Dresden Opera House in the same year (pl. 351, fig. 3). Each large light unit is equipped with two twenty-five ampère arcs. By means of an inner lens the luminous point of the arc, which up to now has defied control by means of a shutter, is here transformed into a luminous vertical line, with the result that the amount of light can be regulated by a shutter, as is the case with other light units carrying incandescent lamps. It is true that later the same model has been built for high wattage incandescent lamps, but the original conception as it is now realized in Dresden called for the arc and not the incandescent bulb. Colour changes are effected by means of glass filters which follow the curve of the metal lamp box. The Dresden Opera House is equipped with forty units of this type disposed in three planes.

For lighting the dome from below a transportable unit is used (pl. 351, fig. 9). Since in all modern constructions the dome is carried down to a point below stage level and provides a sunken space or channel which follows the curve of the inner base line, the lighting from below offers no difficulties. In those cases where no sunken channel exists it is necessary to conceal these horizon lights behind ground rows or other portions of the stage decoration.

The equipment for the illumination of horizontal surfaces, the " Spielflächenbeleuchtung," differs radically in construction from the preceding ones destined for the illumination of vertical surfaces. Here also we find two types in use : one a large diffusing flood light, employing only one colour and the other a unit equipped with three or more colours. The first, carrying lamps ranging from three to fifteen hundred watts (pl. 351, fig. 4) is equipped with slightly rippled parabolic metal reflectors and produces a light with a diffusion of from fifteen to fifty degrees. The rippling of the surface of the reflector prevents the projection of the luminous filament of the lamp. It has a single fixed colour filter or a glass diffusing screen, which may be introduced on the lower side of the hood. The other unit, employing several colours, generally takes the form shown in plate 351, figure 5. These units carry one thousand watt lamps and are equipped with an elliptical reflector. It is well known that the rays from a lamp, placed at the first focal point of an elliptical reflector, converge toward the second focal point, so that consequently it is possible to pass all the rays through a comparatively small colour filtre by placing it near the second focal point. This explains the elongated and converging form of the hood. Colour changes are effected by means of an iron wire transmission. In America, light units of the first type have been built which are equipped with a magazine of colour filters. This, of course, requires more space and may prove cumbersome when compactness is essential.

These light units are suspended above the stage at different points but, since the cone of light is not sharply defined, care must be taken not to place them too close to the sky dome or the cyclorama which, otherwise, will receive the reflected light. To avoid this, the units are equipped with black hoods or maskings, or else lens lights of limited spread are used near the cyclorama.

Often a more concentrated light is required than is produced by the elements just described, and for this purpose lens spot-lights are employed (pl. 351, fig. 6). These are mounted on a swivel and can be turned in all directions. They are fitted with fifteen hundred watt lamps and are generally placed in the stage frame.

On the modern stage, it is usually in the stage frame that the greater number of light elements are assembled. Plate 353 shows a stage proscenium equipped in this way by the Schwabe company. The upper part of the proscenium arch is used as a bridge for the electrician, and is equipped with all necessary floods and projectors placed on accessible platforms, and stands. One reason for adopting this placement is the idea that, in order to obtain certain effects, it is necessary that so far as possible the light should be made to follow the direction in which the spectator is looking. This is also one of the reasons why projectors are sometimes placed in the auditorium itself.

This latter practice is a makeshift which should be avoided if possible, although there are situations in which it is difficult to do without it. This is especially so when it is a question of lighting the fore-stage or that portion of the stage directly under the inset proscenium. Later on we shall see how important this fore-stage as an acting space has become. To light this it is first necessary to enlarge the proscenium and to introduce into it a certain number of light units designed for this purpose. Such an arrangement is only to be found in the very latest theatres, the others being forced to light this space from the auditorium. In some of the more recent theatres, as for example the Kroll Opera and the Ufa-Theater in Berlin the roof of the auditorium has been arranged to carry an equipment of light units completely hidden from the audience. But in the Grosses Schauspielhaus, which is not so very old, the lighting of the orchestra was effected by means of badly masked projectors placed in the auditorium. When the theatre was made over for performances of revues an ugly baldachin had to be constructed to mask the lighting equipment for the fore-stage. At other times the producer has utilized the chandeliers in the auditorium to hide light units, and we have seen in the Redoutensaal in Vienna, lighted by the magnificent candelabra of the time of Maria Theresa, some of the arms of the two crystal chandeliers near the stage cut off by Reinhardt in order to conceal his light units in the remainder.

To all these more or less fixed light elements, modern technique adds others which are transportable. A certain form of construction is imposed on these units by the limitation of weight and the necessity of not developing too much heat in the vicinity of the settings. In all but country theatres, the old type of bunch light, designed to be placed in the wings of the old setting, has been abandoned. When the old system was in use, these took the form of tin wash basins fitted with lamps in several colours. To-day these are replaced by high wattage lamps carried in hoods of various types and mounted in different ways (pl. 352, fig. 13). In order to obtain the full power of the lamp and a sufficient diffusion, and also to avoid spots of light on adjacent portions of the setting, the hoods have been fitted with reflectors of tin plate enamel or with parabolic glass reflectors with a mirror surface. Besides these bunches and reflectors or floods, spot-lights and projectors in various forms and fitted with lenses are needed in modern production, with the result that flood-lights and bunches have been constructed with a lens which now makes it possible to utilize them either as spots or as flood lights (pl. 352, fig. 12). Spot-lights are manufactured which carry lamps up to three thousand watts, but, since the light from these is always slightly yellow, we have seen a return to the use of the arc spot, which produces a pure white light of much greater intensity. The Schwabe concern, for example, builds a one-hundred ampère spot, with which remarkably pure effects of full sunlight can be produced (pl. 352, fig. 14). Modern production demands that, in addition to being able to illuminate particular groups and specific elements of the setting, it shall be possible, if necessary, to light solely the head of a given figure. For this purpose a small pursuit spot is used, with which a small bright light can be concentrated on any point (pl. 352, fig. 15–17).

If a modern installation of this kind be considered as whole, it is apparent that it has introduced certain new conventions into the theatre. It is not so long ago that spot-light effects were considered to belong primarily to Vaudeville and Variety, and a producer of Shakespeare would have been shocked at the thought of employing the lighting methods of the Music Hall and Fairy plays. To-day, producers and public no longer pay any attention to the luminous beams or the diffusion of light produced by projectors placed in the auditorium, accept without question the pools of coloured light which overhead projectors cast on the stage floor, and are no longer astonished to see a spot-light following the tragic hero as he moves about the stage. This collection of new conventions which have supplanted the old theatre traditions— good or bad, depending on the point of view— has, nevertheless, made apparent the weak points of the new system of lighting, and has shown at what points it still needs to be improved. So for instance illumination by means of the new light units, while it accentuates the modelling often in a pleasing way, also casts shadows on the face of the actor which can be very annoying, especially when a nose under the rays of an overhead light suddenly casts a shadow reaching to the chest of the unfortunate hero. Other than the lighting from the sides or from in front, what can be used to correct this ? The footlights again. Here we have an unexpected return to a much reviled element in the stage equipment.

It seems useless to repeat to-day all the arguments which have been brought against the footlights during the last twenty years. Lighting from below has been condemned *en bloc*, without taking into consideration the fact that this means of lighting can be extremely useful, if not indispensable, as a corrective for the other means employed. With the construction of footlights producing an indirect light, they once more assume a position of importance. It is interesting to observe that in the latest installations it is this element in the system which alone makes use of indirect light. In these new footlights the light is thrown on to cycloidal reflectors, which reflect it through a small opening back on to the stage. In addition, the new footlight can be placed well below stage level, a height of two inches being sufficient to permit all the light to pass through. Further, new combination equipments have been built which may be used either for direct or indirect lighting (pl. 352, fig. 10).

The colour of the shadows is another point which does not seem to have been settled. While to-day any desired colour can be thrown on to the stage, the shadows produced always appear dark and hard in comparison with natural ones. In nature the shadow takes on a tone which is the complementary of the colour of the corresponding light. Recently, Gutzeit of Munich has proposed that the light installation be supplemented by additional units for the purpose of regulating the colour of shadows in accordance with this principle of complementaries. While the scheme has not been perfected or applied in practice, the idea should receive the support which it unquestionably merits.

On certain stages a combination of the new lighting with the old is preferred, especially when the repertory of the theatre makes such a combination advisable. Thus, in the large theatre at Wiesbaden, we see the new light units for the sky dome in use with more or less traditional border lights and projectors for overhead use. Since each scene demands its own amount of light, it is impossible to give figures showing the distribution of the illuminating elements.

The whole installation must be controlled from the switchboard and it is apparent that, with so much equipment to be regulated, the emplacement of the switchboard and the attendant master electrician becomes a matter of considerable importance. In the Continental theatre the switchboard is often placed next the prompter's box, in which case, while the operator has the advantage of being able to see the whole stage in front of him, he is out of touch with his assistants and, more important still, with the stage director. In addition, the space is so limited that it is impossible to arrange the board so that it can be handled by one man, who at the same time views the stage. On the other hand, the position at the side of the proscenium, whether raised or on stage level, while it places the operator in direct contact with the stage hands and director, has the disadvantage that for the most part the stage is masked from his view. For the Continental theatres, the installation of a highly compact Majors board in the prompter's box would probably satisfactorily solve the difficulty. With proper telephone communication the presence of the chief operator on the stage is not a necessity.

An installation of illuminating elements as we have just described is completed by the addition of certain " effect " machines. The most important of these are lanterns for projections. Some of these modern Continental devices for the projection of clouds and other effects consist of as many as twenty separate machines designed in two stages around a central axis. Each machine contains a diapositive of a photograph of clouds which are projected by reflection from a mobile mirror, whose movement is combined with the general movement of the whole apparatus as it turns about the central axis (pl. 352, fig. 11). Such naturalistic effects as these, while they still serve the mise en scène of the realistic school (pl. 356) have no great interest for producers of the advanced type, except in those cases when the projected images can be modified in the direction of stylization (pl. 357). While the moderns are not seduced by the possibilities of projecting naturalistic images of clouds and the other phenomena of nature by means of these devices, they are nevertheless quite ready to use them to project entire stage decorations.

As a matter of fact, a whole new procedure seems to have developed with the perfecting of these devices. By means of wide-angle lenses with a short focal length, entire images can be projected from comparatively short distances. For very large planes and curved surfaces, like the dome, certain devices, such as the Richter-Weil, employ two diapositives. The first carries the central portion of the image and is regulated to produce a sharp projection ; the second, producing the outer part of the image, complements the first and can be regulated with equal sharpness. Hagemann's device for projected scenery produces

images of a size almost three times as large as the distance projected. Finally Geyling, Kann and Planer have perfected a machine and a procedure known as the Gekape process, which has solved the problem in an interesting way.

In the Gekape process it is possible to design the diapositives mechanically in such a way that all the deformities resulting from the difficulties of projection—such as the emplacement of the machine either very high above stage or too much to one side, the production of large scale images with a short throw, projections on curved surfaces and the like— are automatically corrected, and an accurate image secured. This preliminary work is carried out on the diapositive, and is combined with certain dispositions of the objective. At the Burgtheater in Vienna, all the stage decorations for Grillparzer's " Der Traum ein Leben " were produced by means of three Gekape machines. One was placed in front at a height of about forty feet and the other two right and left. We reproduce (pl. 359) a decoration for "Peer Gynt" perfected by this Gekape device.

It is apparent that, for the director of the theatre, the luminous projected stage decoration has distinct advantages. First, it makes possible any number of changes of setting without the least technical difficulty. It offers, for the moment at least, a new element of artistic expression, and, above all, where the entire stage decoration consists of a glass plate three and three-quarters by five and a quarter inches, the expenses for settings are reduced to the minimum. When it comes to travelling, all the stage settings for a full repertory can be carried in a case not much larger than a vanity-box.

With these projected settings, we leave stage organization as we have known it to return once more to the old imagery. The projected setting has, it is true, a certain quite special, unreal and fluid character of its own, which distinguishes it from the painted stage decoration ; but it is precisely this curious, intangible quality which separates it even more definitely than painting, from the actor and his world. The setting stands at the back of the stage like an illustration of the action, without ever becoming a part of it. In the production of " Das Mirakel " in Vienna, Reinhardt, using the Gekape device, projected on the first level of a purely naturalistic, architectural arrangement in Gothic style, images of landscapes before which the action on the lower level was supposed to take place. The futility of illustrative indications such as these was here strikingly apparent. Written indications of place, as they were sometimes employed in the Elizabethan theatre, are preferable to such a luminous picture debauch as this. From the instant that the setting is separated in this way from the action, what after all does it represent, if not a written indication transposed into an image ?

It can represent something more—it can present a beautiful image, beautiful in itself, and it is just there that the real danger lies. If we separate the setting from the action, its sole excuse for existence will be its beauty, not scenic but pictorial. And from that moment the projected setting, seeking effects for itself alone, distracts the attention and the interest from the play to which it properly belongs. It is precisely because it is, as it were, of another stuff, another material, than the world of drama that it can seek a new beauty of its own at the side of, and apart from, drama —and let it be noted that if it does not do that its reason for being is gone.

Its presence is apparently justified in plays which are in a certain sense of the same stuff with it, that is to say, dream plays with their fluid visions, or fairy plays and other pieces which have in a way the same intangible quality as the projections. It is here, above all, that projections can be of service to the mise en scène but it seems to us that at this time, when new scenic means appear so seductive, there is a temptation to exaggerate the importance that projections may have for the mise en scène of the future.

It may very well be that the basis of all this new experimentation is that desire for variety and contrast which dominates all human effort. The reaction against naturalism brought with it the so-called stylized stage decoration and, during the period which followed, we have seen all its possibilities expressed in one form or another. After the different applications which we have enumerated, there seems very little left for this tendency to express. Now, finally, the eternal need for variety produces the projected stage decoration, which, after all, is nothing more than a return on another plane to the old type of stage setting long since abandoned.

Projections may also be useful in representing moving elements. In plates 360 and 361 we reproduce two designs by Jorgulesco which represent projects for mobile projections. The idea of projecting Birnam Wood as it moves on Dunsinane in " Macbeth " seems particularly interesting. It is, as it were, externalizing an inner vision. Note also the projections for " Gewitter über Gothland " shown in plate 358.

The problem changes the moment the projection becomes an independent and complete spectacle in itself. Many attempts have been made to create a spectacle of this kind in which colour and sound are corelated. Some of the first of these were made by Luckiesh at the Nela Park laboratory, Cleveland. Here he built a colour organ which was used in New York for the production of the final movement of Scriabine's " Fire Symphony." This did not include any dimming apparatus, with the result that the projections showed merely one colour succeeding another on the screen. In Germany the Hungarian, Laszlo, claims to have created a new mechanism which is also based on the theory of an interdependence between acoustical and optical impressions. His " Farblichtklavier," or colour-light-piano, projects on a screen colours and shadows which are intended to form the accompaniment for a musical composition written expressly for " coloured light and piano." We admit that Laszlo's idea like all such proposals, seems seductive in theory, but his optical compositions as they were shown at the Theatre Exhibition in Magdeburg were not in the least so. These were all the result of the primitive method of superimposing one colour on another and of the employment of a certain number of diapositives treated with banal colours. The projected compositions were in general wholly lacking in expression.

It is quite otherwise in the case of the Clavilux or colour organ invented, perfected and operated by Thomas Wilfred of New York. With this invention we see, for the first time, a successful combination of form, movement and colour. Here it is light itself which creates new and ever-changing forms. By means of a mechanism made up of projectors, colour screens, small motors, moving forms and so on, Wilfred succeeds in decomposing white light in such a way that the different colours of the spectrum are projected on the screen in rhythmic forms. These forms seem to be born under the eyes of the spectator, to grow, to group themselves, to mingle and finally to disappear in the void in accordance with the innate but unknown laws of this new world ; a world of half crystalline, half nebulous forms in eternal movement. He seems actually to create with light, for under his hands an altogether new and beautiful world of moving form and colour seems to come to life. Plates 364 and 365 give only a suggestion of the actual richness and beauty of these creations. Wilfred has never intended that these projections should be an accompaniment to a musical composition. A musician himself, he has perfected an instrument capable of producing a symphonic composition in terms of light, and has devised a system of notation for this light-music which makes it possible for him to repeat at will what he has worked out in the past. These compositions are not improvisations, but the results of creative effort. We can also imagine these projections accompanied by rhythmic dance movements, an experiment

which Wilfred has recently made. We should perhaps recall in this connection the woman who first had the idea of combining rhythmic dance movements with projections in colour, and who, before any of these recent inventions, saw a way through the movement of the dancers and their costumes to animate projections, which up to that time had been without life. It was Loie Fuller who first opened the door on to this new world of purely visual beauty.

Many experiments have been made which deal with the relation existing between the colours used on the stage and the colours of the light sources which illuminate them. Certain colours can be made to disappear as others appear following a change of colour at the light source, so that by painting one setting on top of another, each of which is sensible to a determined light colour, it is possible to make an entire stage decoration disappear as another takes its place. Above all, light of short wave-lengths, the ultra-violet rays and rays close to ultra-violet, produced by special apparatus, have been used to create these effects. By this means costume changes are effected and the well-known trick of changing Whites into Negroes is carried out. So far, such effects have not been employed to any great extent in the legitimate theatre, remaining still the tricks of the Music Hall and Vaudeville stage. It is possible, however, to conceive them as an aid to the production of plays which approach the fairy-play in character. For example, in " The Blue Bird " the sudden transformation of the cemetery into a garden of flowers could easily be realized by such a procedure.

There remain the effects of phosphorescence, effect machines for producing lightning, rainbows, moons, waves and stars. For all these modern technique has new machines, but their operation does not differ greatly from the primitive installations of the older theatre, and to discuss them here would be to enter the field of theatre-tricks and so carry us outside the limits of our study.

CHAPTER XIV

NEW STAGE FORMS AND NEW POSSIBILITIES

THE reforms which we have just passed in review have for the most part taken place within the frame of the traditional theatre, that is to say, on the stereoscopic stage. All that pertains to the image contained within this frame has undergone a change, been renewed, revolutionized even. But throughout it must be remembered that the system of the theatre, bequeathed to us from the long past, which consisted in seating the spectator before a lighted opening, has not been too well adapted to these attempted changes in stage arrangement. It was not only the decorative system which was ailing, but the entire theatre.

Thus the problem for many thinkers interested in this aspect of the theatre, was one of reforming, not only the spectacle, but the relation between the spectacle and the spectator; of creating life, not only on the stage, but of seeking new sources of life in the relation between the public and the actor—between the audience and the stage. With these ideas as a starting point, the necessity for a complete re-organization of the form of the auditorium followed naturally.

The first experiments in this direction were made some time ago. It seems that Antoine was the first to play on a fore-stage, and to him belongs whatever credit there is for thus introducing into the customs of the theatre the fore-stage combined with steps leading to the auditorium. Almost at the same time, Max Reinhardt, whom we find at the beginning of all branches of the modern movement, was experimenting with similar means. In his first performances in the " Schall und Rauch " cabaret, before taking over the direction of the Deutsches Theater, he employed the Japanese " Flowery Way," a runway through the audience over which his actors passed from the auditorium on to the stage. Again, in an effort to break down the barrier between the stage and auditorium and to make the spectators in a way participants in the action, he scattered through the audience a number of actors who, through their interruptions and carefully arranged " business," were to accomplish the liaison. This innovation corresponded excellently with Reinhardt's tendency to create dramatic life by means of the maximum of movement, even at the risk of overdoing it. As early as " A Midsummer Night's Dream," the movement of the elves and fairies on the revolving stage might have been considered excessive, but when we reach some of his later productions, the peopling of the stage with useless figures in a perpetual movement has become an obsession. The " Taming of the Shrew " is an example. Here he tried to maintain an atmosphere of gaiety through the intermezzi of the clowns, who were constantly jumping, climbing and capering on the great stairway.

His overflowing and always restless fancy forced Reinhardt from the outset to look for new stage resources. Thus, in the construction of the " Kammerspiele," he did away with the footlights and tied the auditorium to the stage by three steps. Afterwards this innovation was generalized and from the action on the fore-stage and steps a general amplification of the mise en scène resulted.

In spite of the widespread use of this procedure, the question of carrying the action of the play into the midst of the audience is open to dispute. The adversaries argue that the tendency to mix the real world with the fictitious, to efface the boundaries between reality and art, is prejudicial to that scenic illusion which it is the aim of the theatre to create. The actor, in passing out of the frame of the stage, runs the risk of overstepping the limits of his imaginary world, and this presents a difficulty which is not, after all, always successfully resolved. When we can no longer believe in his actions, illusion in the theatre is threatened.

Moreover, it is argued, history seems to show that art in its great epochs has always been conscious of æsthetic limitations, while in periods of confusion or decadence it has shown a predilection for the abolition of those limits, as well as a desire to obliterate the boundaries between art and life. If this be so, then we must conclude that such experiments as Reinhardt's must be condemned and the stereoscopic stage accepted as a perfect form, since it offers the desired separation between art and life. Other adversaries, less severe, recognize the shortcomings of the stereoscopic stage, but tell us that, since the fore-stage does not offer a solution of the problem defensible from an artistic standpoint, experiments must be made in other directions. Still others smile at the term " decadent " and declare that, from the moment an artistic procedure corresponds to the artistic needs of an epoch, it is perfectly legitimate. And finally, we have the extreme modernists who revolt against the term " scenic illusion," which, in their eyes, discredits in advance all objections of any kind. In the face of all these varied attitudes the question remains open and the problem far from being solved.

The successful use of such means of expression will always depend, in the first place, on the play itself and, secondly, on the tact of the producers ; à propos of which we have the anecdote of the restless actor-manager, always on the look-out for a big effect, who conceived the brilliant idea of delivering the great monologue in " Hamlet " on the lowest step of the fore-stage, in order to be able to put the question, " To be or not to be," in all intimacy to the spectator immediately facing him.

Light seems to be the only means which can keep the actor on the fore-stage within the limits of his make-believe world. If the boundary between the real world and the imaginary world disappears with this new disposition of the action on the fore-stage, it must be restored through the medium of light. Hence we find a quite new organization of the lighting system associated with this reform. In the older theatres, this fore-stage was lighted by projectors hidden in the stage boxes, and sometimes by light units placed at the back or sides of the auditorium. In some of the theatres recently constructed, the architect has widened the proscenium and inserted border lights or high wattage units into the architrave of this deep inset frame. As we have seen, the introduction of a new technique in lighting together with a new disposition and emplacement of the illuminating units brought with them new conventions. If we accept to-day the luminous cone cast by a projector without feeling a lessening of the scenic illusion, why should it be more difficult to accept the acting on the fore-stage ? It seems after all that, with this new disposition of the action, we are dealing, not with an attack on scenic illusion, but with an entirely new conception, which, starting with the introduction of a new convention into the theatre, now carries possibilities of a scenic illusion of its own, similar to that inherent in the traditional conception. We might say further that, strangely enough, this action on the fore-stage seems to fail only when the attempt is made to fit into the frame of the traditional auditorium (that is to say, the theatre of galleries, balconies and boxes) and that as soon as it forms a part of an auditorium conceived in a manner which corresponds to the new concept, stage illusion is in no way prejudiced. Thus we see the amplification of the possibilities for the action completed by a reorganization of the auditorium itself. We have already noted how Georg Fuchs, in his conception of the Künstlertheater realized by Professor Littmann, did away with the boxes and galleries in order to create a closer union between the stage and the auditorium, but, while proclaiming the necessity for this union, he was nevertheless hostile to the idea of acting on the fore-stage for the reasons which we have pointed out above. Here, the old seating plan was replaced by a new disposition in the form of an amphitheatre, or at least what was called amphitheatre, an arrangement which Littmann, Kaufmann and others made use of in many theatres constructed about that time. This disposition corresponded, on the one hand, to the new stage reforms and on the other, to the democratic tendencies of the epoch. We find this amphitheatre—the word is inaccurate, since we have here, not a circular disposition, but a rectangular one in which the rows of seats, widely spaced, mount like a series of terraces, each row being raised considerably above the succeeding one —not only in the theatres intended for the production of Wagnerian Opera like the Prinzregententheater of Munich, but in popular playhouses like the Schillertheater and the Volksbühne.

Here, then, we have a type of modern theatre which has abandoned the tradition. The auditorium with its widely spaced mounting rows of seats is joined by a series of steps to the fore-stage which precedes the stage proper. Sometimes the stage frame is done away with altogether, as in the case of the Vieux Colombier, where the stage is only a part of the small auditorium and hardly separated from it by the curtain rigged between the two supports which sustain the roof—no stage frame, no grand valance or border, and once the curtain is open the steps of the fore-stage and the light alone mark the boundary between stage and auditorium.

As its use extended, the fore-stage has profited by modern technical improvements. To-day, fore-stages are built which have steps functioning mechanically, so that they may assume positions of any height, thus making it possible to change the levels for the action,

not only between play and play, but between scenes as well. With the mobile platform of the fore-stage arranged in sections, the sides can be lowered leaving the centre at stage level, or vice versa, and the different combinations of these sections with the stage itself give greater variety to the action, according to the demands of the mise en scène.

The Redoutensaal in Vienna, transformed for the presentation of plays, serves as another example of a theatre in which stage and auditorium are one. A simple platform at one end of the room serves as a stage, the architecture of the hall being carried across the stage by the curved panels which form the background. A curtain, sliding on an iron wire mid-way to the ceiling, is all that recalls the theatre of yesterday.

An installation such as that in the Redoutensaal in Vienna, set in brilliant and luxurious surroundings, brings to us across the centuries those theatres established by the princes of the Renaissance in the great halls of their palaces ; but the amphitheatre reminiscent of antiquity goes back further still. In fact, the true amphitheatre aims at a renewal of the classic theatre of Greece, a theatre in which great tragedy is played before a great audience.

And here again, we find at the beginning of this movement the imprint of Max Reinhardt. Having realized an entire world on the revolving stage of the Deutsches Theater, and having constructed a Theatre of the Two Hundred, the Kammerspiele, Reinhardt's uneasy imagination was still unsatisfied. He was haunted by the idea of the Theatre of the Five Thousand, that is to say the great amphitheatre of the ancients.

In an auditorium in Munich shaped as an amphitheatre, he revived the classic tragedy "Œdipus Rex," and later, in a circus, he staged a miracle play of the middle ages. Ten years later he saw the theatre of his dreams constructed in iron and cement, the theatre of thousands.

Two factors of necessity co-operate to facilitate illusion in the amphitheatre : the enormous distance and the superhuman grandeur of the plays, dramas, classic tragedies or mysteries of the Middle Ages. But to-day tragedy cannot be played constantly, nor is the distance the same for all spectators ; the actor wears no mask, nor does he move about mounted on the cothurnus. He is only a poor fellow like ourselves, made up and wearing a costume, who tries his best to act the play with the audience seated all about him. In this situation what scenic means can create the world which he demands ?

The existing amphitheatres have been constructed for other ends than the production of plays, namely, for circus and motion pictures. Their unfortunate proportions make it almost impossible for the producer to adapt them to his purposes. The only modern amphitheatre which has been constructed for the performance of tragedy is the Grosses Schauspielhaus opened in Berlin in 1920. We must then consider its arrangements as representing, up to the present, the model amphitheatre.

In principle the modern amphitheatre, with the development of the chorus and crowds in the orchestra, continues the classic tradition. In Reinhardt's great theatre, the orchestra, and by consequence the whole amphitheatre, is elongated in form and, having the advantage of the optical axis of the traditional theatre, the result is that the movement of the actors can be developed on a unique axis (a situation which does not exist in the circus).

In the Grosses Schauspielhaus, the greater part of the action was placed between the orchestra and the upper-stage proper, that is to say on the fore-stage. This fore-stage, which in the circus of to-day is constructed only with the greatest difficulty by means of parallels and platforms, could in Reinhardt's theatre be elevated or lowered as we have described. Operating between the orchestra and the stage proper, it thus provided all the differences of level he required. He had visualized a fore-stage movable in a vertical direction and also mobile in all its parts. This marked a progress of the greatest importance. He then placed the orchestra on a mov-

able platform. All these innovations, and especially the creation of different levels and planes, made it possible for him to give great variety to the rhythm of movement of the actors and he could thus create an imaginary world by developing spatial, or rather three-dimensional rhythm.

As his amphitheatre had no proscenium arch, the curtain being only a continuation of the architecture of the auditorium, Reinhardt was able to play a scene on the fore-stage without actually playing " in front of the curtain." Since the stage-opening was not indicated, he actually played before a wall forming a part of the architecture of the auditorium.

The stage proper, with an opening one hundred feet in width, carried plastic settings and was consequently equipped with a revolving platform and a cyclorama, which served as a sounding-board. If we consider that in the circus of to-day we are forced to act out the play before a single fixed stage decoration, we will grasp at once the advantages offered by this combination of modern stage and amphitheatre. Besides, the height of this great stage space with its revolving platform could be changed ; it could be raised ten feet above the level of the fore-stage or brought down flush with it.

There is a certain danger inherent in the tremendous proportions of a playhouse like the Grosses Schauspielhaus. Only when the space is filled with masses is there contact between the orchestra and the stage, and it is by means of the crowd that this contact is maintained. When the space is no longer filled in this way, there is great danger that the contact will be broken, for the actor alone in the orchestra is too far from the stage, and the theatre divides itself at once into two separate places for the action of the play.

But even in those cases where the contact is not manifestly broken, the stage setting alone is not sufficient to sustain the actor who must play on both the fore-stage and in the orchestra as well. It is only light which can create the imaginary world in which the actor moves and has his being.

If the auditorium is in the shadow, when on the contrary the plane on which the actor is placed is in the light, the difference between the real and the fictitious world becomes at once apparent. The play of light can either accentuate an actor or throw him into the background, and this is equally true for other actors and groups of supernumeraries. The psychological atmosphere or mood of the drama is expressed by means of changes in light and shadow and colour.

In sum, we see that, having eliminated the stage decoration, the amphitheatre has only two means of expression at its disposal ; the first, the rhythm derived from the action on changing planes and, secondly, the variations of the lighting. Naturally, the producer will make the most of groupings and the interplay of masses. This, however, is not sufficient ; the theatre must develop still another factor.

Up to the present time the actor has always appeared in the theatre in the same way ; even if he turns, he shows his profile or his back, for all the spectators are looking at him from the same side. With the new movements and new dispositions of the action imposed by the amphitheatre, the actor found himself surrounded by his audience. There was no longer any such thing as " in front." He was visible from all sides at once and his new creation became plastic by necessity. The actor in the amphitheatre is exposed to the public gaze in much the same way as the bronze David of the Piazza Michelangelo, and he must perforce adjust himself to this monumental unreality through an entirely new form of gesture and bodily movement. He can no longer count on the ambience of the old stage to assist him and so must re-create the imaginary space around him by means which are altogether personal to him as an actor. The true stage setting in the amphitheatre, then, consists in the creation of a physical rhythm by the actor himself, which means the creation of a new form of dramatic art.

The producer, by forcing his actor to play in the amphitheatre before he had acquired a new style adapted to the new conditions, exposed the production to risks which were easily predictable. The speech, the gestures and movements of the actor were not yet adapted to this new form of space and were consequently lost. There remained, however, the movement of chorus and masses, that is to say the spectacle. Hence this alternative was reached ; either to present only dramas built up of masses, in which these mass groups become the real protagonists in the play, such as we saw in Reinhardt's " Danton," which depicted the Paris mobs at the time of the revolution ; or secondly, to reduce the drama to mere spectacle. And so it happened. Already Reinhardt had produced at the Deutsches Theater a pantomime " Sumurun " which was later a great success in Paris, London and America. So he ordered from the playwrights pantomimes for the amphitheatre. And so we see the modern movement, launched by the naturalistic theatre, with its poverty-stricken interiors, passing through the production of stage settings for the classic and modern drama to arrive at last at the pantomime of the circus.

The amphitheatre can never reveal to us its advantages until it develops a new form of dramatic art which meets fully the new conditions. Since a new dramatic form is not created independently of life, it is conceivable that life itself with its new social conditions will provide the inspiration for a new art in general and following that, a great new art of the theatre. Certainly the mass play imposed by the amphitheatre responds to certain social tendencies of our time. But, whenever in the history of the theatre a close communion has existed between the people and the stage, we find that we are in the presence of a cult, that is to say, an ensemble of more or less homogeneous ideas which unite the spectators in the theatre. It is this that the production in the amphitheatre is seeking. The crowd which filled the classic theatre of Greece was the assemblage of an entire people who, animated by the same religious convictions, prayed with the chorus, judged with the

Areopagus, and in a sense participated in the action. This was equally true for the spectators gathered in some market-place in the Middle Ages to watch the performance of a mystery play. But we are not Greeks nor credulous appassionati of the fifteenth century, and so it is somewhat hopeless to revive the classic drama or the mediæval mystery. The theatre of the thousands will only be possible when a new social order has given to us a common cult bringing with it a community of belief, ideals, and values. Then will appear the new tragedy and comedy, and the new dramatic art of the amphitheatre will be born. Until that time, all that is done will be only preparatory, and these projects nothing more than forerunners.

While this is true of all those producers who are to-day seeking, either with or without the amphitheatre, a new style in the theatre, at the time of Reinhardt and his successors in the field of large scale production, the question of a new style of production had not yet been proposed. For them the problem was simply how to fill a vast space with active life and so by this irresistible movement to carry away in rapture thousands of spectators. Reinhardt has always lacked a feeling for style, and this lack of feeling manifests itself just as clearly in a realization like " Œdipus " as it does in " Das Mirakel." For us to-day, severely rhythmic classic tragedy demands something other than a great crowd milling in the arena. When, however, this apparently unorganized movement corresponds to the character of the play, as in the case of " Danton " with its revolutionary crowds, effects are created which reach almost the sublime (pl. 367). And even in plays whose style is more precise, the realization on a large scale has produced arresting moments solely through its vast proportions and through the lighting (pl. 366). Later, Reinhardt continued his large scale productions in Salzburg, producing them both in the cathedral (pl. 368, 369) the Kollegienkirche and in the open air on the steps in front (pl. 373). It is hardly necessary to mention that business enterprise " Das

Mirakel " which during the last fifteen years has overrun Europe and America (pl. 371, 372). Other more modern producers have followed Reinhardt, and we show (pl. 374-375) two productions by Karlheinz Martin realized in the Grosses Schauspielhaus.

While all these producers, all these men of the theatre, who have been thinking, searching, experimenting, have not succeeded in achieving a new and definite form of theatre, they have, nevertheless, through seeking, advanced along the road which leads to a new theatre ; a theatre vaguely imagined, perhaps, of which we know only this—that it will be altogether different from the one bequeathed to us by our fathers. The foremost men are conscious that the theatre as it is to-day has ceased to play a part in the life of the people, and that it must change its aspect if it is to become once more a living organism, participating in life and enriching it, as it formerly did in the great periods of the Art of the Theatre. The theatre of our days has only two choices, either to evolve or to die, and evolution cannot be brought about by mounting cubes and pylons on the stage in place of painted drops. The whole problem of the spectacle in the theatre must be attacked from the foundations up.

Under the impulse of some such ideas as these, new projects have sprung up on all sides. Some of these represent a logical evolution from the ideas announced by the amphitheatre, while others seem born of a desire to do something different at any cost, some seem possible in application, and some are merely amusingly bizarre and altogether impractical.

Neuzil, Loewitsch and Scherer have advanced a project for a plastic stage, a " plastische Bühne," against which such a reproach could hardly be brought. Their scheme follows rather closely the ideas which preceded the plans for the Grosses Schauspielhaus. The most important difference is that in their proposed theatre, the large stage behind the fore-stage is transformed into a relief stage, by bringing the back wall closer to the immense proscenium opening, if one can call it that.

Again the whole stage, the fore-stage, which is here in the middle of the auditorium, and all the separate parts, are movable in a vertical direction. This is combined with another device. The elements which make up the movable sections of the stage floor are in the form of prisms, so that when these prismatic bodies are raised to different heights it is possible to compose with them blocks, stairs, terraces, and even walls, buildings and rocks in landscapes stylized in the form of cubes. The coverings of the cubes being changeable, they can alter colour or even become transparent (pl. 378–380).

A so-called " mystic abyss " surrounds the orchestra, which is here called auditorium stage or " Raumbühne." From this trench, in which light units are placed, the actors may enter on stage from below and from all sides. The stage may also be approached by other entrances at the sides and from the stage at the back. This back-stage is arranged both for the customary settings and for projections. This plan with its combination of a platform, surrounded by the spectators and backed by a relief stage, does not seem to avoid the danger of a separation of the places of action, a danger which we have just pointed out in connection with the Grosses Schauspielhaus. With this in mind, perhaps, the architects have equipped the stage floor of the relief stage, which can be raised in such a way that seats may be placed there, thus completely surrounding the central stage with spectators.

In another chapter we have noted Strnad's project which also has an auditorium arranged in the form of an amphitheatre. In his plans the circular auditorium has the roof carried by pillars, two, four or six of which frame, as desired, a stage of one to five openings (pl. 349–350). Then there is Ernest de Weerth's project which, though employing extremely dubious baroque forms, also combines stage, fore-stage and " mystic abyss " (pl. 382).

The objections to such combinations as these are at once apparent. Treichlinger, the author of still another scheme, states them as follows : The active participation of the spectator in the spectacle is as dangerous for the work of art in the theatre as his complete indifference. Participation may consist either in the presence of spectators on the stage or the presence of actors among spectators. Indifference is produced when the actor retreats behind the frame of the stage and the spectators retire into the boxes. It follows that the actor must come out of the frame, but in placing him outside it is a mistake to employ alternately a framed stage and another placed in front and separated from it. This is to confuse two principles which are distinctly opposed to each other. The platform for the action must be brought into the auditorium, but the opening at the back, if there is a place for one, must not reveal a second stage. This space must be arranged as a great sliding door serving primarily for entrances and exits, though, in addition, it may carry on its surface certain decorative pieces which serve as indications to localize the action ; and, lastly, it may act as a sounding-board. It is variety of movement, different planes of action and play of light which give life to the stage. Here, as in all modern proposals, the different sections of the stage can be displaced in a vertical direction ; the centre portion can be lowered and mounted with settings in the space below stage level. Plate 385 shows a model of the stage and plates 383 and 384 show the stage set and two views of the back wall.

This scheme, while it shows a certain progress toward a new form of theatre, is nevertheless open to criticism. If the stage has already been abolished, why continue a form of auditorium which faces toward an objective which is non-existent ? Replace the stage by a wall, and what is the situation ? The spectators, oriented nearly as they were formerly, now have before them this wall which plays no real part in the ensemble. Is it not better, then, resolutely to abandon the old form and place the spectators in a circle about the stage ? If this is done, there is always the difficulty that the actor must perforce turn his back on a portion of the audience. Proper training for the actor should be able to overcome this apparent difficulty. If, as we have suggested, he be treated as a monument in a public place, it is conceivable that he may finally achieve a physical expression so complete that the play of his back will complement and complete that of his face. It is well to remember that this problem of acting in a circular arena was solved by the circus clown a long time ago. There remains of course, the difficulty involved when several characters are in action and the difficulty of grouping masses.

To educate the actor for this new type of stage, Treichlinger has outlined a supplementary scheme which he calls the school stage. This consists in a construction in different levels open on all sides. Here with the help of these different levels in different colours to act as guides, the pupil must learn to create a spatial form for his dramatic action.

It was only logical that attempts should be made to solve this new problem of the theatre with a stage exposed on all sides. Norman Bel Geddes has proposed several possible solutions. His proposal for a production of Dante's " Divine Comedy " is well known ; a great crater rising in circular terraces (pl. 220, 221). The effects of lighting and grouping, which the artist and especially the remarkable photographer Bruguière, who took the picture of the model, have obtained, are strikingly beautiful. Herman Rosse, for his part, has proposed a circus in which the arena is to be surrounded by a circular decoration on gauze, transparent for the spectators seated behind it, yet always visible as a decoration on the side opposite. This appears to savour a little of the music hall " stunt " and, by consequence, its possibilities are restricted. In some of Geddes' other projects, he abandons the circular form and experiments with different emplacements for the stage. Thus he has invented a theatre in which the stage is placed in the corner of a square auditorium, a sky dome covering with its vault, not only the stage, but the entire auditorium as well. Here the stage floor descends and rises again

carrying a new setting (fig. 25). In his scheme shown in plate 386, we see a long and narrow stage flanked on both sides by an auditorium. With such a disposition, it is evident that the action must be developed as a frieze visible from both sides and presenting the same appearance to the spectators in both auditoriums.

Lastly, certain new forms of the theatre have been proposed which aim to throw into prominence and give expression to what has been termed " scenic dynamism." In these proposals we are told that everything is based on a theory regarding movement in space. This tendency to base the structure of the theatre on a theory of movement in space has led Mahnke to his project for a spiral stage. His theory is that the space of the stage must be transformed as the drama unfolds, just as when reading a piece of literature our imagination develops a never-ending series of changing images. This spatial movement is secured by arranging the stage in spiral form and by the movement of light through a double " light-organ " and control-apparatus. The intention is to have the scenes succeed each other and to be superimposed one on the other, much as they are presented by the technique of the motion picture.

To this end Mahnke has arranged around a square tower four segments of a circle which can be changed in height. Each segment represents a mobile elevator stage, and the entire construction can be turned as desired. These two movements, vertical and horizontal, can take place either separately or together. This stage, by the fact that half the circumference of a circle is outside the frame, represents a compromise between the stereoscopic stage with proscenium and the stage without frame (pl. 387). Entrances for the actors and access for the light is provided by the triple fan-shaped frame, and also by special openings in the orchestra. The backgrounds are formed by several transparent cycloramas. Behind them is a complete equipment of mobile projectors and two motion picture projecting machines. It remains to be seen whether this disposition, when realized, contains as many possibilities as its author claims for it.

But, after all, it is Frederick Kiesler who shows the extreme consequences of this new dynamism. In Vienna, in 1924, he exhibited a " Raumbühne " which consisted in a combination of circular scaffolds arranged on different levels. Another of his projects, called a " Railway Stage for Department Stores," shows a gigantic spiral mounting the different floors of a great shop and fitted in the centre with four elevator platforms provided with gangways, which lead from the different levels to the galleries where the public is seated to watch the show. In his " Endless Theatre," he proposes a sort of endless race-track extending over the roofs of the town and into the country. In this theatre are placed swimming pools, theatres, cinemas, race tracks, stadia for boxing and for football, polo, baseball etc. According to him, in such a theatre the spectator would be able to follow all these spectacles at the same time.

We have to admit that he certainly aims at giving the public its money's worth.

In trying to find in all these experiments and proposals a directing idea, we are struck by the fact that even the most contradictory reforms tend toward a common goal, which is to base the art of the theatre on the actor and on the actor alone. It has been said that, the less the importance given to the stage image, the more the actor profits thereby. On the new stages, it is only the actor who can create about him the ambience he needs. He may be given different levels for his movements and be illuminated in various ways, but for the rest it is he who must, by his own strength, by his own art, create the spectacle as a whole. As we have noted, only after an entirely new method of training will he be able to attain to this. It now remains for us to examine to what extent this new conception corresponds to the idea of the " complete stage spectacle " which was the point of departure for the modern movement.

CHAPTER XV

CONCLUSIONS

IN concluding, we find ourselves far from that complete stage spectacle which we had at our finger-tips in the Reinhardt epoch. Then, the modern movement came into being, animated by the idea that only through an intimate collaboration of all the arts in the work of production could the theatre be saved and the new stage form to which all aspired be created. To-day, there is a very marked tendency which aims at suppressing the majority of details for the proclaimed purpose of giving back to the actor the stage from which many feel he has been crowded out. This even goes further. After twenty years of twentieth-century stage decoration, many serious and sincere reformers are ready to condemn all stage decoration as utterly useless.

This is a perfectly understandable revolt and an attitude for which there is much to be said. Stage decoration, for all the attention which has been paid to it during the last years, is not the most important factor in the theatre. The dynamic force of the theatre resides in the actor. It is the actor who always has been and probably always will be the essential element in the theatre, without which the theatre in any sense in which we understand the word could not exist. Actors were before stage settings. It is said that the mythical Thespis entertained the crowd from the tailboard of a cart. The theatre of Molière was the child of the commedia dell'arte, which was born on a crude platform set up in the public square. The theatre of Shakespeare and Burbage had a similar parentage. In short, the history of the theatre is the history of its actors, and this is as true for the Orient as for the Occident.

And yet this actor and his art are the most ephemeral of all the elements which make up the organism we call theatre. To analyse his art is futile. In the pristine theatre the actor and author were one. When the separation came it was the author who was dependent on the actor to give life to his dreams. The best plays were, and are, written for actors, and the playwright himself is in a way a vicarious actor ; for there is no good playwright who has not something of the actor in him, just as there can be no first-rate producer or scene designer who has not the same feeling for the art of acting. Robert Edmond Jones sees in the relationship of the two a spiritual collaboration. Speaking of the rôle of the scene designer he says : " The designer's sole ambition must be to affirm and ennoble the art of these mystical protagonists. And he (the designer) may rest content only when we say, as the curtain rises on the work of his hands : It is evident that this play we are about to see is no common play. It is evident that these men and women who will appear before us are no common mummers. These are Actors, Seers, Sayers. Let us honour them. For by their inspiration they imitate immortality."

The last generation has seen the old theatre upset and its domain invaded by the painter, the decorator, the architect, the dressmaker, the theorist, the reformer and the expert in this or that field, all jostling one another in their eagerness to make their influence felt. As Arthur Hopkins says in his preface to " Drawings for the Theatre " by Robert Edmond Jones, from which the preceding quotation was taken : " The theatre for the most part has become a medium for man's exploitation of himself." Out of this confusion looms the figure of the producer, the director, the regisseur. The appearance of these others has made his directing presence necessary if not inevitable. In the adjustment to these new conditions, the super-director or producer has usurped the centre of this balanced wheel, while the actor has been pushed toward the periphery. It is the realization of these conditions which has led to the revolt against stage decoration.

At the same time we see men of the theatre, no less modern in their ideas, utilizing forms of visual expression which spring from various tendencies in modern painting, and through them realizing stage settings which represent nothing more than a continuation of the most ancient and traditional forms of the theatre. This co-existence in the same period of such contradictory tendencies is certainly somewhat disconcerting. If they have anything in common, it is to be found in the single fact that both have receded from the complete stage spectacle which was the point of departure for the modern movement. The plastic stage without setting and the painted setting without plastic elements both conformed to the eternal law which demands that all progress be accomplished by repercussions, and all evolution by contrasts rather than in a straight line.

It is evident that the refinement of the stage, even though it often leads to an impoverished stage, is in accord with our æsthetic desires to-day, when the presence on the stage of any too descriptive setting irritates and fatigues us. It is, however, a little premature to conclude that this stripping of the stage springs from a desire to restore the predominance of the actor in the theatre. Usually, this "establishment of the actor in his rights," which we so often have dinned into our ears to-day, is as a matter of fact nothing more than a surface rationalization, hiding the true motives for the movement, which are to be found in our nervous tension, our impatience in the presence of any work of

art which approaches being "complete," and in our psychological need for short-cuts, no matter how facile, in all the arts. The receptivity of the public in 1927 and the receptivity of the artists themselves is such that a piece of negro sculpture is more beautiful than a statue by Rodin, a Picasso more wonderful than a Renoir, and a Meyerhold mise en scène more arresting than one in the Reinhardt manner. This is true, and all the high-sounding words about the " re-establishment of the actor in his rights " only serve to befog the fact that this simplification of the spectacle produces the desired reaction in what the " behaviourists " would call our nervous system of to-day ; a nervous system which in 1927 revolts against the same " complete stage spectacle " to which it responded with satisfaction in 1907. So in these reforms we must recognize that it is not so much a question of the actor as of ourselves, of our nervous system, our " unconscious mind " if you like, of our æsthetic needs and demands. As for the actor, we feel that, in spite of all the vicissitudes to which he has been subjected during the modern evolution, there is only one way in which he can lose his prerogatives in the theatre, and that is by bad acting. If the theatre is to be purified in order to re-establish a world of bad actors, it is better left as it is.

However, if we admit that certain stage decorations can prejudice the impression produced by the acting, we must be precise about what sort of settings we mean, and this definition leads us at once to the recognition of a very curious fact. No one would ever speak of the settings being preponderant in the Reinhardt epoch, and yet it was precisely those settings which were the most descriptive, the most " actual," the most " real." Not only would it have been difficult to efface such actors as Wegener and Moissi, but the setting itself dissolved into the totality of the spectacle and was perceived as a part of a whole, with the result that no outside effort was demanded of the spectator. But, during the modern evolution, the paradoxical fact became evident that the setting, in becoming more and more synthetic, often demands a special attitude on the part of the spectator, who must in this case himself complete what the setting is only concerned with " suggesting." Whenever this setting truly represents a psychological reflection of the action, it becomes one with that action, just as stylized realistic settings have done. It thus becomes a part of a whole, because it is directly emotionalized, as every true stage creation must be. This is not often true, however. The synthetic stage decoration is, on the contrary very often, " intellectualized," and from that moment is addressed to the intelligence rather than to the feelings and emotions. The result of this is that an act of intelligence, outside the apperception of the drama, is required of the spectator. In this way the stage setting draws the attention, monopolizes it and scatters it, and so is a menace to the unity of the spectacle and by consequence a danger to the acting of the players. It is neither the stylized realistic setting nor true psychological expression achieved by synthetic means which is dangerous to the actor and the entire spectacle, but rather the intellectualized setting, a category to which many modern creations belong.

And now we find ourselves at the crux of the whole question of stage decoration. Stage setting is always possible and admissible when it is the result of the imagination of an artist, when it expresses the drama and expresses it by means which conform to our æsthetic demands. It is useless and even irritating when it utilizes those means without achieving expression. Finally, there must be a meeting of the minds on what is meant by this modern " simplification " of which we are always talking. It seems that very often we confuse two sorts of simplification which are really opposed to one another. There is a simplification which is practised in all the arts. This simplification, which is the only one which has value, means that the imagination, the fantasy of the artist, submits itself to law, to the laws of art. This is in fact a striving toward conscious mastery. But to achieve this synthesis there must be something to synthesize ; there must be a certain inner richness and wealth of imagination. Given this inner and unconscious store, synthesis can achieve the maximum of expression by the minimum of means. Synthesis is a goal, the goal of the artist, the goal of the creator. It is never a starting point.

On the other hand, there is a simplification springing from preconceived principles, which is not a " result " but a " starting point " ; a false point of departure. With the minimum of means this simplification succeeds in giving us only a minimum of expression. It is there, it exists *before* the work of creation begins ; it is there to give excuse and a semblance of justification for poverty of fantasy and general lack of imagination. Moreover, the modern art of the theatre, in definitely fixing certain stage means, has provided this type of simplification with a ready-made language of forms, a complete vocabulary ready to be put to use.

Here everything is codified. We have been careful in Chapters VI and VII to present as far as possible the classification of that code, in order that we might now throw into relief all that still remains outside any code ; everything, which over and beyond all adopted language, constitutes a true creation in the field of art. The reduction of the setting to a few elements isolated on the stage ; interiors presented by means of screens ; different levels for the action ; stairs, practicables, curtains, proportions, lines, colours, light ; all these are established, recognized, fixed, and ready waiting to be employed, ready in fact to serve the poor as well as the rich. All this can be transmitted, taught, learned and copied. The question of art, however, begins where all teaching leaves off—it begins before the mysterious door of the artist's imagination.

The plastic imagination of the artist creates a new synthesis for every piece. Poverty of imagination utilizes a preconceived simplification. Simplification by preconceived principles ends by becoming the despair of the spectator.

It is the joy and refuge of every producer who, lacking imagination, can thus hide his poverty of invention behind a recognized and accepted principle.

He also often hides it behind an undeniable technical ingenuity. In fact, in many modern creations, it is " ingenuity " which takes the place of " imagination." We recognize the fact that the restricted means offered by some stages can in certain cases prove the inspiration for a *tour de force*, but in general ingenuity only becomes legitimate when it is in the service of a truly creative imagination. It is, in fact, that balance between creative force and technical invention which constitutes the chief endowment of the true scene designer. But, in many settings composed of fixed elements, curtains, and so on, in place of a real creation all that is presented to us is an ingenious technical solution. We must be suspicious of these, because here ingenuity, instead of serving artistic qualities, has replaced them. The result of this is a synthesis without expressive significance ; from the standpoint of art—nothing. Synthesis has become a point of departure rather than a goal.

Inevitably, those who use this premature simplification end by generalizing it and in this tendency to generalize, so common in the theatre, there is always a certain danger. How often have we seen a principle of production applied to plays to which it was quite unsuited ? Producers, with a leaning toward a certain style of stage presentation, force into their chosen system the most widely dissimilar plays, with little consideration for their fitness. In the final analysis, it is the art of the theatre which suffers by this procedure, and it explains in a measure why we are so ill at ease when we suddenly see a large number of modern productions assembled before us. Such was certainly the unexpected effect of the Theatre Exhibition of Magdeburg, where we had placed before us a collection of some sixteen hundred designs and models for stage decorations. Each of them, taken by itself, seemed more or less successful, often extremely interesting, but in looking at the ensemble

we were forced to conclude that almost all these efforts really resolved themselves into more or less happy applications of certain established principles. Thus, in place of giving us an impression of intense life in the theatre, this exposition ended by creating a feeling of petrifaction, of stagnation, in the art of the stage. And it may very well be that the selection of illustrations which accompany the present study will produce a similar reaction.

It is evident that the producer, in order to avoid the danger of ossification, should realize that he must never attempt to impose a unique and invariable style on all plays without distinction, but should, on the contrary, determine from the character of each play the extent to which the mise en scène can move towards or away from reality. Style is not the indescriminate application of a preconceived idea to any play whatsoever ; it lies in a unity of conception in which all the stage elements represent the work of the author in a manner which satisfies the receptivity of the epoch. Or, again and more exactly, there are two kinds of style. The style of the epoch exists whether we wish it or not, since inevitably we are the children of our time. But the style of the individual play will vary from one production to another. This gives us a great latitude in the establishment of our syntheses.

Assuredly it would be a mistake to impose an extreme stylization on certain naturalistic dramas which still figure in our repertory. Pitoëff understood this when he used for Gorky's " Lower Depths "arrangements which we owe to the naturalism of Stanislavsky. These plays are the product of an epoch and so markedly dated in speech, gesture and whole dramatic make-up that the mise en scène must not damage the impression. Consequently, it has become difficult to give a representation of these plays which aim to bring them more in line with our approach to-day without at the same time endangering their character. However, in certain plays such as " Rosmersholm " and " When We Dead Awaken," it is possible to disengage what they contain of the eternally human and universal and consequently to establish a mise en scène on the same plane. Even so, many details of daily life, much gossip of the little Norwegian village, still strike a discord in an ambience placed outside reality.

The case is quite different for much of modern drama and for the classics. Modern drama in itself responds to our conceptions. As for the classic drama, its universal, human element is able to find a new expression in each new period. Nowhere shall we be so free as before the works of Shakespeare, Racine and Goethe. There is no ground for the contention made by some that the Kamerny Theatre of Moscow falsified Racine's "Phèdre" in its production of that play. It is, on the contrary, by leaving us free to express its beauties by our contemporary means that tragedy offers to the art of the stage the opportunity to show its real strength and its true stature.

Even for classic drama, a great variety of solutions is necessary. We will never be able to synthesize "Romeo and Juliet" in the same way as "Macbeth" or "Hamlet." Some tragedies, like "Macbeth," "Hamlet" and "Lear" which unfold their story outside of time or any epoch, so to speak, demand a synthesis quite different from that for "Richard III" or "The Merchant of Venice." Theatre is only theatre because of this possibility of variation. It is the choice itself of the stage means which in each case produces the expression.

The present-day theatre risks impoverishment when it falls into a formula and attempts to make of the principle of synthesis a thing immutable. And an art which should attest the differentiation in our æsthetic sensibilities ends by making us, if anything, even less differentiated. Modern culture is to be determined by variation, not by regimentation, and it is precisely in the finest sensibilities and the most developed intellects that this differentiation is most marked. But the modern stage, when it shuts itself within the confines of a narrow formula, blunts the sensibilities and damages the very sources from which the art of the theatre springs.

So it is not surprising that we should find that it is actually the best among the men interested in the theatre of our day who are often tempted to consign to the flames all "levels for the action," all effects of light which, some slight variations excepted, are always alike, and to demand of the art of the stage a little less monotony and a little more new life, a little more inner, and by consequence true, life. For them the best scene designer will be he who, gifted with a sensibility sufficiently refined to catch the style necessitated by each piece, will collaborate in the creation of the spectacle by bringing to the common work his own personal expression, free from all formula.

This, then, is the road that evolution must take: by direct inspiration, by sentiment, not by the pursuit of formulas. But the present confusion is such that we cannot tell *where* that road will lead us to-morrow; nor, in terminating this book, should we venture on a prophecy.

PREFACE TO THE LIST OF ARTISTS

OUR aim in adding this list of scene designers has been to furnish the student with a guide to the men who have been identified with the evolution of stage decoration during the last twenty-five years. In preparing it we have followed the same procedure adopted for the collection of the illustrative material. We sent to all artists whose names and addresses we could secure, a printed card, with a request that they give us in condensed form the data we required. These cards, when correctly filled out, contained the name in full, nationality, theatres, early training, three most important productions and, lastly, publications. A very large number returned these cards, and as far as possible we have printed their replies in full.

During the period with which we have dealt, new schools of painting, new ideas in architecture, and to a certain extent new forms of the drama have influenced stage decoration. Many painters have been brought into the theatre for occasional productions or for a very brief period, and have returned again to their painting. Few have been brought up in the theatre, and few remain devoting themselves exclusively to it. This is true of architects as well. Urban is an example. He came into the theatre as an architect, and for fifteen years he worked almost wholly in this field. To-day he is fully occupied with architecture, and only occasionally designs a production. In other words, many of the designers of stage settings have been transients in the theatre. Doubtless many of the names included in our list belong to this category, but obviously it was not within our province to distinguish.

A number of important names in the theatre, especially those associated with the theatre before the War, were inaccessible for one reason or another ; in these cases we have set down the biographical notes ourselves as best we could. We realize fully that this list is not complete, and that it may contain many errors. It is intended only as a beginning, and we shall welcome all additions and corrections in order that we may perfect it in view of a future reprint.

STAGE DECORATORS

Name	Country	Theatres	Three Important Productions	Remarks	No. of Illus.
AAES Eric	Denmark (worked in Germany, Sweden and Denmark)	Theater in der Königgrätzerstrasse, Berlin ; Circus, Stockholm ; Det-nye Theater, Scala and Röde Kro, Copenhagen	Zwischen 9 und 9, Berlin (Sturm) ; Peer Gynt (Ibsen), Copenhagen ; Smil Köbenhaven (revue), Copenhagen	—	—
ADAMS William Bridges	England	Memorial Th., Stratford-on-Avon	Merry Wives of Windsor (Shakespeare), Lyric, London, 1924 ; Much Ado About Nothing (Shakespeare), New Theatre, London, 1926 ; Stratford Shakespeare Festival, 1919-27	Lecturer on Shakespeare and the modern theatre	—
ALIX Yves	France (worked in Belgium)	Théâtre du Marais (Brussels)	Sganarelle (Molière), 1922 ; Le Carosse du Saint Sacrement (Mérimée), 1922 ; Le Menteur (Corneille), 1922	Many illustrated books, lithographs and etchings	—
ALTENKIRCH Prof. Otto	Germany	Sächsische theater	Ring des Nibelungen (Wagner) ; Parsifal (Wagner) ; Faust (Goethe), 1914	—	—
ALTMANN Nathan	Russia	Jewish Theatre, Moscow	Uriel Acosta (Gutzkow), 1922	—	Pl. 170-173
ANDREENKO Michel	Russia (worked in Russia and Czechoslovakia)	Souvorine Th., Petrograd ; Kamerny Th., Odessa ; different theatres, Prague	Menæchmi (Plautus), Kamerny Th., Odessa, 1919 ; Paul I. (Merejkovsky), Théâtre Russe, Prague, 1922 ; Mazanek (. . .) National Theatre, Prague, 1924	Articles in : " Théâtre — Art — Écran," " L'Art Slave," and other magazines	Pl. 284
ANISFELD Boris	Russia (worked in Russia and America)	Ballets Russes ; Pavlova Ballets ; Metropolitan Opera House, New York	The Love for Three Oranges (Prokofieff), Chicago Opera, Chicago	—	Pl. 236

Name	Country	Theatre	Productions	Writings	Plates
APPIA Adolphe	Switzerland	Scala, Milan; Wälterlin, Basel	Tristan und Isolde (Wagner), Scala, 1923; Das Rheingold (Wagner), Basel, 1924–25; Die Walküre (Wagner), Basel, 1924–25	For writings, see Bibliography	Pl. 34–41
ARAVANTINOS Panos	Greece (worked in Greece and Germany)	Staatsoper, Berlin	Die Frau ohne Schatten (Strauss), 1920; Wozzek (Berg), 1926; Don Giovanni (Mozart), 1927	Articles in various Art reviews	—
ARENT Benno von	Germany	Saltenburgbühnen, Berlin	Erich XIV (Strindberg), 1924; Die Nacht der Nächte (Revue), 1926; Romeo and Juliet (Shakespeare), 1925	—	—
ARMFIELD Maxwell	England (worked in America)	Greenleaf Theatre; Greek Theatre, University of California	Miriam (Armfield and Smedley), Greek Theatre, 1919; A Winter's Tale (Shakespeare), Little Theatre, New York	Writings: three One-act Plays; A Text-Book on Design; The Winter's Tale (12 col. plates), Magazine Articles	—
ARONSON Boris	United States	Unser Theater, Bronx, New York; Yiddish Art Theatre; Civic Repertory Theatre	Between Day and Night (Hirschbein); The Bronx Express (Dymov); $2 \times 2 = 5$ (Wied), 1927	—	Pl. 180
BABBERGER August	Germany	Stadttheater, Karlsruhe	Platz (Unruh); Ein Geschlecht (Unruh)	—	—
BABIĆ Ljubo	Yugoslavia	Croatian National Theatre, Zagreb	Richard III (Shakespeare), 1923; Twelfth Night (Shakespeare), 1924; Adam and Eve (Krleia), 1925	—	Pl. 112, 119, 264
BAKST Léon	Russia (worked in Russia and France)	Ballets Russes; Opera, Paris, etc.	Scheherazade (Rimsky Korsakov, 1909; Ballets Russes, 1909; Daphnis et Chloë (Ravel), Ballets Russes, 1912; Istar (d'Indy), Opera, Paris, 1923	See Bibliography	Pl. 230, 231 290, 291, and Colour plates Nos. v, vii
BARANOWSKY Prof. A.	Germany	Städtische Bühnen, Leipzig	Gilles und Jeanne (Kaiser); Fiesko (Schiller); Julius Caesar (Shakespeare)	See Bibliography	—

Name	Country	Theatres	Three Important Productions	Remarks	No. of Illus.
BARRADAS Rafael	Spain	Teatro Eslava, Madrid	Productions for Martinez Sierra	—	—
BÁTO Joseph	Hungary (works in Germany)	Lessing Theater, Berlin	Die Spielereien einer Kaiserin (Dauthendey); Madame Sans-Gêne (Sardou), 1921	—	—
BATY Gaston	France	Comédie Montaigne; La Chimère; Studio des Champs Élysées (Director-producer), Paris	La Cavalière Elsa (Demasy); Têtes de Rechange (Pellerin); Maja (Gantillon)	See Bibliography	Fig. 5
BENOIS Alexander	Russia (worked in Russia, France and England)	Moscow Art Theatre; Alexandrinsky and Mariynsky Theatres, St Petersburg; Opera, Paris, etc.	Petrouchka (Stravinsky), Ballets Russes, Paris, 1911; Le Rossignol (Stravinsky), Drury Lane, London, 1914; Le Malade Imaginaire (Molière), Moscow Art Theatre, 1913	Producer and Scene designer. See Monograph in Russian by Serge Ernst	Pl. 9, 10
BENOIS Nicolas (fils)	Russia (worked in Russia, France and Italy)	Opera, St Petersburg; Opera, Paris; Scala, Milan; Chauve-Souris	Les Quatre Saisons (Glazounoff) St Petersburg, 1924; Kovantchina (Moussorgsky), Milan, 1926; Boris Godounoff (Moussorgsky), Milan, 1927	For Articles on B., see Illustrazione Italiana, 1926, etc.	Pl. 232
BERG Yngwe	Sweden	Intima Theater, Stockholm	Himlens Hemlighet	—	Pl. 139
BERNSTEIN Aline	United States	Neighbourhood Playhouse, New York; Theatre Guild, New York	The Dybbuk (Anski); The Little Clay Cart (Chudraka), Neighbourhood Playhouse; Costumes for Cæsar and Cleopatra (Shaw), Theatre Guild	—	—
BILIBINE Ivan	Russia	Opera, St Petersburg; Ballets Russes; Pavlova Ballet	Russian Ballets	—	—
BILINSKY Boris	Russia (worked in France)	L'Arc en Ciel, Paris; Chauve - Souris (Balieff)	Mostly Cinema	—	Pl. 282, 283

Name	Country	Theatre	Productions	Notes	Plate
BLANKE Hans	Germany	Gera (Reuss)	La Dame de Pique (Tchaikovsky), 1924; Otto und Theophano (Handel), 1925; La Scala (Rosso di San Secondo), 1927	—	
BOGDANOFF Rose	United States	Greek Theatre, University of California; Yale University (Dep. of Costume Design)	Twelfth Night (Shakespeare), 1924	—	
BOGUSLAVSKAJA Xenia	Russia (worked in Denmark, Germany, France)	Douvan - Torzow, Copenhagen; Berlin; Olympia, L'Oiseau Bleu, Paris	—	—	
BOLL André	France	Various Paris Theatres	Hostellerie du Bon Moyne (Dhomont), 1924; Nounette (Duvernois), 1925; Déjeuner de Soleil (Birabeau), 1925	See Bibliography	
BORNHOFEN Heinz	Germany	Stadttheater, Mannheim	Lumpazivagabundus (Nestroy); Carmen (Bizet)	—	
BRAQUE Georges	France	Cigale, Paris	Ballets at " Soirées de Paris "	—	
BRAGAGLIA Anton Giulio	Italy	Argentina, Rome; Manzoni, Turin; Indipendenti, Rome	La Torre Rossa (Sommi), 1925; Sansone (Spaini), 1925	For Writings, see Bibliography	Pl. 156
BRAGDON Claude	United States	Hampden Productions, New York	Cyrano de Bergerac (Rostand), 1925; Hamlet (Shakespeare), 1925; Caponsacchi (A. Goodrich and R. A. Palmer), 1926	See The Theatre of To-morrow, in " Old Lamps for New "	Pl. 136
BREUER Heinrich	Germany	Vereinigte Stadttheater, Düsseldorf	Merchant of Venice (Shakespeare); Henry IV (Pirandello)	—	

Name	Country	Theatres	Three Important Productions	Remarks	No. of Illus.
BREUER Marcel	Germany	Versuchsbühne, Bauhaus, Dessau	"Variété"	—	—
BRUEGMANN W.	Germany	Städtische Bühnen, Leipzig	Jonny spielt auf (Krenek); Arlechino (Busoni); Clavigo (Ettinger)	—	—
BRUYKER A. E. de	Germany	Niederdeutsche Bühne, Hamburg	Klaus Kniephof; Mysterienspiel	—	—
BUCHHOLZ Gerhard T.	Germany	Staatstheater, Wiesbaden	Elektra (Strauss), 1925; Salome (Wilde), 1925; Cardillac (Hindemith), 1927	—	Pl. 214, 215
BURKHARD Emil	Germany	Landestheater, Karlsruhe	Walküre (Wagner); Rheingold (Wagner); Li-Tai-Pe (Frankenstein)	—	—
CAMPENDONCK Heinrich	Germany	Stadttheater, Crefeld	Der Sturz des Apostels Paulus (Lauckner); As You Like It (Shakespeare); Magic (Chesterton)	—	—
ČAPEK Josef	Czechoslovakia	National and Municipal Theatres, Prague	Le Misanthrope (Molière); Le Bourgeois Gentilhomme (Molière); Les Ratés (Lenormand)	Writings: The Insect Comedy (with Karel Čapek); Adam the Creator, etc.	Pl. 146, 147, 274, 357
CHAGALL Marc	Russia	Kamerny and Art Theatres, Moscow; Theatre of the Revolution, Moscow	—	Publications: Illustrations for "Les Âmes Mortes" (Dead Souls), (Gogol); Fables de La Fontaine	—
CHESTAKOFF	Russia	—	Lac Lull	—	—
CHINI	Italy	—	—	—	—

COSAMATI Aldo	Italy (worked in England)	Little Theatre, London	The Tragedy of Mr. Punch, Little Theatre (1920)	—	—
CRAIG Edward Gordon	England	—	Dido and Æneas (Purcell), 1900; Rosmersholm (Ibsen), (for Eleonora Duse), 1906; Hamlet (Shakespeare), Moscow Art Theatre, 1912*	See Bibliography	—
CZESCHKA Prof. Carl O.	Austria (worked in Germany)	Deutsches Theater, Berlin	King Lear (Shakespeare), 1908	See "Max Reinhardt," by S. Jacobson	Pl. 17, 18
CZIOSSEK Felix	Germany	Würtembergisches Landestheater, Stuttgart	Die Sündflut (Barlach); Der blaue Boll (Barlach); König Nicolo (Wedekind)	Publications: see "Bühnentechnische Rundschau"	—
DAHL Loe	Germany	Various Berlin Theatres	Don Carlos (Schiller); Der tote Tag (Barlach); The Playboy of the Western World (Synge)	—	—

* The complete list of Edward Gordon Craig's productions, as reported in Rouché's introduction to the translation of "The Art of the Theatre" is :—

Dido and Æneas	1900, London
The Mask of Love	1901, ,,
Acis and Galatea (Handel) . . .	1902, ,,
Bethlehem (Hausman)	1903, ,,
Sword and Song	1903, ,,
The Vikings (Ibsen)	1903, ,,
Much Ado About Nothing (Shakespeare) .	1903, ,,
Venice Preserved (Otway) . . .	1904, Lessing Theater, Berlin
Elektra (Hofmannsthal), (for Eleonora Duse) .	1905
Rosmersholm (Ibsen), (for Eleonora Duse) .	1906
Hamlet (Shakespeare)	1912, Moscow Art Theatre

Regarding "The Pretenders" (Ibsen), at the Royal Court Theatre, Copenhagen (1926), Craig states that he only assisted at this production.

Name	Country	Theatres	Three Important Productions	Remarks	No. of Illus.
DALSUM Albert van	Holland	Stadschowburg, Amsterdam (producer)	The Only Jealousy of Emer (Yeats), 1924 ; Liliom (Molnár), 1926	—	—
DAMMANN Georg	Germany	Opernhaus, Hannover	Fidelio (Beethoven)	—	—
DANIEL Heinz	Germany	Hamburger Stadttheater and Deutsches Schauspielhaus	Julius Cæsar (Shakespeare), 1925 ; Faust (Goethe), 1926 ; Napoleon (Grabbe), 1926	—	Pl. 191
DARDEL Nils de	Sweden (works in France)	Swedish Ballet, Paris	La Nuit de Saint Jean	—	—
DELAVILLA Franz K.	Austria (works in Germany)	Städtische Bühnen, Frankfurt	Musik (Wedekind) ; Hölle, Weg, Erde (Kaiser) ; Die Sendung Semaels (Zweig)	—	—
DELECLUZE Jean	Belgium	—	Boris Godounoff (Moussorgsky); La Foire de Sorotchini; Marouf	—	—
DEPERO Fortunato	Italy	Indipendenti, Rome ; many other theatres in Italy	Le Rossignol (Stravinsky), 1917 ; Balli Plastici, 1918 ; Anikam de l'an 2000 (Casavola), 1924	—	Pl. 162, 163, 316
DERAIN André	France	Ballets Russes, Opera, Paris	La Boutique Fantasque (Rossini), 1920 ; Jack in the Box, 1926	—	Pl. 263
DETHOMAS Maxime	France	Théâtre des Arts and other Paris theatres	Le Carnaval des Enfants (St. Georges de Bouhélier), 1910 ; Les Frères Karamazov (Dostoievsky), 1911 ; Thésée (Lully), 1913	—	—
DIEZ Prof. Julius	Germany	Künstlertheater, Munich	Judith (Hebbel)	—	—
DINSE Walter	Germany	Städtische Bühnen, Frankfurt	Rain (Somerset Maugham) ; Florian Geyer (Hauptmann) ; Sakara (S. Bucharoff)	—	—

Name	Country	Theatres	Productions	Publications	Plate
DOBUJINSKY Mstislav	Russia (worked in Russia, Germany, and France)	Moscow Art Theatre; Ballets Russes; Opera, Paris, Dresden and Kovno; Chauve - Souris (Balieff)	Un Mois à la Campagne (Turgenieff), Moscow Art Theatre, 1909; Eugène Onegin (Tchaikovsky), Dresden, 1924; Dame de Pique (Tchaikovsky), Kovno, 1925.	Publications on D., see Comoedia illustré, May, June, 1914; Art et Décoration, November 1923. Monographs and Designs, Berlin and Petrograd, 1923	Pl. 7, 8, and Colour plate No. ii
DOBUJINSKY Rostislav (fils)	Russia (worked in France)	Chauve-Souris (Balieff)	L'Enlèvement du Sérail (Archangelsky), 1926	—	Pl. 268
DOBRA Wilhelm	Germany	Städtische Bühnen, Leipzig	Ariadne auf Naxos (Strauss); Evangelimann (Kienzl); Oberon (Weber)	—	—
DOLLIAN Guy	France	—	La Nuit; Andromaque (Costumes)	Wood-engraver	—
DOMERGUE Jean Gabriel	France	Théâtre Femina, Paris	Arlequin; Sin	—	—
DRABIK Vincent	Poland	Teatr Polski, Opera National and Theatre, Warsaw	La Comédie non Divine (Krasinski); Miséricorde (Rostovowski); Pan Twardowski	—	Pl. 239
DRESA	France	Théâtre des Arts; Opéra; Comédie Française; Gymnase, Paris	Le Sicilien (Molière), Arts, 1910; Castor et Pollux (Lully), Opéra, 1918; Fantasio (Musset), Français, 1926	Illustrations for "Bonplaisir" (H. de Regnier), Kieffer, Paris, 1918	—
DUFY Raoul	France	—	—	—	—
EDWARDS Norman de Kalb	United States	Greek Theatre, Cal.; Orchestra Hall F, Detroit; Eastman Th., Rochester	Henry IV (Shakespeare), Greek Th., 1920; Merry Wives of Windsor (Shakespeare), Detroit, 1921; Pelléas et Mélisande (Maeterlinck), Detroit, 1921	—	Pl. 376, 377

NAME	COUNTRY	THEATRES	THREE IMPORTANT PRODUCTIONS	REMARKS	NO. OF ILLUS.
EGOROFF V. E.	Russia	Moscow Art Theatre	L'Oiseau bleu (Maeterlinck), Bataille de Dames (Scribe)	—	—
ENGELS Robert	Germany	Prinzregententheater, Munich	Oberon (Weber)	—	—
ERLER Prof. Fritz	Germany	Künstlertheater, Munich	Hamlet (Shakespeare) ; Faust (Goethe)	See Bibliography	Pl. 57-60
ESSMANN Manuel	United States	—	Masks	—	—
EXTER Alexandra	Russia	Kamerny Theatre, Moscow ; Moscow Art Theatre	Thamiro of the Cithern (Annensky), Kamerny Th., 1916 ; Salome (Wilde), Kamerny, 1917 ; Romeo and Juliet (Shakespeare), 1921	See Bibliography under " Tugendhold "	Pl. 152, 153
FALK Robert	Russia	Jewish Kamerny Th., Moscow	A Night in the Old Market (Peretz)	—	Pl. 103
FANTO Prof. E.	Germany	Staatsoper, Dresden	Turandot (Puccini)	—	Pl. 356
FAUCONNET	France	Vieux Colombier, Paris ; Art et Action, Paris	Les Dits des Jeux du Monde (Meral and Honegger), Vieux Col., 1918 ; Le Bœuf sur le Toit (Cocteau), (Masks), Art et Action, 1920	See Album du Vieux Colombier	—
FEDOROWSKY	Russia	Moscow Art Theatre	Carmen (Bizet) ; Sanin (Artzibasheff)	—	—
FERDINANDOFF	Russia	—	Œdipus (Sophocles)	—	—
FEUERSTEIN Bedrich	Czechoslovakia	National and Municipal Theatres, Prague	Edward II (Marlowe) ; Le Malade Imaginaire (Molière) ; L'Amour et la Mort (Vrchlicky)	See Bibliography	Pl. 202, 203, 244, 245
FINETTI Gino de	Italy (worked in Germany)	Lessing Theater, Wallner Theatre, Berlin	The Mirror of the Virgin (Stolitsa), 1920 ; Die Tanzgräfin (Stolz), 1922 ; Nixchen (Strauss), 1923	—	—

Name	Country	Theatres	Productions	Notes	Plates
FONTANELS Manuel	Spain (worked in Spain and Italy)	Teatro Eslava, Madrid; Teatro d'Arte del Convegno, Milan	Don Juan de España (Martínez Sierra); Il Pavo Real (Marquina); Dona Francisquita (Vives)	—	Pl. 199
FOSSKO Joseph	United States	—	Judith (Hebbel)	—	—
FRASER Claude Lovat (dec. 18th June 1921)	England	Lyric Theatre, Hammersmith, London	The Beggar's Opera (Gay), Lyric, Hammersmith, London, 1920; La Serva Padrona (Pergolesi), same 1919; If (Dunsany), Ambassadors, London; As You Like It (Shakespeare), Lyric, Hammersmith	See Bibliography and "Characters from Dickens," drawn by Cl. L. Fraser, Jack, Nelson & Sons, London	Colour plate, No. i
FREY Maxim	Germany	Volksbühne, Neues Volkstheater, Berlin	Götterprüfung (Eisner); St. Jacobsfahrt (Dietzenschmidt); Pericles (Shakespeare)	—	—
FRITZ Hans	Austria	Innsbrucker Kammerspiele	Invention of standardized cube-stage	See Bibliography under Rochowanski	Pl. 53
FRYCZ Karol	Poland	—	Hamlet (Shakespeare), and many other important productions	—	—
FUERST Walter René	Austria and Yugoslavia (worked in Germany, Austria, Greece and France)	Deutsches Theater, Berlin; Volksbühne, Berlin; Théâtre National de l'Odéon, Paris	Alles um Geld (Eulenberg), Vienna, 1913; Emperor Jones (O'Neill), Paris, 1923; L'Homme et ses Fantômes (Lenormand), Paris, 1924	For writings, see Bibliography	Pl. 110, 111, 208, 218, 219, 223, 265, 266, 267, 329 and Fig. 4
GABO N.	Russia (worked in France)	Ballets Russes, Paris	La Chatte (Sauguet), 1927	—	Pl. 165
GADE Svend	Sweden (worked in Germany)	Different theatres, Berlin	Nach Damaskus (Strindberg)	—	Pl. 210, 211
GALITZINE Prince Nicolas	Russia (worked in England)	Drury Lane, London; principal provincial theatres of Great Britain	The Wooing of Catherine Parr (W. Devereux), 1926; The Desert Song (O. Harbach, O. Hammerstein and F. Mandel), 1927	Lecturer on Stage Designing at R.A.D.A., London. See Bibliography under "Robes of Thespis"	—

Name	Country	Theatres	Three Important Productions	Remarks	No. of Illus.
GARSIDE John	England	The Old Vic, London	A Midsummer Night's Dream (Shakespeare), 1924; Antony and Cleopatra (Shakespeare), 1925	—	—
GEDDES Norman Bel	United States	Opera, New York; Opera, Chicago; Various New York theatres	Shanewis (Cadman), Metropolitan Opera, New York, 1918; The Miracle (Vollmoeller), Reinhardt, New York, 1924; Jehanne d'Arc (de Acosta), Paris, 1925	See Bibliography	Pl. 69, 70, 94, 220, 221, 333, 386, and Fig. 25
GERGELY J.	Russia	—	Beim Rabbi; Mai Ko Maschime	—	—
GEYLING Remigius	Austria	Burgtheater, Vienna	Die Nibelungen (Hebbel); Peer Gynt (Ibsen); Cæsar and Cleopatra (Shaw)	—	Pl. 359
GLIESE Rochus	Germany	—	Macbeth (Shakespeare); Don Giovanni (Mozart); Die Piccolomini (Schiller)	—	—
GLUMAC Sergius	Yugoslavia	—	Faust (Goethe)	—	—
GOLOVINE Alexander	Russia	Alexandrinsky Theatre, St Petersburg	Don Giovanni (Mozart); Orphée (Gluck); L'Oiseau de Feu (Stravinsky)	—	—
GONTCHAROVA Nathalie	Russia (worked in France)	Ballets Russes; Kamerny Theatre, Moscow	Coq d'Or (Stravinsky), Ballets Russes, Paris, 1914; Les Noces (Stravinsky), Ballets Russes, Paris, 1923; L'Oiseau de Feu (Stravinsky), Ballets Russes, London, 1926	See Bibliography and "Le Jeu Infernal," Moscow, 1911; "La Guerre," Moscow, 1914; "Ombre Transparente," Paris, 1920, and numerous other publications	Pl. 258, 304, 305

Name	Country	Theatre	Works	Publication	Plates
GORELIK Mordecäi	United States	Various New York theatres	King Hunger (Andreyev), Philadelphia, 1925; Processional (Lawson), Garrick Theatre, New York, 1926; Loud Speaker (Lawson), 52nd Street Theatre, New York, 1927	Publication: "Some Observations on the New Stagecraft," in "The Arts," New York, April 1926	—
GRANOWSKI Tadeusz	Poland	—	Von Morgen bis Mitternacht (Kaiser)	—	—
GRANVAL Charles	France	Comédie Française, Paris; Opéra, Monte Carlo	On ne badine pas avec l'amour (Musset), 1924; Les Fourberies de Scapin (Molière), 1922; Catherine the Great (Shaw), Monte Carlo, 1926	—	Pl. 250
GRAY Terence	Ireland (worked in England)	Festival Theatre, Cambridge	Oresteia (Æschylus); Heraclitus (Ellis); On Baile's Strand (Yeats)	See Bibliography and "Cuchulain," "And in the Tomb were found," "The Life of Hathepsut"	Pl. 65-68, 114, 115
GRETHE Heinz	Germany	Stadttheater, Mannheim	Jungfrau von Orleans (Schiller); Peer Gynt (Ibsen); Prince Igor (Moussorgsky)	—	—
GRIS Juan (dec.)	France	—	Les Tentations del la Bergère (Monteclair)	—	—
GROSZ George	Germany	—	Das trunkene Schiff; Cleopatra (Gliere), (Costumes); Methusalem (Goll), (Costumes)	—	Pl. 310, 311
GRÜNEWALD Isaac	Sweden	Royal Opera, Stockholm	Samson et Dalila (Saint-Saëns); Sakuntala (Kalidasa); Oberon (Weber)	—	Pl. 222, 296, 297
GSCHWIND Max	Germany	Stadttheater, Coblentz	Contes d'Hoffmann (Offenbach)	—	—
GUDERIAN Paul Gerd	Germany	—	Wandlung (Toller); Gas (Kaiser)	—	—

NAME	COUNTRY	THEATRES	THREE IMPORTANT PRODUCTIONS	REMARKS	NO. OF ILLUS.
GUTZEIT Kurt	Germany	Munich Theatres	Faust (Goethe); Leonce und Lena (Büchner); Der Tor und der Tod (Hofmannsthal)	See Bibliography	Pl. 193
HACKER	Germany	Vereinigte Stadttheater, Düsseldorf	Wilhelm Tell (Schiller); Belphegor (Denneay), Ivas Turm	—	—
HAMMOND Aubrey	England	Haymarket, Wyndhams, Vaudeville, London, New Liverpool Repertory Theatre	The Man with a Load of Mischief (Dukes), 1925; Masses and Men (Toller), 1925; The Rose and the Ring (Thackeray), 1925	—	Pl. 227, 288, 289
HANCOCK Caroline	United States	—	The Man of Destiny (Shaw); The Crack of Doom	—	—
HARKER Joseph C.	England	His Majesty's Theatre, London, and various others	Kismet (Knoblock), 1911; Chu Chin Chow (Asche), 1916; Mecca (Asche), New York, 1920	See Bibliography	—
HASAIT Max	Germany	Opera, Dresden (Technical Director)	Turandot (Puccini); Zauberflöte (Mozart); Aïda (Verdi)	—	Pl. 353, 356
HAUSER Cary	Austria	—	Die rote Strasse (Czokor)	—	—
HAY Julius	Germany	—	The Tempest (Shakespeare); Julius Cæsar (Shakespeare)	—	—
HECHT Torsten	Germany	Stadttheater, Mainz; Landestheater, Karlsruhe	Gyges und sein Ring (Hebbel); Georges Dandin (Molière); Listiges Füchslein (Janaček)	—	Pl. 132
HECKROTH Heinrich	Germany	Frankfurter Schauspielhaus; Stadttheater, Münster, and many others	Theodora (Handel); Salome (Wilde); Alexander Balus (Handel)	—	Pl. 120, 121, 148, 217
HERWIG Curt	Germany	Stadttheater, Hildesheim and Magdeburg	Peer Gynt (Ibsen), 1925; Herodes und Mariamne (Hebbel), 1926; Don Juan und Faust (Grabbe), 1927	—	Pl. 278, 279

Name	Country	Theatre	Works	Bibliography	Plates
HEYTHUM Antonin	Czechoslovakia	National Theatre and Theatre Libre, Prague	L'Autre Messie (Soumagne); Desire under the Elms (O'Neill); Thesmophoriazusæ (Aristophanes)	—	Pl. 102
HILER HARZBERG	United States	Philadelphia University Theatre	Acrobatic Ballet; Great Klaus and Little Klaus (Hans Andersen); Chu Chin Chow (Asche)	See Bibliography	—
HIRSCH Karl Jacob	Germany	—	Gas (Kaiser)	—	—
HOFFMANN Prof. Ludwig von	Germany	Deutsches Theater, Berlin	Aglavaine et Sélysette (Maeterlinck), 1907; Die Büchse der Pandora (Wedekind), 1909	—	Pl. 15, 16
HOFMAN Vlastislav	Czechoslovakia	National and Municipal Theatres, Prague	Queen Christine (Strindberg), 1922; The Hussites (Dvořák), 1919; Žižka (Lom), 1925	—	Pl. 98, 99, 144, 145, 240, 241, 243, 270, 271, 272, 362
HRABY	Germany	Stadttheater, Cologne	Julius Cæsar (Handel); Cosi fan tutte (Mozart); Boris Godounoff (Moussorgsky)	—	—
HRSKA Alexander Vladimir	Czechoslovakia	Municipal and National Theatre, Prague, National Theatre, Brno	Don Juan (Molière), Municipal Theatre, Prague; The Insect Play (Čapek), National Theatre, Brno; St Joan (Shaw), National Theatre, Prague	—	Pl. 91, 246
HUGO Jean	France	Ballets Suédois; Soirées de Paris (Théâtre de la Cigale); L'Atelier; Théâtre des Champs Élysées, Paris	Roméo et Juliette (Shakespeare-Cocteau), Cigale, 1924; The Silent Woman (Jonson), L'Atelier, 1925; Olive chez les Nègres (Falk and Wiener), Champs Élysées, 1926	See Bibliography under "Cocteau"	Pl. 113, 256, 257, 298, 299, 318-323, and Colour plate No. iii
HUHNEN F.	Germany	Stadttheater, Crefeld	The Merry Wives of Windsor (Shakespeare); Zweimal Oliver (Kaiser); Colportage	—	—
HUME Samuel J.	United States	Arts and Craft Theatre, Detroit; Greek Theatre, University of California	Helena's Husband (Moeller), Detroit, 1917; Doctor Faustus (Marlowe), Detroit, 1917; Œdipus Rex (Sophocles), Greek Theatre	—	Pl. 62-64, 376, 377

Name	Country	Theatres	Three Important Productions	Remarks	No. of Illus.
HUNZIKER G. and W.	Switzerland	—	Orphée (Gluck); The Tempest (Shakespeare); Carmen (Bizet). (Projects only)	—	—
HUSSMANN Heinrich	Germany	Städtische Bühnen, Leipzig	Louis Ferdinand von Preussen (Unruh); Henry IV (Pirandello); Le Temps Viendra (R. Rolland)	—	—
HYDE James	United States	Pasadena Community Theatre	The Sunken Bell (Hauptmann); Lazarus Laughed (O'Neill), 1928	—	—
IDELSON Vera	Russia	Taroff Productions	The Tempest (Shakespeare); Jouchewitch History; Angoscia delle Machine (Vasari)	—	—
IHRKE Oswald	Germany	Städtische Bühnen, Leipzig	Nozze di Figaro (Mozart); Samson et Dalilah (Saint-Saëns)	—	—
ISLER Albert	Switzerland	Stadttheater, Zürich	Ratcliff (Volkmar), 1916; Don Ranudo (Schock), 1917; Ilsebill (Klose), 1922	—	Pl. 88
JACOULOFF Georges	Russia	Kamerny Theatre, Moscow; Bolshoi Theatre, Moscow; Ballets Russes	Giroflé — Girofla (Lecocq); Princess Brambilla (Hoffmann); Rienzi (Wagner)	—	Pl. 164, 166
JAROCKI Stanislas	Poland	Opera, Poznán Théâtre Dramatique, Poznán	La Comédie non Divine (Krasinski); La Légende de la Baltique; Le Festin d'Hérodias	—	Pl. 82–85
JONES Robert Edmond	United States	Various American theatres	The Man Who Married a Dumb Wife (France), Wallacks, 1915; Macbeth (Shakespeare), Apollo Theatre, New York, 1921; Skyscrapers (Carpenter), Opera, New York, 1925	See Bibliography	Pl. 96, 97, 196, 201, 204, 242
JONES (3rd) William Frederick	United States	Various New York theatres	The Idiot (Dostoievsky), 1920; Cæsar and Cleopatra (Shaw), New Guild Theatre, New York, 1925; Hamlet (Shakespeare), Booth Theatre, New York, 1926	—	—

Name	Country	Theatre	Productions		
JONSON Raymond	United States	Chicago Little Theatre	Grotesques (Head), Chicago Little Theatre, 1915; The Trojan Women (Euripides), National Tour, 1915; Medea (Euripides), Theatre Guild, New York, 1920	—	—
JORGULESCO Jonel	Rumania (worked in America)	Boston Repertory Theatre	Arms and the Man (Shaw); The Wild Duck (Ibsen); Loyalties (Galsworthy)	—	Pl. 212, 213, 360, 361
JOUVET Louis	France	Vieux Colombier, Paris; Comédie des Champs Élysées (Director)	La Mort de Sparte (Verhaéren), Vieux Colombier, 1921; Twelfth Night (Shakespeare), Vieux Colombier; Knock (Romains), Champs Élysées, 1924	—	Pl. 48, 49 and Fig. 2, 8
KAINER Ludwig	Germany (worked in Germany and Austria)	Staatsoper, Vienna; Reinhardt Bühnen, Berlin; Staatsoper and Haller-Revue, Berlin	Die Zauberflöte (Mozart), Berlin, 1920; Scheherazade (Rimsky-Korsakov), Vienna, 1922; Coppelia (Delibes), Vienna, 1922	—	—
KALMAKOFF N. K.	Russia	Kamerny Theatre, Moscow	Life is a Dream (Calderón), 1915	—	—
KEMPIN Curt	Germany	Hoftheater, Darmstadt	Lohengrin (Wagner), 1914; Tasso (Goethe); Nibelungen (Hebbel)	—	—
KIESLER Frederick	Austria (worked in Austria, Germany and U.S.A.)	Theater am Kurfürstendamm, Berlin	R.U.R. (Čapek)	—	Pl. 158, 159
KLEIN Bernhard	Germany	Theatre, Königsberg in Preussen	Der tote Tag (Barlach); Und Pippa tanzt (Hauptmann); Erde (Zech)	—	—
KLEIN Prof. César	Germany	Staatstheater, Lessingtheater, Theater in der Königgrätzerstrasse, Berlin	Napoleon (Grabbe); Wallenstein (Schiller); Twelfth Night (Shakespeare)	See Bibliography under "Knudsen"	Pl. 92, 93, 252, 253
KOCH Hermann	Germany	Stadttheater, Bremen	Die Soldaten (Lenz), 1925; Joseph (Aelml), 1926	—	—
KOLTER-TEN HOONTE, K.	Germany	Stadttheater, Freiburg	Fidelio (Beethoven); Judith (Hebbel); Gas (Kaiser)	—	—

NAME	COUNTRY	THEATRES	THREE IMPORTANT PRODUCTIONS	REMARKS	NO. OF ILLUS.
KOMARDENKOFF A.	Russia	—	Eugen der Unglückliche ; Anna Christie (O'Neill) ; Facétie	—	—
KONTCHALOVSKY Pierre	Russia	—	—	—	—
KOROVINE Constantin	Russia	Imperial Opera, St Petersburg	Productions of Imperial Opera during twenty-five years	—	—
KREHAN Hermann	Germany	Theater in der Königgrätzerstrasse and Deutsches Theater, Berlin	Manon Lescaut, 1922 ; Clown Gottes (Philipp), 1924 ; Scherz, Satire, Ironie (Grabbe), 1925	—	Pl. 89, 275
KROP Hildo	Holland	Stadschowburg, Amsterdam	Masks for The Only Jealousy of Emer (Yeats), 1925	Sculptor	Pl. 324-327
KUGA Janis	Latvia	New Theatre and National Opera, Riga	Fire and Night (Rainis), 1911 ; Tannhäuser (Wagner) ; Der fliegende Holländer (Wagner)	—	—
KUSNETSOFF Pavel	Russia	Kamerny Theatre, Moscow	Sakuntala (Kalidasa), 1914 ; The Playboy of the Western World (Synge), 1914 ; The Pentecost of Toledo (Kuznim), 1915	—	—
LAGLENNE Jean Francis	France	—	Le Misanthrope (Molière)	—	—
LAGUT Irène	France	Théâtre des Champs Élysées, Paris	Les Mariés de la Tour Eiffel (Cocteau), 1921	—	Pl. 259
LAMEY Richard	Germany	Schauspielhaus, Bremen	Rheinische Rebellen (Bronnen) ; Back to Methuselah (Shaw)	—	—
LAPRADE Pierre	France	—	Arlequin ; Ballet of the XVIIIth Century	—	—
LARIONOFF Michel	Russia (worked in France)	Ballets Russes, Paris	Soleil de Minuit, 1915 ; Contes Russes, 1917 ; Chout (Prokofieff), 1921	See Bibliography and "Pomade," Moscow, 1911 ; "Polou Jivoï," Moscow, 1911 ; "Les Douze," London, 1921	Pl. 300-303

Name	Country	Theatre	Productions	Notes	Plates
LASKE Oskar	Austria	Burgtheater and Josefstädtertheater, Vienna	Much Ado About Nothing (Shakespeare); Il Servitore di due Padrone (Goldoni)	—	—
LAURENCIN Marie	France	Soirées de Paris, Théâtre de la Cigale, Paris	Les Biches (Poulenc)	—	—
LEFFLER Heinrich	Austria	Opera, Vienna	Pelléas et Mélisande (Debussy)	—	—
LÉGER Fernand	France	Swedish Ballet at Théâtre des Champs Élysées, Paris	Skating Rink (Canudo); La Création du Monde (Cendrars-Milhaud)	—	Pl. 260, 261, 306, 307
LENSVELT Fritz	Holland	Het Nederlandsch Tooneel, Amsterdam	Gysbrecht van Aamstel, 1913; Twelfth Night (Shakespeare), 1916; Faust (Goethe), 1918; The Merry Wives of Windsor (Skakespeare), 1916	—	—
LENTULOFF G.	Russia	Tairoff Productions	The Demon (Lermontov)	—	—
LEPAPE Georges	France	Théâtre Mogador, Paris	L'Oiseau Bleu (Maeterlinck)	—	—
LEWY Fritz	Germany	Theatres of Düsseldorf and Weimar	The King of the Dark Chamber (Tagore); Clavigo (Goethe)	—	—
LIBERTS Ludolf	Latvia	National Opera and National Dramatic Theatre, Riga	Judith (Hebbel); Kovantchina (Moussorgsky); Carmen (Bizet)	—	Pl. 248, 249
LINNEBACH Prof. Adolf	Germany	Staatstheater, Munich; Opera, Dresden	Jedermann (Hofmannsthal), Dresden, 1913	Theatre - architect and engineer	Pl. 188, 341, 342, 344, Fig. 13–16, 24
LISSIM Simon	Russia (worked in France, Belgium, and Spain)	Théâtre de l'Œuvre, Paris, Th. Royal de la Monnaie, Brussels; Liceo Theatre, Barcelona	L'Autre Messie (Soumagne), Paris, 1923; La Farce des Encore (Ghéon), Paris, 1924; Tsar Saltan, Barcelona, 1924	—	Pl. 233, 292, 293

Name	Country	Theatres	Three Important Productions	Remarks	No. of Illus.
LOEFFLER Dr Eduard	Austria (worked in Germany)	Grosse Volksoper, Berlin; Friedrich Theater, Dessau; National Theater, Mannheim	Orphée (Gluck), 1925; Traum-spiel (Strindberg), 1926; Zau-berflöte (Mozart), 1925	—	—
LOZOWICK Louis	United States	—	Gas (Kaiser)	—	—
MACDERMOTT Norman	England	Everyman Theatre and various London theatres	At Mrs Beams (Munro); The Mask and the Face (Chiarelli); The Vortex (Coward)	—	Pl. 77, 78
MAHNKE Adolf	Germany	Staatsoper and Schauspielhaus, Dresden; Les-singtheater, Berlin	L'Aiglon (Rostand), Berlin, 1925; Der Protagonist (Weill), Dresden, 1926; Anarchie auf Silian (Bronnen), 1926	See Bibliography under "Bara-nowsky"	Pl. 160, 343, 346, 387
MARCHI Virgilio	Italy	Indipendenti, Rome	Circe (Reggio), 1925; Il Carosello (Patti), 1925; Nella Steppa (Borodine), 1925	See Bibliography	—
MARTERSTEIG Max	Germany	Stadttheater, Leip-zig; Hoftheater, Mannheim (In-tendant)	Herodes und Mariamne (Hebbel), Leipzig, 1914; Die Nibelun-gen (Hebbel), 1913	See Bibliography	—
MARTIN Karlheinz	Germany	Kammerspiele, Frankfurt; Les-singtheater, Berlin (Director)	Wandlung (Toller), 1919; Fran-ziska (Wedekind), 1925; Henry IV (Pirandello), 1927	—	Pl. 176, 281, 374, 375
MASRIERA Louis	Spain	Compania Belu-guet, Barcelona	Els Zapitos de Maria Cristina; Vitrals de Santa Rita; Pasto-rale Comique	Complete Works (Plays), Barce-lona, 1926	—
MEDGYES Ladislas	Hungary	Theatre Jiriza	—	—	—
MEESTER, Jr., J. de	Belgium	Het Vlaamsche Volkstoneel	Malborough; Tijl; Where the Star Stood Still (de Meester)	Actor and stage-director	—

Name	Country	Theatre	Works	Bibliography	Plates
MESSEL Oliver	England	—	Masks	—	Pl. 328, 335, 336
MESTCHERSKY Boris	Russia (worked in France)	La Chimère and various Paris theatres	La Belle d'Haguenau, Com. des Champs Élysées, 1921; L'Etrange Épouse du Prof. Stierbecke (Albert-Jean), Studio des Champs Élysées, 1924	—	—
MIELZINER Jo	United States	Theatre Guild and various N.Y. Theatres	Lucky Sam McCarver (Sidney Howard); The Wild Duck (Ibsen); Faust (Goethe); Strange Interlude (O'Neill), 1928	—	Pl. 95
MITZSCHEKE-COLLANDE, von	Germany	—	Gas (Kaiser); Der Arme Heinrich (Hauptmann); Othello (Shakespeare)	—	—
MOHOLY-NAGY G. L.	Hungary (worked in Germany)	Versuchsbühne, Bauhaus, Dessau	Mechanical Eccentrics	See Bibliography under "Schlemmer"	—
MOLNÁR Farkas	Hungary	—	"U-Theatre," Project in "Die Bühne im Bauhaus"	—	—
MOSER Prof. Koloman (dec.)	Austria	Opera, Vienna	Der Musikant (Bittner); Der Bergsee (Bittner)	See Deutsche Kunst und Dekoration XXVII	—
MOULAERT Rêné	Belgium	Théâtre du Marais, Brussels; Het Vlaamsche Volkstoneel	Malbrough s'en va-t'-en Guerre (Achard), Marais, 1921; La Passion, 1926; Vie de St François (Alost), Volkstoneel, 1927	—	Pl. 50, 52, 179
MÜLLER Traugott	Germany	Volksbühne, Staatstheater and Piscatorbühne, Berlin	Segel am Horizont (Leonhard), 1924; Herodes und Marianne (Hebbel), 1926; Gewitter über Gothland (Welk), 1927	—	Pl. 125, 358
MUNCIS Jean	Latvia	Art Theatre, Riga	Antony and Cleopatra (Shakespeare), 1915; Macbeth (Shakespeare), 1915; Ligatura (Abeles)	—	—

Name	Country	Theatres	Three Important Productions	Remarks	No. of Illus.
Nash Paul	England	Coliseum, London	Designs for the Players' Shakespeare; The Truth about the Russian Dancers (Barrie), 1921	See Players' Shakespeare, Benn, London, 1927	Pl. 198
Neher Caspar	Germany	Staatstheater and Deutsches Theater, Berlin	Lulu (Wedekind); Hamlet (Shakespeare); Mann ist Mann (Brecht)	—	Pl. 105
Neilson Kay	Denmark	Royal Theatre, Copenhagen	The Tempest (Shakespeare); Aladdin	—	—
Neppach Robert	Germany	Tribüne, Berlin	Wandlung (Toller)	—	—
Nitsche Franz	Germany	Schauspielhaus, Leipzig	Das Neugierige Sternlein (Bethe-Kuhn)	—	—
Nivinsky I.	Russia	—	Turandot (Gozzi); Les Comédies de Mérimée; The Invisible Lady	—	Pl. 167
Ockel Reinhold	Germany	Theatres of Bonn, Aachen, Augsburg, etc.	L'Annonce faite à Marie (Claudel), Aachen, 1925; Bauernzorn (Reinacher), 1926; Cosi fan tutte (Mozart), 1926	Actor and stage-manager	Pl. 137
Oenslager Donald Mitchell	United States	Actors Theatre and Neighbourhood Playhouse, New York; Yale University Theatre	A Bit o' Love (Galsworthy), Actors Theatre, 1925; Morals (Thoma), 1926; Pinwheel (Faragoh), Neighbourhood Playhouse, 1927	Instructor in Scene Design, Yale University	Pl. 181, 381
Orlik Prof. Emil	Czechoslovakia and Germany	Deutsches Theater, Berlin	Merchant of Venice (Shakespeare), 1905; Winter's Tale (Shakespeare), 1906; Die Räuber (Schiller), 1908	Professor Kunstgewerbeschule, Berlin	Pl. 11, 12, 13, 14
Ott Paul	Germany	Reussisches Landestheater, Gera; Stadttheater, Munich	Contes d'Hoffmann (Offenbach); Don Giovanni (Mozart); König Nicolo (Wedekind)	—	Pl. 194, 195

Name	Country	Theatre	Productions	Notes	Plate
PAELTZ A.	Germany	Staatsoper, Dresden	Aïda (Verdi); Josephslegende (Strauss); Feuersnot (Strauss)	—	—
PANAGGI Ivo	Italy	Indipendenti, Rome	Ballo Meccanico, 1922; L'Angoscia delle Machine (Vasari); Pierrot Fumiste (Laforgue), 1925	—	Pl. 312, 313
PANKOK Prof. Bernhard	Germany	Opera, Stuttgart	Nozze di Figaro (Mozart); L'Enlèvement du Serail (Mozart), 1914	Prof., Art Academy, Stuttgart. For Publications, see Bibliography under "Gerhäuser"	—
PARR Mme	France	Swedish Ballet, Champs Élysées, Paris	L'Homme et son Désir (Claudel)	—	Pl. 122, 314
PASCAR Henriette	Russia	Children's Theatre, Moscow	—	—	—
PASSETTI Leon	Russia (worked in Germany)	Various theatres in Munich, Berlin, Hamburg; Pavlova Ballets	As You Like It (Shakespeare), Munich, 1916; Parsifal (Wagner), Munich, 1924; Turandot (Puccini), Berlin, 1926	Publications: Illustrations for many books; articles in various periodicals	—
PERDRIAT Helène	France	Swedish Ballet, Champs Élysées, Paris	Marchand d'Oiseaux (Taillefer)	—	—
PETERS Rollo	United States	Cowl Productions; various New York theatres	Madame Sand (Moeller); John Ferguson (St John Ervine); Romeo and Juliet (Shakespeare)	—	—
PEVSNER Nat	Russia	Ballets Russes	La Chatte (Sauguet), 1927	Professor, Moscow Art School	Pl. 165
PICABIA Francis	France	Swedish Ballet, Champs Élysées, Paris	Relâche (Picabia)	—	Pl. 155
PICASSO Pablo	Spain (worked in France)	Ballets Russes, Paris	Parade (Satie), 1920; Pulcinella (Stravinsky), 1920; Le Tricorne (de Falla), 1920	—	Pl. 262

NAME	COUNTRY	THEATRES	THREE IMPORTANT PRODUCTIONS	REMARKS	NO. OF ILLUS.
PILLARTZ T. C.	Germany	Staatstheater, Wiesbaden; Stadttheater, Crefeld	Kean (Al. Dumas, père); Troilus and Cressida (Shakespeare); Der Befreite Don Quichote (Lunacharsky)	—	Pl. 138, 228
PIOT Réné	France	Théâtre des Arts; Opéra, Paris	Le Chagrin dans le Palais de Han (Laloy), Arts, 1911; Idomeneo (Mozart), Arts, 1912; La Péri (Dukas), Opéra, 1921	—	—
PIRCHAN Emil	Germany	Oper and Schauspielhaus, Berlin	Othello (Shakespeare), 1920; Josefslegende (Strauss), 1921; Empörung des Lucius (Bluth), 1923	See "Das Werk der Staatsoper"	Pl. 90, 106, 107, 123, 124, 126-129, 251, 337-340
PITOËFF Georges	Russia (worked in France)	Comédie des Champs Élysées; Théâtre des Arts, Paris (Director)	Les Ratés (Lenormand); St Joan (Shaw), 1926; Hamlet (Shakespeare), 1927	Actor and producer	Pl. 117, 200, 216
PLATT Livingston	United States	Toy Theatre, Castle Square, Boston; Anglin Productions	Toy Theatre and Anglin Productions	—	—
POELZIG Hans	Germany	Oper, Grosses Schauspielhaus and Dramatisches Theater, Berlin	Don Giovanni (Mozart); Gilles und Jeanne (Kaiser); King Lear (Shakespeare)	—	—
POHL Arthur	Germany	Deutsches Theater, Berlin; Hessisches Landestheater, Darmstadt	Bonaparte (Unruh); Edward II (Marlowe); Macbeth (Shakespeare)	—	—
POLUNIN Vladimir	Russia (worked in England)	Various theatres in Great Britain	Ouverture, 1812 (Tchaikovsky), 1914; Otello (Verdi), 1915	—	—

Name	Country	Theatre	Repertory	Bibliography	Plates
POMPEI Mario	Italy	Odescalchi, Pirandello's Teatro d'Arte and Teatro dei Piccoli, Rome	Paulette (Giovanetti); Parisina (D'Annunzio); Le Voyage de M. Perrichon (Labiche)	—	Pl. 285
POPOVA L.	Russia	Meyerhold Theatre, Moscow	Le Cocu Magnifique (Crommelynck)	—	Pl. 174
POREP Heinz	Germany	Schauspiele, Baden-Baden	Cæsar and Cleopatra (Shaw); R.U.R. (Čapek); Geschichte vom Soldaten	—	—
PRAMPOLINI Enrico	Italy (worked in Italy, Czechoslovakia and France)	Argentina and Indepentdenti, Rome, Svando-theatre, Prague	Lo Schiavo (Ricciardi); Chitra (Tagore), Rome; Romeo and Juliet (Shakespeare), Prague	See Bibliography	Pl. 157, 308, 309, 334
PRETORIUS Emil	Germany	Staatstheater and Künstlertheater, Munich; Opera, Berlin	Iphigénie en Aulide (Gluck); Faust (Goethe), Munich; Cosi fan tutte (Mozart), Berlin	—	—
PRENTICE Herbert	England	Sheffield Repertory Theatre; Festival Theatre, Cambridge	The Machine Wreckers (Toller), Sheffield, 1927; Oresteia (Æschylus), (Masks), Cambridge, 1926; Heraclius (Ellis), 1927	—	—
PRITZEL Lotte	Germany	—	Costumes for: Kreidekreis (Klabund), Tartuffe (Molière), Anja and Esther	—	—
PRONASZKO André and Zbigniew	Poland	Teatr Boguslawsky, Warsaw	Von Morgen bis Mitternacht (Kaiser); Achilles	—	—
QUEDENFELD Harald	Germany	Düsseldorf	King Hunger (Andrejev); Der fröhliche Weinberg; Clown Gottes (Philipp)	—	—
RABINOVITCH Isaac	Russia	Moscow Art Theatre; Stanislavsky Studio; Meyerhold Theatre; Central Jewish Theatre; Bolshoi Theatre, Leningrad	Lysistrata (Aristophanes), Moscow Art Theatre; The Inspector General (Gogol); Don Carlos (Schiller), Meyerhold Theatre; The Love for Three Oranges (Prokofieff)	—	Pl. 168, 169, 178, 183

Name	Country	Theatres	Three Important Productions	Remarks	No. of Illus.
REE Max	Denmark (worked in Germany)	Reinhardt production, Berlin	Orphée aux Enfers (Offenbach)	—	—
REIGBERT Otto	Germany	Kammerspiele, Munich	Spiel des Lebens (Hamsun); Kaiserin von Neufundland (Wedekind); Trommeln in der Nacht (Brecht)	—	Pl. 254, 255
REIMAN Walter	Germany	Staatstheater, Berlin	Macbeth (Shakespeare)	—	Pl. 130, 131
REMISOFF Nicolas	Russia (worked in United States)	Chauve-Souris; Bolm Ballets, Chicago	Souvenirs of Other Days, Chauve-Souris, 1924; Tragedy of the 'Cello, Bolm Ballets, 1927; Pierrot Lunaire (Schönberg), 1926	—	Pl. 315
RÉMOND Fritz	Germany	Vereinigte Stadttheater, Cologne (General Intendant)	Zauberflöte (Mozart), etc.	—	—
REYNOLDS James	United States	Various New York theatres	The Last of Mrs Cheney (Lonsdale), Fulton, 1925; The Last Night of Don Juan (E. Rostand), Greenwich Vill., 1926; L'Aiglon (Rostand), Washington	—	Pl. 294, 295
RICHTER Arno	Germany	Staatstheater, Berlin	Edward II (Marlowe); Sintflut (Barlach); Ostpolzug (Bronnen)	—	—
RICHTER Prof. Klaus	Germany	Freie Volksbühne, Berlin, and others	Leidenschaft (Eulenberg), 1911; Grüne Felder (Warschauer Jüdisches Theater), 1921; Turandot (Schiller), Königsberg, 1925	Professor of Theatre Craft, Königsberg University. Publication: "Calderón's Stage" in "The Mask," 1926	Colour plate No. vi

Name	Country	Theatre	Productions	Publication	Plates
RICKETTS Charles	England	Various theatres London	Eumenides (Æschylus); Salome (Wilde); King Lear (Shakespeare)	Publication: "The Prado and its Masterpieces"	—
ROERICH Nicolas (dec.)	Russia (worked in the United States)	Ballets Russes; Chicago Opera	Prince Igor (Borodine); Snegourotchka (Rimsky-Korsakov); The Three Kings (Mystery), Starinnyi Theatre, Moscow, 1907	See Bibliography	—
ROLLER Hofrat Prof. Alfred	Austria	Deutsches Theater, Berlin; Hofoper, Vienna	Faust (Goethe), Deutsches Theater, Berlin, 1909, 1911; Don Giovanni (Mozart), Vienna, 1905; Tristan und Isolde (Wagner), Vienna, 1903	Director, Kunstgewerbeschule, Vienna	Pl. 19-21, 24, 25, 55, 56, 186
ROOS J. R. B. de	Holland	—	Pelléas et Mélisande (Maeterlinck)	—	—
ROSSE Herman	Holland (worked in United States)	Rivoli Theatre, Empire Theatre, Princess Theatre, New York; Auditorium Theatre, Chicago	Madame Chrysanthème (Loti); Chicago; Casanova (de Azertis-Howard); Mandragola (Machiavelli), New York	—	Pl. 86, 143
RUTHERSTON Albert Daniel	England	Granville - Barker, Shakespeare Season, Savoy Theatre, 1912-14; Various London theatres	A Winter's Tale (Shakespeare); Androcles and the Lion (Shaw); Le Mariage Forcé (Molière)	See Bibliography	Pl. 142
RYBACK Soukher Ber	Russia	Jewish Kamerny Theatre, Moscow; Jewish State Theatre of Ukraine	On the Confessional Chair (Peretz); Purim	—	—
SALTER Georg	Germany	Theatres of Barmen-Elberfeld	Aïda (Verdi); Zweimal Oliver (Kaiser); Don Giovanni (Mozart)	—	—
SALZMANN Alexander	Russia (worked in Germany and France)	Theatres Dresden, Hellerau (Dalcroze); Champs Élysées, Paris	Pelléas et Mélisande (Debussy), Paris	—	—

Name	Country	Theatres	Three Important Productions	Remarks	No. of Illus.
SANLAVILLE Charles	France	La Chimère, Paris	Farce de Papa Gheorge (Orna)	—	—
SAPOUNOFF Klaudius	Russia	Moscow Art Theatre	Tsar Féodor (Tolstoy), 1912	—	Pl. 6
SCAIOLI Alberto	Italy	Various theatres: Milan, Turin, Rome, Buenos Ayres	Pelléas et Mélisande (Debussy), Scala, Milan, 1924; Aïda (Verdi) Regio, Turin, 1921; Fidelio (Beethoven), Buenos Ayres, 1927	—	—
SCHAWINSKY Alexander	Germany	Versuchsbühne, Bauhaus, Dessau	Konstruktive Raumbühne; Varieté-scenes	See "Die Bühne im Bauhaus"	—
SCHEURICH Paul	Germany	Schauspielhaus, Berlin	Der Kronprinz	—	—
SCHLEMMER Oskar	Germany	Versuchsbühne, Bauhaus, Dessau	Don Juan und Faust (Grabbe), Weimar, 1925; Mörder, Hoffnung der Frauen (Kokoschka-Hindemith) Stuttgart, 1921; Triadisches Ballett, Dessau, 1912–27	See Bibliography	Pl. 154, 317, and Fig. 9–12
SCHLONSKI	Germany	Stadttheater, Düsseldorf	Tannhäuser (Wagner); Meistersinger (Wagner)	—	—
SCHMITT Karl Hugo	Germany	Theater Nuremberg	Œdipus Rex (Sophocles); Geisha (Jones); Salome (Wilde)	—	—
SCHOEN Reinhold	Austria (worked in Austria and Germany)	Theater am Schiffbauerdamm, Berlin; Raimundtheater, Vienna	Die Jüdische Wittwe (Kaiser); Franziska (Wedekind)	—	—
SCHOUKHAEFF Vassily	Russia	Chauve-Souris; Imperial Theatre and National Theatre, St Petersburg	La Pastourelle; La Traviata (Verdi); The Arrival at Bethlehem, 1924	—	Pl. 234, 235

Name	Country	Theater	Works	Notes
SCHRAMM Werner	Germany	Schauspielhaus, Düsseldorf	Comrades (Strindberg); Spiegelmensch (Werfel)	—
SCHREYER Lothar	Germany	Kampfbühne, Hamburg; Sturmbühne, Berlin	Kreuzigung; Mann; Kindsterben	—
SCHROEDER Johannes	Germany	Vereinigte Stadttheater, Hamburg, Bochum-Duisburg and Kammerspiele, Hamburg	Ring des Nibelungen (Wagner), Duisburg, 1925; Kingdramas at German Shakespeare Week, Bochum, 1927; Edward II (Marlowe), Hamburg, 1927	Pl. 269
SCHROEDER Rudolf	Germany	Staatstheater, Dresden	Le bon petit diable (Rostand, fils); Die Räuber (Schiller); Wozzek (Büchner)	Actor
SCHUBERT Helmut	Germany	Kleines Theater, Kassel	Der arme Vetter (Barlach)	—
SCHÜTTE Ernst	Germany	Deutsches Theater, Berlin	Juarez und Maximilian (Werfel); Fahrt nach der Südsee (Blume), Staatstheater, 1926; Bonaparte (Unruh), Deutsches Theater, 1927	Publications: illustrated books, etc. Pl. 31
SCHUHMACHER Fritz	Germany	Theater, Cologne	Macbeth (Shakespeare)	—
SCHULTZ H.	United States	—	Salome (Wilde); The Tempest (Shakespeare); The Merchant of Venice (Shakespeare)	—
SCHWARZ Robert	Germany	Schauspielhaus, Godesberg	Le Tombeau sous l'Arc de Triomphe (Raynal); Penthesilea (Kleist); Eber Lichtenstein (Reinacher), 1926–27	—
SHARPE Robert R.	United States	Pasadena Community Theatre	The Makropoulos Secret	—

NAME	COUNTRY	THEATRES	THREE IMPORTANT PRODUCTIONS	REMARKS	NO. OF ILLUS.
SHELVING Paul	England	Birmingham Repertory Theatre; various London theatres	Back to Methuselah (Shaw), Birmingham, 1925; The Immortal Hour (Rutland Broughton), Regent Theatre, London, 1922; The Marvellous History of St Bernard (H. Ghéon), Kingsway, 1926	—	Pl. 226
SHERINGHAM George	England	Lyric Theatre, Hammersmith; London Coliseum	The Duenna (Sheridan); Midsummer Madness (Bax); Swinburne Ballet	See Bibliography	—
SHERVASHIDZE Prince Alexander	Russia (worked in Russia, France and Belgium)	Imperial Theatres, St Petersburg (Chief Stage Designer, 1907–1918); Ballets Russes	Tristan und Isolde (Wagner), Theatre Marie, 1910; Tantris der Narr (Hardt), Alexandrovsky Theatre, 1911; Hamlet (Shakespeare), Alexandrovsky Theatre, 1913	—	Pl. 51
SIEVERT Ludwig	Germany	Städtische Bühnen, Frankfurt-am-Main	Der Sohn (Hasenclever), Mannheim, 1916; Die grosse Landstrasse (Strindberg). Frankfort, 1923; Nozze di Figaro (Mozart), 1924	Publications: see Bibliography under "Wagner"; "Das Bühnenbild der Oper," in "Die Musik"	Pl. 118, 205–207
SIMONSON Lee	United States	Garrick, Guild and New Guild Theatre, New York	Back to Methuselah (Shaw); Peer Gynt (Ibsen); Bocksgesang (Werfel); Marco Millions (O'Neill), 1928	See Bibliography	Pl. 61, 75, 76, 100, 101, 108, 363
SINCLAIR Walter	Canada	Hart House Theatre, Toronto (Producer)	Les Romanesques (Rostand); The Rivals (Sheridan); Twelfth Night (Shakespeare), 1927	—	—
SLEVOGT Prof. Max	Germany	Staatstheater, Dresden	Don Giovanni (Mozart)	—	—
SLIWINSKI Stanislas	Poland	Teatr Polski and Maly, Warsaw	Danton (Rolland), 1925; Le Roi Dagobert, 1926; Samuel Zborowski (Slowacki), 1927	—	Pl. 209, 238
SMYTH Owen P.	England	Maddermarket Theatre, Norwich	A Midsummer Night's Dream (Shakespeare); The Man with a Load of Mischief (Dukes)	—	—

				Publications	
SOMOFF Constantin	Russia	Moscow Art Theatre; Kamerny Theatre, Moscow	The Cherry Orchard (Tchekoff), 1904; Costumes for Colombine, Pavlova, 1908, and Tamar Karsavina, 1924; Le Mariage de Figaro (Beaumarchais), 1915	Publications: Constantin Somoff, a Monograph, Berlin, 1907; many illustrated books	—
SOUDEIKINE Serge	Russia	Chauve-Souris; Ballets Russes; Kamerny Theatre, Moscow	Soir d'Hiver, 1924; Autour du Chariot, 1926; Dans une Vieille Campagne Russe, 1926	—	Pl. 237
STAHL Walter	Germany	Stadttheater, Frankfurt a. d. Oder	Le Médecin malgré lui (Molière)	—	—
STEINER Bernd	Austria (worked in Germany)	Stadttheater, Bremen	Zauberflöte (Mozart); Golem	—	—
STEINER-PRAG Prof. Hugo	Germany	Städtische Bühnen, Leipzig	Die Macht des Schicksals; John Gabriel Borkmann (Ibsen); Wer niemals einen Rausch gehabt	—	—
STEINHOF Prof. Eugen	Austria	Opera, Vienna, and various others	Die glückliche Hand (Schönberg), Volksoper, 1925; Die Walküre (Wagner)	Publications in various Paris, Vienna and Zürich periodicals	—
STENBERG W. and G.	Russia	Kamerny Theatre, Moscow	Saint Joan (Shaw); with K. Medounetsky, Thunderstorm (Ostrovsky); Lawyer from Babylon	—	—
STERN Prof. Ernst	Germany	Deutsches Theater and Theater am Kurfürstendamm, Berlin; Grosses Schauspielhaus, Berlin	Penthesilea (Kleist); Macbeth (Shakespeare); Danton (Rolland); the greater part of Reinhardt's productions	See Bibliography	Pl. 22, 23, 26-29, 345, Fig. 18-22, and colour plate No. iv
STERN Ernst Erich	Germany	Münchener Schauspielhaus	Juaréz und Maximilian (Werfel); Fahrt nach der Südsee (Blume); Saint Joan (Shaw)	—	—

NAME	COUNTRY	THEATRES	THREE IMPORTANT PRODUCTIONS	REMARKS	NO. OF ILLUS.
STOBBAERTS M.	Belgium	—	Rien qu'un Homme ; R.U.R. (Čapek)	—	—
STRNAD Prof. Oskar	Austria	Burgtheater and Josefstädtertheater, Vienna	King Lear (Shakespeare), Josefstädtertheater ; Peripherie (Langer), Josefstädtertheater ; Das Mirakel (Vollmoeller), Zirkus Renz	See Bibliography	Pl. 30, 32, 33, 71, 72, 192, 197, 349, 350, 371, 372
STROEM Knut	Sweden (worked in Sweden and Germany)	Schauspielhaus, Düsseldorf ; Lorensbergteatern, Göteborg	Macbeth (Shakespeare) ; Rausch (Strindberg)	—	—
STROHBACH Hans	Germany	Volksbühne, Berlin	King Lear (Shakespeare) ; Masse Mensch (Toller)	—	—
STUNZ H.	Sweden	Intima Teatern, Stockholm	—	—	—
STURM Eduard	Germany	Schauspielhaus, Düsseldorf	Kaiser und Galiläer (Ibsen), 1924 ; Prinz von Homburg (Kleist), 1925 ; Maria Stuart (Schiller), 1926	See Stage Year-book, London, 1913 ; Hellweg, July 1926 ; Die Première, Oct. 1925	Pl. 133, 190, 347, 348 and Fig. 23
SUHR Edward	Germany	Volksbühne, Berlin ; Schauspielhaus, Düsseldorf	Kätchen von Heilbronn (Kleist), Düsseldorf, 1918 ; Fahnen (Paquet), Berlin, 1924 ; Traumspiel (Strindberg), Berlin, 1927	—	Pl. 104, 280
TÄUBER Harry	Austria	Burgtheater, Deutsches Volkstheater, Raimundtheater, Vienna	Spiegelmensch (Werfel) ; Götz von Berlichingen (Goethe) ; Kreidekreis (Klabund)	—	Pl. 134, 135, 161
TESCHNER Richard	Germany (worked in Czechoslovakia)	Deutsches Theater, Prague	Pelléas et Mélisande (Debussy) ; Bastien und Bastienne (Mozart)	See Deutsche Kunst und Dekoration, 1911, and Oesterreichs Bau-und Werkkunst, Jahr 2, Heft 3	—

Name	Country	Theatre	Productions	Notes	Plates
THESING Paul	Germany	Stadttheater, Mainz	Penthesilea (Kleist)	—	—
THIERSCH Prof. Paul	Germany	Altes Stadttheater, Leipzig	Saint Joan (Shaw), 1924; Kabale und Liebe (Schiller), 1926; Geisterbann (Volbrandt), 1926	Director Kunstgewerbeschule Halle	Pl. 276, 277
THIRIAR James	Belgium	Théâtre Royal de la Monnaie, Brussels	Boris Godounoff (Moussorgsky), 1921; L'Enfant et les Sortilèges, 1926; Turandot (Puccini), 1927	—	—
THOMPSON Woodman	United States	Seven Seasons Little Theatres; Six Seasons various New York theatres	Beggar on Horseback (Kaufmann and Connelly); Iolanthe (Gilbert and Sullivan); Deep River (Stalling)	—	Pl. 73, 74, 87, 177
THOMSON Carl	England	Unnamed Society, Manchester; Playroom Six, London; David Lewis Theatre, Liverpool	The Immortal Hour (Boughton), 1925; Savitri (Holst), 1926; At the Boar's Head (Holst), 1926, Liverpool	—	—
THROCKMORTON Cleon	United States	Provincetown Players and various New York theatres	The Verge (Glaspell); The Hairy Ape (O'Neill); The Emperor Jones (O'Neill)	—	—
THUM Erich	Germany	Various theatres in Stuttgart, Berlin, Dresden, Vienna	Otello (Verdi), Staatsoper, Dresden; Sakuntala (Kalidasa), Josefstadt, Vienna; Euryanthe (Weber), Dresden	—	—
TOUCHAGUES	France	L'Atelier, Paris	Huon de Bordeaux; Celui qui vivait sa Mort; Pygmalion (Shaw)	—	—
TREICHLINGER Dr Wilhelm	Austria	Bühne der Jungen, Vienna	Xerxes (Handel), Schönbrunner Schlosstheater, 1925; Wiedergeburt in Kain (Haidvogel), Bühne der Jungen, 1927	See Bibliography	Pl. 383–385
TRAPP, SCHENK VON Lothar	Germany (worked in Switzerland, United States and Germany)	Landestheater, Darmstadt	Cardillac (Hindemith), Darmstadt, 1927; Don Giovanni (Mozart), Chicago, 1927; Zauberflöte (Mozart), Zürich, 1926	—	Pl. 109

NAME	COUNTRY	THEATRES	THREE IMPORTANT PRODUCTIONS	REMARKS	NO. OF ILLUS.
TREPCE Jossip	Yugoslavia	National Theatre, Zagreb	—	—	—
THE UNNAMED SOCIETY (Lilian Reburn, William Grimmond, Eric Newton, Margaret Nicholls)	England	The Unnamed Little Theatre, Manchester	St Simon Stylites (Sladen-Smith), 1919; Chimp (Sladen-Smith); The Hairy Ape (O'Neill); The Cortège (Barber), 1921; The Tower of Babel (Sladen-Smith), 1900	—	—
URBAN Joseph	Austria (worked in Austria and United States)	Opera and Burgtheater, Vienna; Champs Élysées, Paris; Boston Opera House; Metropolitan Opera, New York	Cosi fan tutte (Mozart), New York, 1924; Pelléas et Mélisande (Debussy), New York, 1925; Fidelio (Beethoven), New York, 1927	Publications: Many illustrated books	Pl. 189, 224, 225
VALDO-BARBEY	France	Opéra, Paris	Sept Chansons (Malipiero), 1920; Padmavati (Roussel), 1924; Arlequin (d'Ollone), 1925	See Bibliography	—
VESNINE Alexander	Russia	Kamerny Theatre, Moscow	Phèdre (Racine); L'Annonce faite à Marie (Claudel); The Man Who Was Thursday (Chesterton)	—	Pl. 150, 151, 175
VOELCKERS Otto	Germany	Munich Theatres	Tristan (Geiger)	—	—
WACIK Franz	Austria	Burgtheater and Komödienhaus, Vienna	Und Pippa tanzt (Hauptmann), Burgtheater; Die gefesselte Phantasie (Raimund), Komödienhaus	—	—
WALSER Karl	Germany	Deutsches and Lessingtheater, Berlin	Romeo and Juliet (Shakespeare), Deutsches Theater; Cyrano de Bergerac (Rostand); Leonce und Lena (Büchner)	See Bibliography	Pl. 286, 287

Name	Country	Theatres	Productions	Position	Plate
WECUS Prof. Walter von	Germany	Theatres Düsseldorf, Munich, Bonn	Gaukler, Tod und Juwelier (C. Hauptmann); Düsseld., 1920; Titus Andronicus (Shakespeare), Munich, 1924; Hannibal (Grabbe), Bonn, 1925	Stagecraft Teacher, Art Academy, Düsseldorf	Pl. 116, 149, 229
WEERTH Ernest de	United States (worked in United States and Austria)	Various theatres	King Lear (Shakespeare), Vienna, 1925; Midsummer Night's Dream (Shakespeare), Vienna, 1925; Kuan Yin (Carroll Lunt), Neighbourhood Playhouse, New York, 1926	—	Pl. 382
WENGER John	United States	Various New York theatres	Petrouchka (Stravinsky), Metropolitan Opera, New York, 1919; Bridge of Distance, Morosco Theatre, 1925; Aïda (Verdi), Mun. Open Air Opera, New York, 1925	—	—
WENIG Josef	Czechoslovakia	Municipal and National Theatre, Prague; Liceo, Barcelona	The Bartered Bride (Smetana); Troilus and Cressida (Shakespeare); Bajazet (Racine)	—	Pl. 273
WERNER	Germany	Stadttheater, Magdeburg	Schatzgräber; 1001 Nacht (Strauss); Zauberflöte (Mozart)	—	—
WIELAND Hans Beatus	Germany	Künstlertheater, Munich	Tanzlegendchen	—	—
WIJDEVELD H. Th.	Holland	Municipal Theatre, Amsterdam	Hamlet (Shakespeare), 1918; Saint Joan (Shaw), 1924	Editor of "Wendingen," Amsterdam	Pl. 79–81
WILDEN Egon	Germany	Theater Hagen i. W.	Turandot (Gozzi); König Nicolo (Wedekind)	—	—
WILDERMANN Prof. Hans	Germany	Stadttheater, Breslau	Tristan und Isolde (Wagner), Cologne Festival, 1910; Zauberflöte (Mozart), Nüremberg, 1922; Die Gezeichneten (Schrecker), Munich, 1919	—	Pl. 187

Name	Country	Theatres	Three Important Productions	Remarks	No. of Illus.
WILKINSON Norman	England	Frohman Repertory, Duke of York's, London, 1910; Granville-Barker's Shakespeare - Season, Savoy Theatre, London, 1912–14	Midsummer Night's Dream (Shakespeare); Winter's Tale (Shakespeare); Twelfth Night (Shakespeare)	—	Pl. 140–141
WINCKLER-TANNENBERG Friedrich	Germany	Städtische Oper, Berlin; Stadttheater, Breslau, etc.	The Persians (Æschylus); Herbstvögel; Hermannsschlacht (Kleist)	—	—
WISCHNEROWSKY Johann M.	Germany	Stadttheater Frankfurt a. d. Oder	Der Schwätzer (Engel); Das Goldene Vliess (Grillparzer)	—	—
WUNDERWALD G.	Germany	Opera, Charlottenburg	Iphigenia (Goethe), 1914; Fidelio (Beethoven), 1914; Nibelungen (Hebbel)	—	—
ZACK Léon	France	Ballets Romantiques	Gisele; Trapèze; Eau de Cologne Magique	—	—
ZUCKERMANDL Ludwig	Germany	—	Coriolanus (Shakespeare); Christus (Strindberg); Peer Gynt (Ibsen)	—	—

HAND-LIST OF BOOKS, PAMPHLETS, ETC.

ALEXANDRE, Arsène : L'Art Décoratif de Léon Bakst. Essai critique par Arsène Alexandre. Notes sur les Ballets par Jean Cocteau. De Brunoff, Paris, 1913.
(English Translation by Harry Melville, " The Decorative Art of Léon Bakst." Fine Art Society, London, 1913).

ALT, Theodor : Das " Künstlertheater," Kritik der mod. Stilbewegung. C. Winter, Heidelberg, 1909.

ALTERDINGER, J.: Handbuch für Theatermalerei und Bühnenbau. 1904.

AMUNDSEN, F : Die neue Shakespearebühne des Münchner Hoftheaters. Volksbühnenverlag, Munich, 1912.

APPIA, Adolphe : La Mise en Scène du Drame Wagnérien. Challey, Paris, 1895.
—— Die Musik und die Inszenierung. Deutsche Ausgabe besorgt von Prinzessin Elsa Cantacuzène. Mit 18 Lichtdrucktafeln. Bruckmann, Munich, 1899.
—— L'Œuvre d'Art Vivant. Ill. Editions Atar, Geneva, 1921.
—— Art Vivant ou Nature Morte ? Ill. Bottega di Poesia, Milan 1923.
—— Comment reformer notre mise en scène : in *La Revue*. Paris, 1904.
—— Numerous articles in periodicals and reviews.

APUSHKIN, J.: The Kamerny Theatre. Kinopechat, Moscow, 1927.

ARNOLD, Robert F. : Bibliographie der deutschen Bühnen seit 1830. K. J. Täubner, Strassburg, 1909.

AROLA Y SALA, Francisco : Escenografia. Madrid and Barcelona, 1922.

BAB, Julius : Wesen und Weg der Berliner Volksbühnenbewegung. Ill. Wasmuth, Berlin, 1920.
—— Neue Wege zum Drama. Oesterheld, Berlin, 1911.
—— —— Re-issued in enlarged form as Die Chronik des Deutschen Dramas. Berlin, 1922.
—— Die Volksbühne in Berlin. Wasmuth, Berlin, 1919.
—— Der Mensch auf der Bühne. Oesterheld, Berlin, 1923.

BAKSHY, Alexander : The Path of the Modern Russian Stage and Other Essays. Palmer & Heywood, London, 1916.
—— The Theatre Unbound. Palmer, London, 1923.

BAKST, Léon : Le Ballet de Léon Bakst. St Petersburg, 1912.
—— Balletskizzen : in *Deutsche Kunst und Dekoration*, vol. xxxi. p. 309. Koch, Darmstadt, 1912–13.
—— Collection des plus beaux Numéros de Comoedia Illustré et des Programmes consacrés aux Ballets et Galas Russes depuis le début à Paris, 1909–21. De Brunoff, Paris, 1922.
—— The Designs of Léon Bakst for the Sleeping Princess ; Preface by A. Levinson. Benn Bros., London, 1923.
—— Unpublished Works of Bakst : Essays on Bakst, by Louis Réau, Denis Roche, V. Svyetlov and Tessier : Brentano, New York, 1927.
—— Bakst. See ALEXANDRE.
—— See COCTEAU.
—— See LEVINSON.
—— See SVYETLOV.

BAPST, Constant Germain : Essai sur l'histoire du Théâtre ; La Mise en Scène, le Décor, le Costume, l'Architecture, l'Eclairage, l'Hygiène. Ill. Hachette, Paris, 1893.

BARANOWSKY, A., and MAHNKE, Adolf : Neuzeitliche Bühnenmalerei. Portfolio of 30 Plates in Black and White, and Colours. Jüstel & Göttel, Leipzig, 1926.

BARDOS, Artur : Az uj szinpad : Nyugat Kiadasa, Budapest, 1911.

BARKER, Harley Granville : The Exemplary Theatre. Chatto & Windus, London, 1922.

BATY, Gaston : Le Masque et l'Encensoir : Introduction à une Esthétique du Théâtre. Preface par Maurice Brillant. Bloud & Gay, Paris, 1926.

BAUMGARTEN, Fritz : Zirkus Reinhardt. Tilgner, Potsdam, 1920.

BELASCO, David : The Theatre through the Stage-door. Harper, New York and London, 1919.

BERGMANN, E. : Der Fall Reinhardt, oder der künstlerische Bankrott des Deutschen Theaters. Berlin.

BIE, Oscar : Der Tanz. S. Fischer, Berlin, 1913.
—— Die Oper. S. Fischer, Berlin, 1923.
—— Der Architekt Oskar Kaufmann. Ill. Ernst Pollak Verlag, Berlin, 1928.
—— See WALSER.

BIRKMIRE, William Harvey : The Planning and Construction of American Theatres. Wiley, New York, 1896.

BIRMINGHAM REPERTORY THEATRE : The Story of the Birmingham Repertory Theatre. Chatto & Windus, London, 1924.

BOEHM, Hans : Die Wiener Reinhardtbühne im Lichtbild, 50 Illustrations. Amaltheaverlag, Vienna, 1926.

BOEHN, Max von : Das Bühnenkostüm in Altertum, Mittelalter und Neuzeit. Cassirer, Berlin, 1920.

BOLL, André : Du Décor de Théâtre. Chiron, Paris, 1926.

BRAGAGLIA, Anton Giulio : La Maschera Mobile. Campitelli, Foligno, 1926.

BRILLANT, Maurice. See BATY.

BRUECKNER, Max : Bayreuther Bühnenbilder. Greiz, 1890.

BÜHNENBELEUCHTUNG, Bühnenbeleuchtung, System Fortuny. Allgemeine Elektrizitäts-Gesellschaft. Berlin, 1910.

BUEHNENTECHNISCHE BIBLIOTHEK DER VOLKSBUEHNE. Volksbühnenverlag, Munich.

BUNING, J. W. F. Werumeus : Het Tooneldecor. Brusse, Rotterdam, 1923.

BURCKHARDT, Max : Das Theater. Rütten & Löhning, Frankfurt a. d. M., 1907.

CAMPBELL, Lily : Scenes and Machines on the English Stage : Cambridge University Press, Cambridge, 1923.

CARTER, Huntly : The New Spirit in Drama and Art, Ill. Kennerley, New York ; Palmer, London, 1913.
—— The Theatre of Max Reinhardt, Ill. Palmer, London, 1914.
—— The New Spirit in the European Theatre, Ill. Ernest Benn, London, 1925.
—— The New Theatre and Cinema of Soviet Russia, Ill. Chapman & Dodd, London, 1926.

CHENEY, Sheldon : The New Movement in the Theatre, Ill. Mitchell Kennerly, New York, 1914.
—— The Art Theatre, Ill. Knopf, New York, 1925.
—— Modern Art and the Theatre. Sleepy Hollow Press, Scarborough on Hudson, 1921.

COCTEAU, Jean : Notes sur les Ballets, dans L'Art Décoratif de Léon Bakst, par Arsène Alexandre. De Brunoff, Paris, 1913.
—— et HUGO, Jean : Roméo et Juliette. With Scenes and Costume-designs. Au Sans Pareil, Paris, 1926.

CRAIG, Edward Gordon : Book of Penny Toys, Sign of the Rose. Hackbridge, Surrey, 1899.
—— Henry Irving and Ellen Terry : a Book of Portraits. H. J. Stone, Chicago, 1899.
—— The Art of the Theatre : Preface by Graham Robertson. Ill. Foulis, Edinburgh and London, 1905.
—— —— Later Editions : Heinemann, London, 1911, 1924, 1926.
—— —— Translations and foreign editions : Die Kunst des Theaters ; Vorwort von Harry Graf Kessler. Berlin and Leipzig, 1905.
—— —— De Kunst van het theater Ventaling van D. van Elten, etc. Bauer, Amsterdam, 1906.
—— —— On the Art of the Theatre : Brown's Book Store. Ill. Chicago, 1911.
—— —— Shingeki Genron. Japanese Translation, by Heimin Wataru. Bunsen Book Store, Tokio, 1912.
—— —— De l'Art du Théâtre : Traduction française par Geneviève Seligman-Lui ; Introduction de Jacques Rouché. Ill. Nouvelle Revue Française, Paris, 1916.

CRAIG, Edward Gordon : Etwas über den Regisseur und die Bühnenausstattung in *Deutsche Kunst und Dekoration*, vol. xvi. p. 596. Koch, Darmstadt, 1905.
—— A Note on " Rosmersholm " (English and Italian). Florence, 1906.
—— Catalogue : Ontwerpen voor Tooneel-decors en Tooneel-costumes, en studies over beweging en verlichting (English—Dutch). Rotterdam, 1906.
—— Towards a New Theatre, 40 Illustrations. Dent, London and Toronto, 1912.
—— A Living Theatre : The Gordon-Craig School (Articles on Craig). *The Mask*, Florence, 1913.
—— The Theatre Advancing. Constable, London, 1921.
—— Puppets and Poets : *The Chap Book*, No. 20. Poetry Bookshop, London, 1921.
—— On Stage Lighting : *The Chap Book*. Poetry Bookshop, London, 1922.
—— Scene : Foreword and Poem, by John Masefield. Oxford University Press, Oxford, 1923.
—— Nothing, or the Bookplate. Chatto & Windus, London, 1924–25.
—— Books and Theatres. Dent, London and Toronto, 1925.
—— Woodcuts and Some Words : Introduction by Campbell Dodgson. Dent, London, 1926.
—— See *The Mask*.

DEUTSCHE THEATER-AUSSTELLUNG MAGDEBURG, 1927, DIE : Eine Schilderung iherer Entstehung und ihres Verlaufes. Herausgegeben von der Mitteldeutschen Ausstellungsgesellschaft m. b. H. 180 Ill. Magdeburg, 1928.

DIEBOLD, Bernhard : Anarchie im Drama : 3 Auflage, mit einem Kapitel : *Das Bühnenbild*. Frankfurter Verlagsanstalt, Frankfurt, 1925.

DRACH, Erich : Ludwig Tiecks Bühnenreformen. Berlin, 1909.

DRINKWATER, John. See FRASER.

EATON, W. P. : The American Stage of To-Day. Boston, 1918.

ECKERT, Victor : Litteratur und Theater : 1. Deutsche Theaterkunst ; 2. Die Städtische Bühne. Gutsch, Karlsruhe, 1914.

EFROS, Nicolas : The Moscow Art Theatre, 1898–1923 (Moskovsky Khudožestvenny Teatr.). Moscow and Leningrad, 1924.

EMMEL, Felix : Das Ekstatische Theater. Vienna, 1924.

ENGEL, Alfred : Beleuchtungseinrichtungen am Theater. Hachmeister & Thal, Leipzig, 1916.
—— Bühnenbeleuchtung : Entwicklung und neuester Stand der Lichttechnik. Hachmeister & Thal, Leipzig, 1926.

ENGELMUELLER, Karel : see OTTNY DIVADELNI SLOVNIK.

EPSTEIN, M. : Max Reinhardt. Winckelmann, Berlin, 1920.

ERLER, Fritz : Ausstellung der Bühnenentwürfe. Brakls Moderne Kunsthandlung, Munich, 1909.

ERNST, SERGE : Nicholas Roerich, A Monograph. Commune of St Eugenie, Petrograd, 1918.

EVREINOV, N. : Les Novations Théâtrales : Troisième Garde, Petrograd, 1922.

FALKENFELD : Sinn der Schauspielkunst. Lehmann, Stuttgart, 1918.

FAUCONNET : Album du Vieux Colombier. Paris.

FERRARI, Carlo : Scenografia, 30 Plates. Crudo, Turin.
—— Five Volumes of Reproductions of Stage Settings of the Last Century. Hoepli, Milan.

FEUERSTEIN, Bedrich : Stage Setting, Architecture. Tokio, 1927.

FILIPOV, V. : The Moscow Small Theatre. Mezhdunarodnaya Kniga, Moscow, 1927.

FILSER, B. : Das Theater der Zukunft : Vierteljahrshefte des Bühnenvolksbundes, Ill. Augsburg, 1921.

FISCHEL, Oscar : Das Moderne Bühnenbild, 155 Ill. in Black and White and Colours. Wasmuth, Berlin, 1923.

FORNARO, Carlo de. See WENGER.

FRANK, Rudolf : Das Moderne Theater : Sammlung, *Wege zum Wissen*. Ullstein, Berlin, 1927.

FRANK, Waldo : The Art of the Vieux Colombier, 1918.

FRASER, Claude Lovat : The Beggar's Opera, by J. Gay : Preface and Illustrations by Cl. L. Fraser : Biographical Notice by John Drinkwater. Heinemann, London, 1921.
—— The Same, without Preface. Scenes and Costumes by Lovat Fraser. Heinemann, 1921.

FRASER. See MACFALL.

FRISCH, Efraim : Von der Kunst des Theaters : Ein Gespräch. Müller, Munich, 1910.

FUCHS, Georg : Die Schaubühne der Zukunft. Schuster & Loeffler, Berlin.
—— Die Revolution des Theaters. Ill. Müller, Munich, 1909.
—— Die Sezession in der dramatischen Kunst und das Volksfestspiel. Müller, Munich, 1911.

FUELOEP-MILLER, René. See GREGOR.

FUERST, Artur : Das elektrische Licht. Langen, Munich.

FUERST, Walter René : Du Décor, 20 Ill. : La Douce France, Paris, 1925.
—— Dekorationen : In *Der Strom*, Dec. 1912. Oesterheld, Vienna, 1912.
—— Der Schauspieler und sein Raum : In *Theaterkalender*, 1913. Oesterheld, Berlin, 1913.
—— Kallitechnia kai Skini : Nea Hellas, Athens, Feb. 1916.
—— Du Décor. In *Choses de Théâtre*. Roussou, Paris, April 1923.
—— Décors. In *Le Cap*. Hiver, Paris, April 1924.
—— Les Tendances actuelles du Décor Théâtral. In *Journal de Psychologie*. Alcan, Paris, March 1926.

GAEHDE, Christian : Das Theater. Teubner, Leipzig, 1921.

GALITZINE, Prince. See ROBES OF THESPIS.

GAMBLE, W. B. : Stage Scenery. A List of References on about 2000 Ill. of Stage Scenery. New York Public Library, New York, 1917.
—— The Development of Scenic Art and Stage Machinery : A Bibliography. New York Public Library, New York, 1920.

GAY, J. See FRASER.

GEDDES, Norman Bel : A Project for a Theatrical Production of Dante's Divine Comedy. Theatre Arts Inc., New York.

GEHRIG, Oscar : Hiler, Theater-und Ballet Entwürfe. Hiler, Berlin, 1922.

GERHAEUSER, E., and PANKOK, Bernhard : Stuttgarter Bühnenkunst : 50 Colour-plates by Pankok, numerous Sketches, Photogravures and Drawings. Deutsche Verlagsanstalt, Stuttgart, 1917.

GIRRANE, G., and GROBAN, Cesar : Nouvelle Machine Théâtrale, la "Double Scène." Rey, Lyons, 1917.

GOLDSCHMIDT, Rudolf K. : Eduard Devrients Bühnenreform am Karlsruher Hoftheater. Leipzig, 1921.

GONTCHAROVA, Nathalie: Liturgie. Album de 18 Costumes au Pochoir. Povolotzky, Paris, 1927.
—— Album de 14 Portraits Théâtraux. St Sebastian, Lausanne, 1915-16.
—— and LARIONOFF : L'Art Théâtral Décoratif Moderne. La Cible, Paris, 1919.
—— and LARIONOFF : Monography. Münster, Moscow, 1914.
—— See THE RUSSIAN BALLET.

GRAY, Terence : Dance Drama. Experiments in the Art of the Theatre. Heffer, Cambridge, 1925

GREGOR, Joseph : Wiener Szenische Kunst. Amaltheaverlag, Vienna.

      1. Die Theaterdekoration, Ill., 1924.
      2. Das Bühnenkostüm, 1925.
      3. Dramaturgie, 1926.
      4. Regie, 1927.

—— Der Umbau des Theaters in der Josefstadt. In *Oesterreichs Bau-und Werkkunst*, Heft 1. Krystalsverlag, Vienna, 1924.
—— and FÜLÖP-MILLER, René : Das Russische Theater. Mit besonderer Berücksichtigung der Revolutionsperiode. About 300 Ill. in Black and White and Colours. Amaltheaverlag, Vienna, 1927.

HAND-LIST OF BOOKS, PAMPHLETS, ETC. 171

GREGORI, Ferdinand : Deutsche Bühnenkunst. Tagewerkverlag, Donauwörth, 1925.

GROBAN, César. See GIRRANE.

GROOM, H. R. Lester : Modern Developments of Stage Lighting. Reprint from *Contact*, January 1925. *Contact*, London, 1925.
—— Stage Lighting. Reprint from *The Illuminating Engineer*, April 1926. *Illuminating Engineer*, London, 1926.

GRUBE, Max : Geschichte der Meininger. Deutsche Verlagsanstalt, Stuttgart, 1926.

GUENTHER, Johannes : Vom Werden und Wesen der Bühne. Dürnhaupt, Dessau.

GUTZEIT, Dr Kurt : Das Problem des Raums im Drama. In *Die Form*, 1 Jahr, Heft 3. Reckendorf, Munich-Berlin, 1922.

HAGEMANN, Carl : Spiele der Völker. Berlin, 1919.
—— Schauspielkunst und Schauspielkünstler. Schuster & Loeffler, Berlin-Leipzig, 1903.
—— Der Mime.
—— Regie. Die Kunst der szenischen Darstellung. Schuster & Loeffler, Berlin-Leipzig, 1912.
—— —— Japanese Translation : Kindaiengeki no Riron to Jissai, by Tamizo Shimamura. Genbunsha, Tokio.
—— Moderne Bühnenkunst : Schuster & Loeffler, Berlin-Leipzig, 1916–18.

HAMMITZSCH, Martin : Der Moderne Theaterbau. Ill. E. Wasmuth, Berlin, 1906.

HANNSEN, Hans : Beiträge zur Technik der Bühnenregiekunst. Ill. Xenien-Verlag, Leipzig, 1908.

HARKER, Joseph : Studio and Stage. Nisbet, London, 1924.

HEMARDINGUER, Charles. See VANLABELLE.

HERALD, Heinz : Max Reinhardt. Ein Versuch über das Wesen der modernen Regie. Lehmann, Berlin, 1915.
—— and STERN, Ernst : Reinhardt und seine Bühne. Eysler, Berlin, 1920.
—— —— Das grosse Schauspielhaus. Berlin, 1920.

HERRIG, Hans : Die Meininger. Von Grumbkow, Dresden, 1880.

HILER HARZBERG : Four Stunts for Clowns. Project executed for the Ringling Brothers' Shows. With 20 original Water-colour Plates. Hiler, Paris, 1924.
—— Great Klaus and Little Klaus. 17 original Designs and 5 Photos. Hiler, New York, 1920.
—— Portfolio of Photos of 6 modern Masks. Hiler, Berlin, 1922.
—— and MOSS, Arthur : Slapstick and Dumbell. Hiler, New York, 1924.
—— See GEHRIG.

HORST, Walter Alfred : Das Bühnenkunstwerk. Schildberger, Berlin, 1911.

HUGO, Jean. See COCTEAU.

JACOBSON, Siegfried : Max Reinhardt. Reiss, Berlin, 1914.

JHERING, H. : Regisseure und Bühnenmaler. Goldschmidt, Berlin, 1921.

JONES, Robert Edmond : Drawings for the Theatre : Theatre Arts. New York, 1925.
—— See MACGOWAN.
—— See MACKAYE.

JOURDAIN, E. F. : The Drama in Europe in Theory and Practice. Methuen, London, 1924.

KAMINKA, Karel. See OTTNY DIVADELNI SLOVNIK.

KAPP, Julius : Die Staatsoper zu Berlin, 1919–1925. Deutsche Verlagsanstalt, Stuttgart, 1926.

KEMENDY, Jenö : A. Huszodik szárad Szinpadja. Muvészet, Budapest, 1907.

KERŽENTSEV, P. M. : Tvorcheskii Teatr. Petrograd, 1920.

KILLIAN, Eugen : Goethe's " Götz " und die neueingerichtete Münchner Bühne. Munich, 1890.

KINSILA, E. B. : Modern Theatre Construction. Ill. Moving Picture World, New York, 1917.

KLETTE, W. : Ueber Theorien und Probleme der Bühnenillusion. Müller, Munich, 1911.

KNUDSEN, Dr Hans : Der Bühnenmaler Cesar Klein (Cesar Klein, scenic artist), German and English Text. Ill. in " Gebrauchsgraphik," 3 Jahr, Heft 11. Phoenixverlag, Berlin, 1927.

KODIČEK, Josef, and RUTTE, Miroslav: Nové České Divadlo, 1918–26. (The New Czech Theatre.) Ill. Aventinum, Prague, 1926.

KRAMPEN, W., and SPIELMAYER, W.: Almanach Dessauer Theater: Selbstverlag, Dessau, 1923–24.

KRANICH, Dr Friedrich: Die moderne Bühnentechnik. Oldenburg, Munich, 1928.

KROLL, Max: Das Deutsche Theater der Gegenwart. 21 Portraits and 12 Stage-decorations. Rösl, Munich, 1923.

KROWS, Arthur Edwin: Play Production in America. Ill. Holt, New York, 1916.

KRUEGER, Max: Ueber Bühne und Bildende Kunst. Ill. Piper, Munich, 1913.
—— Ueber das Verhältnis von Bühne und Bildender Kunst. Vienna, 1911.

LARIONOFF, Michel. See GONTCHAROVA.

LAVER, James, and SHERINGHAM, George: Design in the Theatre; with over 100 Illustrations of Modern Stage-sets and Costumes in Europe and America. Studio, London, 1927.

LASZLO, Alexander: Die Farblichtmusik. Ill. Breitkopf & Härtel, Leipzig, 1925.

LAUTENSCHLAEGER, Karl: Die Münchner Drehbühne im Residenztheater, nebst Beschreibung einer vollständig neuen Bühneneinrichtung mit elektrischem Betrieb. Munich, 1896.

LEBEDE, Hans: Vom Werden der Deutschen Bühne. 1923.

LEFEVRE, Julien: L'Electricité au Théâtre. Grelot, Paris, 1894.

LEGBAND, Paul: Das Deutsche Theater in Berlin. Müller, Munich, 1909.

LENSVELT, F.: Over die Nieuwe Kunst van het Theater. In " Socialistische Gids," March, April, 1922. Soc. Gids, Amsterdam, 1922.

LEVINSON, André: Bakst. The Story of the Artist's Life. Bayard Press, London, 1923.

LITTMANN, Max: Das Münchner Künstlertheater. Ill. J. Werner, Munich, 1908.
—— Die Königlichen Hoftheater in Stuttgart. Ill. Koch, Darmstadt, 1912.
—— Das Grossherzogliche Hoftheater in Weimar. Ill. L. Werner, Munich, 1908.
—— Das Prinzregententheater in Munchen. Ill. L. Werner, Munich, 1901.
—— Das Stadttheater in Hildesheim. Ill. L. Werner, Munich, 1909.
—— Das Stadttheater in Posen. Ill. L. Werner, Munich, 1910.

LOEWITSCH, Franz. See NEUZIL.

LOEWY, Siegfried: Deutsche Theaterkunst von Goethe bis Reinhardt. Vienna, 1923.

LOSSOW, William: Das Neue Königliche Schauspielhaus, Dresden. Ill. A. Koch, Darmstadt, n.d.

LUCKIESH, M.: Colour and its Applications (Section on Colour Effects for the Stage). Constable, London, 1915.

LUX: Moderne Theaterbeleuchtung.

MACFALL, Haldane: The Book of Claude Lovat Fraser. 200 Ill. in Black and White and Colour. Dent, London, 1924.

MACGOWAN, Kenneth: The Theatre of To-morrow. Ill. Boni & Liveright, New York, 1923; Unwin, London, 1923.
—— and JONES, Robert Edmund: Continental Stagecraft. Ill. Harcourt Brace, New York, 1922; Benn, London, 1923.
—— and ROSSE, Hermann: Masks and Demons. Harcourt Brace, New York, 1925.

MACKAYE, Percy: Exhibition of Stage Models and Designs by R. E. Jones. New York, 1920.

M'CANDLESS, Stanley R.: Glossary of Stage Lighting. Theatre Arts, New York, 1926.

MAHLBERG, Paul: Schinkels Theaterdekorationen. Düsseldorf, 1916.

MAHNKE, Adolf. See BARANOWSKY.

MARCHI, Virgilio: Architettura e teatro. Campitelli, Foligno, 1926.

MARINETTI, F. T.: Proclama sul teatro futurista.

MARKOV, P. A.: Noveischaia Teatralnaia Technika. Moscow.

MARSOP, P. : Weshalb brauchen wir die Reformbühne ? Ein Versuch. Munich, 1907.

MARTERSTEIG, Max : Die Protokolle des Mannheimer Hoftheaters. Mannheim.

—— Das Theater im neuen Staat. De Gruyter, Berlin, 1920.

MASEFIELD, John. See CRAIG.

MELOY, Arthur S. : Theatres and Motion Picture Houses. Ill. Architects' Supply and Publishing Co., New York, 1916.

MESTRES, Apeles : Colección de treinta y tres decoraciones del escenógrafo Salvador Alarma. Ill. Barcelona, 1919.

MEYERHOLD, Vsevolod : O Teatre. (Contribution à la technique du Théâtre.) " Prosveschenie," St Petersburg, 1913.

MICHAEL, Friedrich : Deutsches Theater. Hirt's Verlag, Breslau, 1923.

MODERWELL, Hiram Kelly : The Theatre of To-day. Ill. Lane, New York and London, 1914 ; Dodd Mead, New York, 1925.
—— —— Japanese Translations : Kindaigaki Konku, by Yusaku Yokoyama. Dainihon Bunmeik-yokai Pub. Gendaino Gekijo, by Shinichiro Kikuoka. Wasedashippanbu Pub.

MOHOLY-NAGY, L. : see SCHLEMMER.

MORITZ, Eduard : Das antike Theater und die modernen Reformbestrebungen. Ill. Wasmuth, Berlin, 1910.

MOSCOW SMALL THEATRE (Moskovskii Maly Teatr) : History of this Moscow Theatre from 1824–1924. State Printing, Moscow, 1924.

MOSER, Prof. Koloman : Bühnenbilder und Kostümentwürfe zu Bittners " Musikant " in *Deutsche Kunst und Dekoration*, xxvii. p. 388 ff. Koch, Darmstadt, 1910.

MOUSSINAC, Léon : La Décoration Théâtrale. Ill. Rieder, Paris, 1921.

MURILLEJO, Joaquin Muñoz : Escenografia Española. Ill. Blass, Madrid, 1923.

NATIONAL THEATRE, PRAGUE (Dejinij Narodniho Divadla v Praze) 1883–1900. Fr. Subert, Prague, 1910.

NEMETH, Anton. See SZINESZETI LEXICON.

NICHOLL, Allardyce : The Development of the Theatre. A Study of Theatrical Art from the Beginnings to the Present Day. Ill. Harrap, London ; Harcourt Brace, New York, 1927.

NIESSEN, Carl : Das Bühnenbild, 80 Plates and 10 Colour-plates. Klopp, Bonn, 1926–27.

NEUE SCHAUBUEHNE, DIE : eine Forderung. Kaemmerer, Berlin, 1920.

NEUZIL, Walter, LOEWITSCH, Franz, and SCHERER, Rudolf : Plastische Bühne. In : " Oesterreichs Bau-und Werkkunst," 2 Jahrgang, Heft 3. Krystallverlag, Vienna, 1925.

OTTNY DIVADELNI SLOVNIK (A Dictionary of the Theatre), edited by KAMINKA, Karel, and ENGEL-MUELLER, Karel. 33 Numbers to the letter G. Prague, 1919.

PANKOK, Prof. Bernhard : see GERHAEUSER.

PETERSON, Georg : Ueber antike und moderne Theaterbaukunst, sowie über das Theaterwesen. Ill. Franke Habelschwerdt, 1911.

PICHEL, Irving : Modern Theatres. Ill. Harcourt Brace & Co., New York, 1925.

—— On Building a Theatre. Ill. Theatre Arts, New York, 1920.

PIRKER, Max : Die Salzburger Festspiele. Amaltheaverlag, Vienna.

PLAYFAIR, Nigel : Story of the Lyric Theatre, Hammersmith. Chatto & Windus, London, 1925.

PLOTKE, Georg : Deutsche Bühne (Jahrbuch der Frankfurter Städtischen Bühnen), vol i. Rütten & Löhning, Frankfurt, 1919.

POLISH THEATRE (Teatr Polski w Warzsawie), 1913-1923. Towarzystwo Wydawnicze " Ignis," Warsaw.

POUPEYE, Camille : La Mise en Scène Théâtrale d'Aujourd'hui. 20 Linoleum-cuts by Flouquet. Éditions l'Equerre, Brussels, 1927.

PRAMPOLINI, Enrico : La Scenografia Futurista. 1915.
—— L'Atmosfera Scenica Futurista. *Noi*, Roma, 1924.
—— Teatro della Rivolta. *Impero*, Roma, 1924.
—— Studi sul Teatro.
—— Articles in *Impero* and *Noi*.

RAPP, Dr Franz : Das Deutsche Bühnenbild unserer Zeit. In *Die Form*, 1 Jahr, Heft 3. Reckendorf, Munich and Berlin, 1922.

REAU, Louis. See BAKST.

REDKO, A. E. : Teatr i evolutsia teatralnykh form. Sabaschnikoff, Leningrad, 1926.

RICCIARDI, Achille : Scritti Teatrali. Gobetti, Turin, 1926.

RIEZLER, Walter : Das Bühnenbild im " Gesammtkunstwerk." In *Die Form,* 1 Jahr, Heft 3. Reckendorf, Munich and Berlin, 1922.

ROBES OF THESPIS : Costume Designs by Modern Artists. Edited by George Sheringham. 100 Plates. Section on Scenic Design by Prince Galitzine. Benn, London, 1928.

ROCHE, Denis. See BAKST.

ROCHOWANSKI, L. : Die Würfelbühne. In *Oesterrichs Bau-und Werkkunst*, 1 Jahr, Heft 5. Krystallverlag, Vienna, 1925.

ROERICH, Nicholas : Himalayah. Ill. Brentano's, New York, 1927.

ROESSLER, Artur : Richard Teschner's Figurenbühne. In *Oesterreichs Bau-und Werkkunst*, 2 Jahr, Heft 3. Krystallverlag, Vienna, 1925.

ROETTGER, Carl : Zum Drama und Theater der Zukunft. Ill. Leipzig, 1921.

ROMAINS, Jules : Souvenirs du Vieux Colombier. 55 Dessins. Claude Aveline, Paris, 1926.

ROSENBAUM, Fritz : see TREICHLINGER.

ROSE, A. : Scenes for Scene Painters. Ill. Routledge, London, 1925.

ROSENTHAL, Fr. : Wanderbühnen. Vienna, 1922.

ROSSE, Herman : Designs and Impressions. 24 Ill. Seymour, Chicago, 1920.
—— See MACGOWAN.

ROUCHÉ, Jacques : L'Art Théâtral Moderne. Ill. Cornely, Paris, 1910. 2nd Edition. Bloud & Gay, Paris, 1924.

RUSSIAN BALLET : The Russian Ballet in Western Europe, 1909–1920. Lane, London, 1921.

RUTHERSTON, Albert Daniel : Decoration in the Art of the Theatre. Monthly *Chap Book*, vol. i. No. 2. Ill. Poetry Bookshop, London, 1919.

SACHS, Edwin O., and WOODROW, A. E. : Modern Opera Houses and Theatres, 3 vols. Ill. Batsford, London, 1897–98.
—— —— Stage Construction. A Supplement. Ill. Batsford, London, 1898.

SAYLOR, Oliver M. : Max Reinhardt and his Theatre. A Collection of Essays, translated from the German. Edited by O. M. Saylor. Ill. Brentanos, New York and London, 1924.

—— The Russian Theatre. Brentanos, New York and London, 1923.
—— Our American Theatre. Brentanos, New York and London, 1923.
—— Inside the Moscow Art Theatre. Brentanos, New York and London, 1926.

SAVITS, Josza : Das Naturtheater. Piper, Munich, 1910.

SCHINKEL, C. F. : Sammlung von Theaterdekorationen. Ernst & Korn, Berlin, 1862.

SCHERER, Rudolf. See NEUZIL.

SCHLEMMER, Oskar, and MOHOLY-NAGY, G. L. : Die Bühne in Bauhaus. Ill. Bauhausbücher, No. 4. Langen, Munich, 1924.

SCHNACKENBERG : Ballet und Pantomime. 1928.

SELL, Henry B. : What is it all about ? A Sketch of the Movement in the Theatre. Laurentian Press, Chicago, 1914.

SEMPER, Manfred : Theater. (Handbuch der Architektur, Teil 4, Halbband 6, Heft 5). Bergsträsser, Stuttgart, 1904.

SHAWN, Ted : American Ballet. New York, 1926.

SHERINGHAM, George : The Duenna. Costumes and Scenic Designs. Constable, London, 1925.
—— See ROBES OF THESPIS.
—— See LAVER.

SIERRA, Gregorio Martinez : Un Teatro de Arte en Espagna, 1917–1925. Esfinge, Madrid, 1925.

SIMONSON, Lee : Minor Prophecies. Harcourt Brace, New York.

SPIELMAYER, W. : see KRAMPEN.

STAATSOPER BERLIN, DAS WERK DER, 2 vols. Gurlitt, Berlin, 1926.

STANISLAVSKY, Constantin : My Life in Art. Bles, London, 1924.

STARK, Eduard : Starinny Teatr. Troisième Garde, Petrograd, 1922.

STERN, Ernst : Ariadne auf Naxos. Oper von H. von Hofmannstal, Musik von Richard Strauss. Skizzen für die Kostüme und Dekorationen. Fürstner, Berlin, 1921.
—— See HERALD.

STORCK, Willy F. : Litterarische Randbemerkungen (Moderne Theaterkunst). Freibund, Mannheim, 1913.
—— Freibund, Mannheim. Katalog der Ausstellung Moderner Theaterkunst. Freibund, Mannheim.

STREIT, Andreas : Das Theatre. Ill. Nehmann und Wentzel, Wien, 1903.

STRNAD, Prof. Oskar: Projekt für ein Schauspielhaus. Der Architekt, xxiii. Nos. 7–8. Schroll, Vienna.

STUEMCKE, Heinrich : Die Deutsche Theaterausstellung, Berlin, 1910. Selbstverlag, Berlin, 1911.

SVYETLOV, Vladimir : Le Ballet Contemporain. Ouvrage édité avec la collaboration de Léon Bakst. Traduction Française de M. D. Calvocoressi. De Brunoff, Paris, 1912 ; de Brunoff, St Petersbourg, 1912.

SZINÉSZETI LEXICON (Scientific Theatre Lexicon) : edited by Anton Nemeth. Stage Decoration and Costume Section : Dr Wilhelm Treichlinger. Gyözö Andor, Budapest, 1928.

TAIROFF, Alexander : Zapiski Rejissera. Moscow, 1922.
—— Das entfesselte Theater. Authorized Translation from the Russian. Ill. Kiepenheuer, Potsdam, 1923.

TESSIER, A. See BAKST.

THEATRE LIGHTING, PAST AND PRESENT : Ward Leonard Electric Co. Ill. Mount Vernon, New York, 1923.

TREICHLINGER, Dr Wilhelm : see SZINÉSZETI LEXICON.
—— Theaterprojekt. In Oesterreichs Bau-und Werkkunst, April 1926. Krystallverlag, Vienna, 1926.

TRUDELLE, V. : La Lumière Electrique et ses différentes applications au Théâtre. Paris, 1914.

TUGENDHOLD, Jacques : Alexandra Exter. Translation from the Russian Manuscript. Ill. Saria, Paris, 1922.

VANLABELLE, A., and HEMARDINGUER, Charles : La Science au Théâtre. Paulin, Paris, 1908.

VERNON, Frank : The Twentieth Century Theatre. Harrap, London, 1924.

VITOUX, Georges : Le Théâtre de l'Avenir : Mise en Scène, Machinerie, etc. Schleicher, Paris, 1903.

WAGNER, Ludwig : Der Szeniker Ludwig Sievert. Ill. Bühnenvolksverlag, Berlin, 1926.

WALSER, Karl : Das Theater. Bühnenbild und Kostüm. Text von Oscar Bie 28 Colour-plates and 8 Plates in Black and White. Cassirer, Berlin, 1912.

WAUER, William : Der Kunst eine Gasse. Berlin, 1906.
—— Die Kunst im Theater. Berlin, 1909.
—— Theater als Kunstwerk. Der Sturm, Berlin, 1919.

WEIL, Th. : Die Elektrische Bühnen-und Effektbeleuchtung. Hartleben, Vienna, 1914.

WENGER, John : A Collection of Sketches. Ill. Text by Carlo de Fornaro. Lawren, New York, 1925.

WESTHEIM, Paul : Wege und Ziele der Bühnenausstattung. In " Deutsche Kunst und Dekoration," xxviii. Koch, Darmstadt, 1911.

WIDMANN, W. : Theater und Revolution : Oesterheld, Berlin, 1920.

WINDS, Adolf : Der Schauspieler in seiner Entwicklung von den Mysterien zum Kammerspiel. Deutsche Verlagsanstalt, Berlin and Leipzig, 1919.

—— Geschichte der Regie. 145 Ill. Deutsche Verlagsanstalt, Berlin and Leipzig, 1925.

—— Quer über die Bühnen. Schuster and Loeffler, Berlin, 1919.

—— Das Theater. Einblicke in sein Wesen. Minden, Dresden and Leipzig, 1926.

WOLFF, J. F. : Das Bühnensystem des neuen kgl. Schauspielhauses zu Dresden. Reiss, Berlin.

WOODWARD, E. A. : see SACHS.

YOUNG, Stark : Glamour. Essays on the Art of the Theatre. Scribners, New York, 1925.

ZABEL, Eugen : Moderne Bühnenkunst. Velhagen und Klasing, Berlin.

ZNOSKO-BOROVSKY, Evr. A. : Russkij Teatr Natchala 20 Veka. Isdatelvo Plamja, Prague, 1927.

ZUCKER, Paul : Theater und Lichtspielhäuser. Ill. Wasmuth, Berlin, 1926.

REVIEWS, PERIODICALS, ARTICLES.

L'ART DÉCORATIF. Paris.
> Oct. 1912 : " L'Art Décoratif au Théâtre des Arts " (R. L'Estrange).

ART ET DÉCORATION : Librairie des Beaux Arts, Paris.
> Feb. 1911 : " Léon Bakst " (J. L. Vaudoyer).
> April, May, 1911 : " L'Exposition du Théâtre au Salon d'Automne " (Georges Mouveau).
> January, 1912 : " Maxime Dethomas " (Georges Mouveau).
> April, May, 1920 : " Les Peintres Modernes et le Théâtre " (Valdo-Barbey), etc.

BILDUNGSANSTALT GARTENSTADT HELLERAU : Prospectus.

BLAETTER DES STADTTHEATERS ZU BAMBERG. Bamberg, 1925–26.

BLAETTER DES DEUTSCHEN THEATERS. Deutsches Theater, Berlin.

BUEHNE, DIE : Magazin für Theater, Litteratur, Film, Mode, Kunst, Gesellschaft, Sport. Vienna, 1923 ff.

BUEHNEN-JAHRBUCH DER GENOSSENSCHAFT DEUTSCHER BUEHNENANGEHOERIGEN. F. A. Günther & Sohn, Berlin, 1889 ff.

BUEHNENTECHNISCHE RUNDSCHAU : Zeitschrift der Berufsgruppe " Technische Bühnenvorstände." Stuttgart, 1917 ff.

CAHIERS DU THEATRE, LES : Organe de la Société Universelle du Théatre, Paris. French, English and German Edition. Four numbers until now.

CAHIERS DU VIEUX COLOMBIER, LES. Paris.

CHOSES DE THEATRE : Cahiers Mensuels de notes, d'études et de recherches théâtrales. Mattei Rousseau, Dir. Paris, 1922–24.

COMOEDIA : (Daily Theatre newspaper). Paris.
> Vols. ix.–xi. : " Enquète sur l'Evolution du Décor " (Raymond Cogniat).

COMOEDIA ILLUSTRÉ. Ill. Paris, 1908–22.

COMOEDIA, LA. Edizioni Mondadori. Milano, 1918 ff.

DEKORATIVE KUNST : F. Bruckmann, Munich.
> 1913 : Special issue : Mannheim Theatre Exhibition.

DEUTSCHE BUEHNE, DIE. Oesterheld & Co., Berlin.

DEUTSCHE BÜHNE (Lübeck).

DEUTSCHE KUNST UND DEKORATION. Alexander Koch, Darmstadt, 1894 ff.
> Vol. vi. : " Dekoration der Bühne " (Peter Behrens).
> „ xvi. : " Ueber Bühnenausstattung " (Gordon Craig).
> „ xxviii. : " Wege und Ziele der Bühnenausstattung " (P. Westheim).
> „ xxxi. : " Bühnenmasken." Ibid. : " Balletskizzen."
> „ xxxvii. : " Bühne und Malerei."
> „ xliii. : " Vom Bühnenbild " (Al. von Gleichen-Russwurm).
> „ li. : " Das Bühnenbild als Gemälde."

DRAMA, THE. Ill. Chicago, 1910 ff.

DRAMATISCHE THEATER, DAS : Eine Monatsschrift für Theater, Musik, Litteratur und Künste. Herausg. : F. A. Angermayer und Paul Zech., Leipzig, 1924.

FORM, DIE : Organ der Deutschen Gewerbeschau, München. Hermann Reckendorf, Munich and Berlin, 1922.
> Heft 3 : Special Number : Theater Exhibition, Munich, 1922.

MASK, THE : Illustrated Quarterly Review. Florence, 1908 ff.

MASKE : Organ der Deutschen Theaterausstellung Magdeburg, 1926. See " Die vierte Wand."

MASKEN. Ill. Copenhagen, 1910 ff.

MASKER, HET : Amsterdam.

MASQUES : Cahiers d'Art Dramatique. Gaston Baty, Paris, 1927.

MONATSHEFTE FUER BAUKUNST. Wasmuth, Berlin.
>   Jahr 5, Hefte 1–2 : " Das grosse Schauspielhaus."
>   „ 5, „ 9–10 : " Das Salzburger Festspielhaus."
>   „ 6, „ 6 : Strnad's " Projekt für ein Schauspielhaus."

NERVIE, LA. Brussels.
>   Dec. 1923 : Special Number : Le Théâtre du Marais.

NEUE SCHAUBUEHNE, DIE. R. Kaemmerer Verlag, Berlin.

NEUE WEG, DER : Organ der Genossenschaft Deutscher Bühnenangehörigen. Berlin.

NOI : Rivista d'Arte Futurista. Roma.
>   Anno 1–2, Seria 6–9 : Special Number : Teatro e Scena Futurista.

OESTERREICHS BAU-UND WERKKUNST. Krystallverlag, Vienna, 1924 ff.
>   Jahr 1, Heft 1 : " Der Umbau des Theaters in der Josefstadt " (Gregor).
>   „ 1, „ 5 : " Die Würfelbühne " (Rochowanski).
>   „ 2, „ 3 : " Plastische Bühne " (Neuzil, Löwitsch, Scherer).
>   „ 2, „ 3 : " Richard Teschner's Figurenbühne " (Roessler).
>   „ 2, „ 7 : " Theaterprojekt " (Treichlinger-Rosenbaum).

REVUE DE L'ŒUVRE, LA : Revue Internationale des Arts du Théâtre. Dir., A. F. Lugné-Poe. Ass.-Dir., Simon Lissim. Maison de L'Œuvre, Paris.

RUSSLAND, DAS NEUE : Berlin, 1925. 2 Jahrgang, Hefte 3–4 : Special Number : Russisches Theater.

SCHAUBUEHNE, DIE : Herausgeber Siegfried Jacobson and Eric Reiss. Oesterheld & Co., Berlin.

STAGE YEAR-BOOK, THE. Editor, Lionel Carson. The Stage, Publishers, London.
>   1908–14 : Pre-war German Stage Decoration.
>   1914 : " Modern Scenic Art," by Craig, Rothenstein, Wilkenson, etc.

STROM, DER : Organ der Wiener Freien Volksbühne. Herausgeber : Pernerstorfer, Grossmann, Rundt. Oesterheld & Co, Vienna-Berlin, 1911–14.

SCENE, DIE : Blätter für Bühnenkunst. Ill. Vita, Berlin. 1900 ff.

THEATER, DAS : Eine Revue, Herausgegeben von Arthur Kirchner. Theaterverlagsgesellschaft m. b. H. Berlin.

THEATRE, THE : Monthly Illustrated Review. New York, 1901 ff.

THÉÂTRE, LE. Paris.

THEATRE-CRAFT. London.

TEATRUL : Revista de Teatru şi Arta. Dir., Soare Soare. Bucharest, 1923.

THEATER, HET. Amsterdam.

THEATRE ARTS MONTHLY : Formerly, Theatre Arts Magazine. Edith J. R. Isaacs, Editor. John Mason Brown, Assistant. New York, 1916 ff.

THEATERKALENDER AUF DAS JAHR 1913. Oesterheld & Co., Berlin, 1913.

VIERTE WAND, DIE : Organ der Deutschen Theaterausstellung. Magdeburg, 1927. Mitteldeutsche Ausstellungsgesellschaft. Magdeburg, 1927.

VISTE, JE (Stage, The) : Czech Theatre Review. Out of print.

WENDINGEN : Editor, H. Th. Wijdeveld. Ill. Amsterdam.
>   1921, Nos. 9–10 : Special Number : International Theater Exhibition, Amsterdam. Other Numbers on Stage Decoration, Masks, and Marionettes. Special Number on the Flemish Folk Theatre. 1928.

INDEX

(N.B.: For references to specific dramatic works, consult alphabetical listing under title of play.)

i   *Claude Lovat Fraser, " King Henry IV " (Shakespeare) : London.*

TWENTIETH-CENTURY
STAGE DECORATION

WALTER RENÉ FUERST

AND

SAMUEL J. HUME

WITH AN INTRODUCTION BY ADOLPHE APPIA

VOLUME TWO: ILLUSTRATIONS

BENJAMIN BLOM, NEW YORK

This edition, first published in 1967, is an unabridged and corrected republication of the work originally published by Alfred A. Knopf, Ltd., in 1929. This edition contains a newly prepared Index, and a detailed List of Plates and full captions under all illustrations replace the separately printed Hand-List of Plates that accompanied the original edition.

This new edition is published in paperback by Dover Publications, Inc., 180 Varick Street, New York, N. Y. 10014, and in hardcover by Benjamin Blom, Inc., 4 West Mt. Eden Avenue, Bronx, N. Y. 10452.

Library of Congress Catalog Card Number (paperbound): 65-24021

Library of Congress Catalog Card Number (clothbound): 67-28846

Manufactured in the United States of America

ii

ii Mstislav Dobujinsky, " Le Régiment qui passe " : Chauve-Souris, 1927.

iii

iv

iii *Jean Hugo, " The Silent Woman " (Jonson): L'Atelier, Paris, 1925.*

iv *Ernst Stern, " Don Carlos " (Schiller): Deutsches Theater, Berlin, 1909.*

v

vi

v *Léon Bakst, Prologue to " La Pisanella " (D'Annunzio–Ildebrando da Parma) :*
Théâtre du Châtelet, Paris, 1913.

vi *Klaus Richter, Setting for the Warsaw Jewish Theatre, Berlin, 1921.*

vii

vii   *Léon Bakst, Costume design for " Scheherazade " (Rimsky-Korsakov):*
Ballets Russes, 1909.

PREFACE TO THE ILLUSTRATIONS

IT must be clear to every one, as it is to us, that the reproductions of photographs and designs for stage decorations are bound to be not only deceptive and inadequate, but often actually false. The mise en scène is a living organic whole in which the stage decoration plays its part, and no photograph and no design can ever give more than a hint of what that mise en scène, and more particularly its scenic environment, were like in actuality. If the stage setting could be considered as something apart, a finished work finding its justification within itself, the case would be different ; but stage decoration, apart from the living drama for which it was created and which it was designed to complement and serve, loses its very reason for being. The moment the artist separates his design from the stage and asks us to judge it on its own merits, irrespective of the stage, it passes into another category. In this sense it may be considered as a work of art and judged accordingly ; so long as it remains a design for a stage setting to be realized on a living stage, it cannot stand alone as a work of art for, properly speaking, the stage setting does not enter into the domain of art ; it is an environment for the action of the drama, and without that action it is unfulfilled, sterile and dead.

It is the actor telling his story in word and gesture who animates the theatre, and so the photograph of the setting without the actors who should people it is likewise dead. No setting can be truly judged unless we can watch it as it environs the action, unfolding from moment to moment in a continuous, consecutive and unbroken stream. Those photographs taken with the people and the lighting are better, but after all they are " stills," a given moment in the stream arrested and crystallized on the photographic plate. It is true that these selected moments may be good, but what of the others ? The setting, if it is anything, is not for the moments of a play. It must follow and serve the play at all times.

If we remember that these reproductions in black and white invariably represent an original in the theatre which was more or less abounding in colour and animated by the power of living light, we shall realize how far short they fall of giving even a hint of what that original was like. It is true that in the photographs of that master of stage photography, Francis Bruguière, we often get results which are arresting in themselves ; so arresting, in fact, that we are tempted to believe that he has succeeded in suggesting to us a visual image more beautiful and more provocative than the original. Apropos of which, there is the story of how one very well-known American scene designer once said to another equally well-known : " You know, X——, your productions are never as fine as your drawings for them." To which the other replied : " That may be true, but it is a certainty that your productions are never as good as Bruguière's photographs of them."

The colour plates made from original designs are perhaps better, but after all they give us only the artist's intent and tell us nothing of the realization ; nothing of how the ensemble appeared when animated with its people moving in the light of the stage. They say nothing about this light nor its resultant shadows, nor of the changes in colour in both light and shadow which the living mise en scène contained. Beautiful in itself, an intimation of the artist's vision, the design, even in colour, is false when considered as a document for a book of this kind. It is a record of what the eye of the imagination saw, but how seldom does the realization even approach the dream ! But here we are concerned with the concrete realization of the dream in terms of the stage, and for us these charming designs, until they are actualized, must remain only designs—unfulfilled and by consequence somewhat apart.

It is clear that only those artists who understand the technical means by which the design is to be realized and to become a part of the organization of the stage, and who are conscious of those means at the moment the design is set down, can successfully create the scenic environment for the play and, at the same time, meet the conditions of the stage. With the artist who has this consciousness the design is often no more than a rough sketch-note, so to speak, in black and white and colour, which has little or no meaning for anyone other than the artist himself. Thus a series of designs for stage decorations, charming and suggestive in themselves, are often the very ones which are least capable of being transferred to the stage and when actualized, least resemble the realization.

On the other hand, designs which in themselves are of no particular interest, intended only as a record for the artist, often result in the very best and most expressive stage decorations.

To assemble the illustrative material for reproduction in this book we have written to all the important scene designers of Europe and America, whose names and addresses we could secure, giving them the necessary information and inviting them to send us examples of their work. We have received replies from artists representing fifteen countries of Europe, and from America. On all sides we have been met with courtesy, interest, and a great willingness to co-operate, for all of which we here express our great appreciation. The material forwarded to us has been of all kinds, and in every form. We have received original designs in black and white and in colours, photographs of designs, models, and actual stage settings in all imaginable sizes and of every conceivable quality. Many interesting documents were rejected because of the impossibility of reproducing them properly, as for example pastels, and other designs in delicate colours, which without the colour would have meant nothing ; photographs so small or so badly taken that a good cliché was impossible, and so on. It would have been comparatively easy to arrange a series of reproductions of beautiful photographs, but we have put this temptation aside and have tried throughout to choose those documents which would best illustrate the subject matter contained in the text, and so as far as possible to correlate the two. We have, in addition, tried to compose the individual pages, putting side by side those photographs and designs which seemed most alike in spirit, and aiming, if possible, never to mix photographs and designs on the same page. Again, in illustrating a given tendency, we have tried to select our examples from the work of different artists in Europe and America in order that the general showing might be as representative as possible. Naturally, it has not been possible to carry out these aims to the letter.

For the purposes of our study we needed certain pre-War material, which proved extremely difficult to secure, because the originals themselves were no longer in existence. For assistance in this matter, as well as in many others, we wish to thank Mr Norman Macdermott, Founder of the Everyman Theatre, London, an able and gifted Director, who was one of the first men in England after the War to put into practice the modern principles of the mise en scène. We here also acknowledge the courtesy of the Amalthea Verlag of Vienna in permitting us to use the four clichés of early settings by Alfred Roller (Pl. 24, 25, 55, 56).

In glancing through the list of illustrations, the first thing that will be noted is the omission of any illustrations of the work of Gordon Craig. We feel that such an omission in a book of this kind is of sufficient importance to justify a word of explanation. We requested Mr Craig, as we did all other important artists in Europe, for permission to reproduce some of his designs. Unfortunately, Mr Craig did not see his way to granting the desired permission. The result has been to leave a gap which renders our book, as a record, imperfect. We regret this exceedingly, but we cannot remedy it.

It is with great pleasure that we turn to give in closing a brief, and what must appear an altogether inadequate, expression of our appreciation of the help and advice we have received in so many different quarters, from so many different individuals, and in so many different ways.

First, our warmest thanks to Adolphe Appia for his interest and co-operation throughout. As our study of twentieth-century stage decoration begins with the appearance of his book, we felt it fitting that he should write the Foreword and, with great generosity, he consented to do this. We here testify to our appreciation. Next our thanks to Huntly Carter, who has generously allowed us to use photographs of the Russian theatre from his extensive and valuable collection. We are particularly indebted to Mrs Edith J. R. Isaacs, the Editor, and John Mason Brown, the Assistant Editor of the *Theatre Arts Monthly*, N.Y., for the use of numerous clichés of subjects otherwise unobtainable, and for advice and assistance in ways too varied to enumerate. It is with pleasure that we acknowledge the many favours shown us by Simon Lissim, Assistant Editor of *L'Oeuvre*, Paris, who has not only assisted us in obtaining important documents, but has shown us many personal kindnesses as well. We also extend our thanks to Mrs Claude Lovat Fraser for permission to use an example of her late husband's work, and to Mr James Laver of the Victoria and Albert Museum for assistance in the same connection ; to Mr Max Radin, of the University of California, who has assisted with the correction of manuscript and proofs ; to the *Gebrauchsgraphik, Die Bühne*, Krystall Verlag, and Amalthea Verlag of Vienna for permission to use photographs and clichés and, lastly, to Messrs Ruckert & Company, photo-engravers, Paris, whose interest and care have made possible the present volume of illustrations.

LIST OF PLATES

COLOUR PLATES

HALF-TONE PLATES

CHAPTER ONE: CLEARING THE GROUND

FIRST ASPECT OF THE NATURALISTIC SETTING

SECOND ASPECT OF THE NATURALISTIC SETTING

CHAPTER TWO: THE NEW IDEAS AND THE NEW MAN

NO ILLUSTRATIONS

CHAPTER SEVEN: THE PLASTIC SETTING

NO ILLUSTRATIONS

CHAPTER EIGHT: THE EVOLUTION OF THE MODERN SETTING

CHAPTER TWELVE: TECHNICAL DEVICES

CHAPTER THIRTEEN: STAGE LIGHTING

CHAPTER FOURTEEN: NEW STAGE FORMS AND NEW POSSIBILITIES

CHAPTER FIFTEEN: CONCLUSIONS

NO ILLUSTRATIONS

TWENTIETH-CENTURY
STAGE DECORATION

I

CLEARING THE GROUND	LE THÉATRE AVANT L'ÈRE MODERNE	VORSTUFEN DER ENTWICKLUNG

1

2

1 Constantin Stanislavsky, " A Doll's House " (Ibsen) : Philharmonic School,
later the Moscow Art Theatre, 1890.

2 Constantin Stanislavsky, " The Seagull " (Tchekoff) : Moscow Art Theatre, 1898.

3

4

3-4 *André Antoine, " King Lear " (Shakespeare) : Théâtre de l'Odéon, Paris, 1904.*

5

6

5 *Constantin Somoff (Stanislavsky), " The Cherry Orchard " (Tchekoff) : Moscow Art Theatre, 1904.*

6 *Klaudius Sapounoff (Stanislavsky), " Tsar Féodor " (Tolstoy) : Moscow Art Theatre, 1898–1912.*

7

8

7–8 *Mstislav Dobujinsky (Stanislavsky), " A Month in the Country "*
(Turgenieff): Moscow Art Theatre, 1909.

9

10

9-10   *Alexander Benois (Stanislavsky), " La Locandiera " (Goldoni) : Moscow
Art Theatre, 1914.*

II

THE NEW IDEAS	NOUVELLES IDÉES	DIE NEUEN AUFGABEN
AND		UND
THE NEW MEN	HOMMES NOUVEAUX	DER NEUE BÜHNENBILDER
No illustrations	*Pas d'illustrations*	*Keine Abbildungen*

III

MAX REINHARDT

11

12

11–12 *Emil Orlik (Reinhardt), " The Merchant of Venice " (Shakespeare):
Deutsches Theater, Berlin, 1905.*

13

14

13 *Emil Orlik (Reinhardt), " Die Räuber " (Schiller): Deutsches Theater, Berlin, 1908.*

14 *Emil Orlik (Reinhardt), " The Winter's Tale " (Shakespeare): Deutsches Theater, Berlin, 1906.*

15

16

15-16 *Ludwig von Hoffmann (Reinhardt), " Aglavaine et Sélysette " (Maeter-linck): Kammerspiele, Berlin, 1907.*

17

18

17-18 *Carl Czeschka (Reinhardt), " King Lear " (Shakespeare): Deutsches Theater, Berlin, 1908.*

19

20

21

19–21   *Alfred Roller (Reinhardt), " Faust " (Goethe) : Deutsches Theater,*
Berlin, 1909.

22

23

22–23 *Ernst Stern (Reinhardt), " Don Carlos " (Schiller) : Deutsches Theater, Berlin, 1909.*

24

25

24-25 *Alfred Roller (Reinhardt), " Faust," 2nd Part (Goethe) : Deutsches Theater, Berlin, 1911.*

26

27

26 *Ernst Stern (Reinhardt), " Georges Dandin " (Molière) : Deutsches Theater, Berlin, 1912.*

27 *Ernst Stern (Reinhardt), " Much Ado About Nothing " (Shakespeare) : Deutsches Theater, Berlin, 1912.*

28

29

28–29 *Ernst Stern (Reinhardt), "Le Bourgeois Gentilhomme" (Molière):*
Deutsches Theater, Berlin, 1918.

30

31

30 *Oskar Strnad (Reinhardt), " Oesterreichische Komödie " (Lernet–Holenia):
Josefstädtertheater, Vienna, 1927.*

31 *Ernst Schütte (Reinhardt), " Bonaparte " (Unruh): Deutsches Theater,
Berlin, 1926.*

32

33

32–33 *Oskar Strnad (Reinhardt), " The Merchant of Venice " (Shakespeare):*
Josefstädtertheater, Vienna, 1927.

IV

ADOLPHE APPIA

34

35

34 *Adolphe Appia, " Tristan und Isolde " (Wagner) : 1896.*
35 *Adolphe Appia, " Die Walküre " (Wagner) : 1892.*

36

37

36 *Adolphe Appia, Oblique Shadows, a setting for rhythm, 1909.*
37 *Adolphe Appia, Setting for Rhythm, 1901.*

38

39

38 *Adolphe Appia* (*Jaques-Dalcroze*), " *Orphée* " (*Gluck*) : *Hellerau, 1906.*

39 *Adolphe Appia,* " *Die Walküre* " (*Wagner*) : *1923.*

40

41

40-41 *Adolphe Appia, " King Lear " (Shakespeare) : 1926.*

V

EDWARD GORDON CRAIG
No illustrations—Pas d'illustrations—Keine Abbildungen

VI

ARCHITECTURAL STAGES	LES SCÈNES	DIE
AND	À	ARCHIETEKTONISCHE
PERMANENT SETTINGS	ARCHITECTURE FIXE	BÜHNE

42

43

42 *Karl Immermann, " Twelfth Night " (Shakespeare) : reconstructed Shakespeare stage, Düsseldorf, 1852.*

43 *Freiherr von Perfall, " King Lear " (Shakespeare) : reconstructed Shakespeare stage, Munich, 1884.*

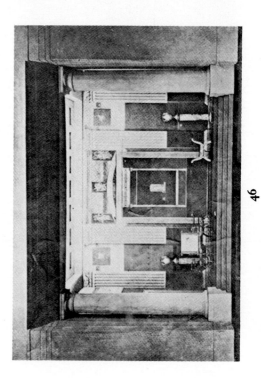

44-45 *Julius Klein and Eugen Killian,* "*Hamlet*" (*Shakespeare*): *Hoftheater, Munich, 1913.*

46-47 *Julius Klein and Eugen Killian,* "*Julius Caesar*" (*Shakespeare*):
Hoftheater, Munich, 1913.

48

49

48 *Jacques Copeau and Louis Jouvet, " Les Surprises de l'Amour " (Marivaux):*
Théâtre du Vieux Colombier, Paris, 1920.

49 *Jacques Copeau and Louis Jouvet, " Twelfth Night " (Shakespeare):*
Théâtre du Vieux Colombier, Paris, 1920.

50

51

52

50 *Rêné Moulaert (Delacre), " A quoi rêvent les jeunes filles " (de Musset):
Théâtre du Marais, Brussels, 1923.*

51 *Alexander Shervashidze (Delacre), " A Month in the Country "
(Turgenieff): Théâtre du Marais, Brussels, 1923.*

52 *Rêné Moulaert (Delacre), " L'Amour Médecin " (Molière): Théâtre du
Marais, Brussels, 1923.*

53

54

53 *Hans Fritz, Würfelbühne, Stage settings composed of interchangeable blocks, Innsbruck, 1927.*

54 *August Perret, Théâtre de l'Exposition des Arts Décoratifs, Paris, 1925.*

55

56

55-56 *Alfred Roller, " Don Giovanni " (Mozart) : Hofoper, Vienna, 1905.*

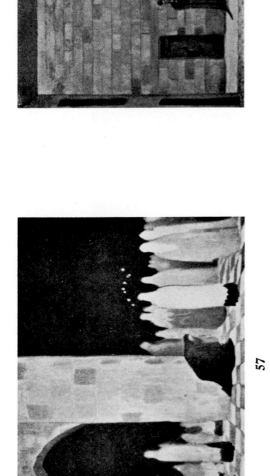

57-58 *Fritz Erler (Fuchs), " Faust " (Goethe) : Relief stage, Künstlertheater, Munich, 1909.*

59 *Fritz Erler (Fuchs), " Hamlet " (Shakespeare) : Relief stage, Künstlertheater, Munich, 1909.*

60 *Fritz Erler (Fuchs), " Faust " (Goethe) : Relief stage, Künstlertheater, Munich, 1909.*

61

62

61 *Lee Simonson, " L'Annonce faite à Marie " (Claudel) : Theatre Guild,
New York, 1922.*

62 *Samuel J. Hume, " The Golden Doom " (Dunsany) : Permanent setting,
Arts and Crafts Theatre, Detroit, 1917.*

63

64

63 *Samuel J. Hume, " Doctor Faustus " (Marlowe): Permanent setting, Arts and Crafts Theatre, Detroit, 1917.*

64 *Samuel J. Hume, " The Doorway " (Brighouse): Permanent setting, Arts and Crafts Theatre, Detroit, 1917.*

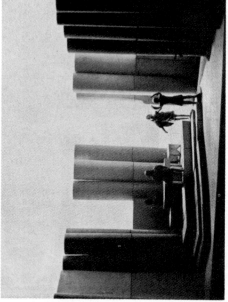

66

68

65

67

65–68 *Terence Gray, System of hollow blocks or boxes, Model, Cambridge, England, 1926.*

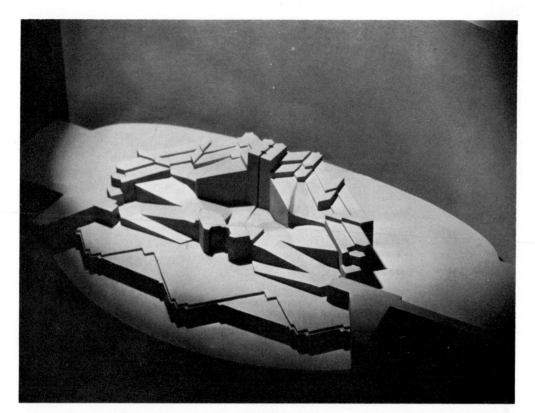

69

70

69 *Norman Bel Geddes, " Lazarus Laughed " (O'Neill) : Model, New York, 1926.*

70 *Norman Bel Geddes, " Jehanne d'Arc " (de Acosta) : Model, Paris, 1925.*

71

72

71-72 *Oskar Strnad, " Hamlet " (Shakespeare) : Burgtheater, Vienna.*

73

74

73 *Woodman Thompson, " Malvaloca " (J. and S. Quintero) : Unit setting,
first phase ; 48th Street Theatre, New York, 1922.*

74 *Woodman Thompson, " Malvaloca " (J. and S. Quintero) : Unit setting,
second phase ; 48th Street Theatre, New York, 1922.*

75

76

75-76   *Lee Simonson, " As You Like It " (Shakespeare): Semi-permanent
setting using telari, American National Theatre, New York, 1923.*

77

78

77 *Norman Macdermott, " Romeo and Juliet " (Shakespeare) : Permanent setting, Everyman Theatre, London 1921.*

78 *Norman Macdermott, " Arms and the Man " (Shaw) : Permanent setting, Everyman Theatre, London, 1922.*

79

80

81

79–81 *H. Th. Wijdeveld, " Hamlet " (Shakespeare): Permanent setting,*
Amsterdam, 1918.

83

85

82

84

82-85 *Stanislas Jarocki, " La Comédie-non Divine " (Krasinski) : Teatr Polski, Poznán.*

VII

THE PLASTIC	LE DÉCOR	DER SCHAUSPIELER
SETTING	SPATIAL	UND SEIN RAUM
No illustrations	*Pas d'illustrations*	*Keine Abbildungen*

VIII

THE EVOLUTION	L'ÉVOLUTION DE	DER ENTWICKLUNGSGANG
OF	L'ART THÉATRAL	DER MODERNEN
MODERN SETTING	MODERNE	BÜHNENKUNST

86

87

86 *Herman Rosse, " Casanova " (de Azertis–Howard): Belmont Theatre, New York, 1923.*

87 *Woodman Thompson, " The Firebrand " (Mayer): Morosco Theatre, New York, 1924.*

88

89

88   Albert Isler, " Arlechino " (Busoni) : Stadttheater, Zurich.

89   Hermann Krehan, " Die Jüdische Wittwe " (Kaiser) : Landestheater,
Meiningen.

90

91

90   Emil Pirchan, " Boris Godounoff " (Moussorgsky) : Opernhaus, Berlin.

91   Alexander Vladimir Hrska (Hilar), " As You Like It " (Shakespeare) :
National Theatre, Prague, 1923.

92

93

92 *César Klein, " Faust " (Goethe) : Staatstheater, Berlin.*

93 *César Klein (Jessner), " Napoleon " (Grabbe) : Staatstheater, Berlin, 1921.*

94

95

94 *Norman Bel Geddes, " King Lear " (Shakespeare): Model of a project, New York, 1926.*

95 *Jo Mielziner, " Faust " (Goethe): Model of a project, New York, 1927.*

96

97

96–97   *Robert Edmond Jones, " Beyond " (Hasenclever): Provincetown Playhouse, New York, 1925.*

114

115

114-115 *Terence Gray, Model for a system of luminous screens, Cambridge, England, 1926.*

116

117

116   *Walter von Wecus, " Demetrius " (Lernet–Holenia) : Stadttheater, Bonn.*

117   *Georges Pitoëff, " Macbeth " (Shakespeare) : Theatre Pitoëff, Geneva.*

118

119

118   *Ludwig Sievert, " Penthesilea " (Kleist) : Schauspielhaus, Frankfurt.*
119   *Ljubo Babić, " Richard III " (Shakespeare) : National Theatre, Zagreb.*

120

121

120–121   *Heinrich Heckroth, " Theodora " (Handel) : Stadttheater, Münster, 1925.*

122

123

122   *Madame Parr, " L'Homme et son Désir " (Claudel) : Swedish Ballet, Paris.*

123   *Emil Pirchan (Jessner), " Richard III " (Shakespeare) : Staatstheater, Berlin, 1921.*

124

125

124 *Emil Pirchan (Jessner), " Empörung des Lucius " (Bluth) : Staatstheater, Berlin, 1924.*

125 *Traugott Müller, " Segel am Horizont " (Leonhard) : Volksbühne, Berlin, 1924.*

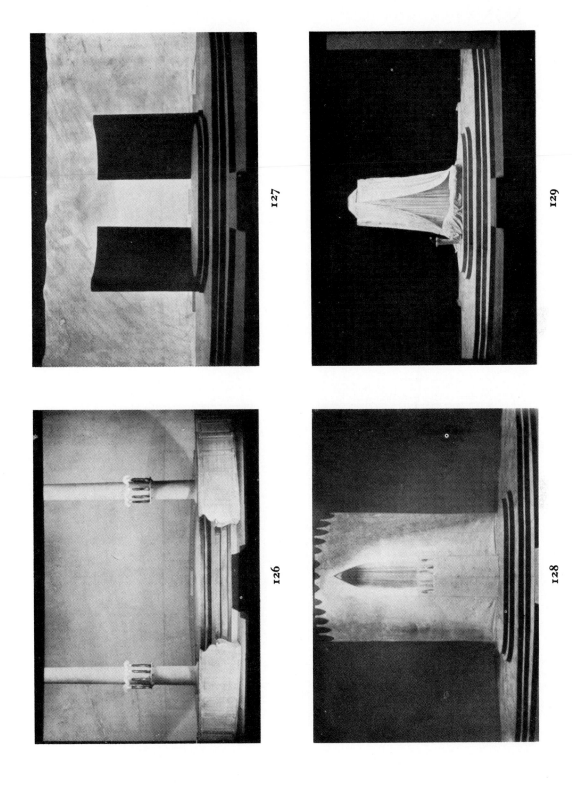

127

129

126

128

126–129 *Emil Pirchan (Jessner), "Othello" (Shakespeare): Staatstheater, Berlin, 1921.*

130

131

130-131 *Walter Reiman (Jessner), " Macbeth " (Shakespeare): Staatstheater, Berlin, 1923.*

132

133

132 *Torsten Hecht, " Gyges und sein Ring " (Hebbel) : Staatstheater, Mainz.*

133 *Eduard Sturm, " Prinz von Homburg " (Kleist) : Schauspielhaus, Düsseldorf, 1925.*

134

135

134-135 *Harry Täuber, " When We Dead Awaken " (Ibsen): Akademietheater, Vienna, 1925.*

136

137

136 *Claude Bragdon, " Cyrano de Bergerac " (Rostand) : Hampden Theatre,
New York, 1924.*

137 *Reinhold Ockel, " Bauernzorn " (Reinacher) : Stadttheater, Aachen, 1926.*

138

139

138   *T. C. Pillartz, " Der Befreite Don Quichote " (Lunacharsky) : Stadttheater, Crefeld.*
139   *Yngwe Berg (Colijn), " Himlens Hemlighet : Intima Teatern, Stockholm.*

141

143

140

142

140–141 *Norman Wilkinson (Granville-Barker), " A Midsummer Night's Dream " (Shakespeare) : Savoy Theatre, London, 1912–13.*

142 *Albert Rutherston (Granville-Barker), " Androcles and the Lion " (Shaw) : Savoy Theatre, London, 1912–13.*

143 *Herman Rosse, " South Sea Island Fantasy " : J. Murray Anderson Revue, New York, 1926.*

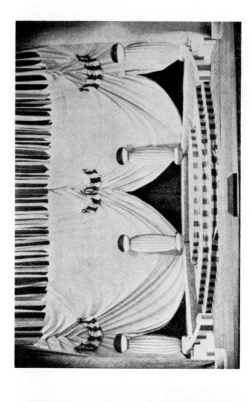

145

147

144

146

144 *Vlastislav Hofman (Hilar),* " *The Bacchantes* " *(Euripides)* : *National Theatre, Prague, 1921.*
145 *Vlastislav Hofman (Hilar),* " *Columbus* " *(Hilbert)* : *National Theatre, Prague, 1924.*
146 *Josef Čapek,* " *Le Misanthrope* " *(Molière)* : *National Theatre, Prague, 1923.*
147 *Josef Čapek,* " *Le Bourgeois Gentilhomme* " *(Molière)* : *National Theatre, Prague, 1926.*

148

149

148 *Heinrich Heckroth, " Salome " (Wilde) : Stadttheater, Münster.*
149 *Walter von Wecus, " Salome " (Wilde) : Stadttheater, Düsseldorf.*

150

151

150 *Alexander Vesnine (Tairoff), " L'Annonce faite à Marie " (Claudel) :
Kamerny Theatre, Moscow, 1920.*

151 *Alexander Vesnine (Tairoff), " Phèdre " (Racine) : Kamerny Theatre,
Moscow, 1921.*

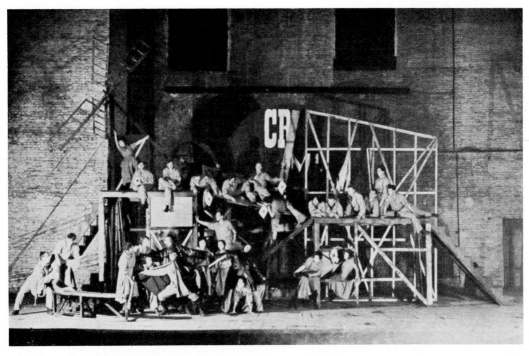

174

175

174 *Lubov Popova (Meyerhold), " Le Cocu Magnifique " (Crommelynck):*
Meyerhold Theatre, Moscow, 1922.

175 *Alexander Vesnine (Tairoff), " The Man Who Was Thursday "*
(Chesterton): Kamerny Theatre, Moscow, 1923.

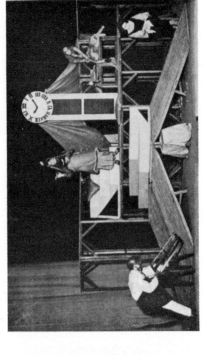

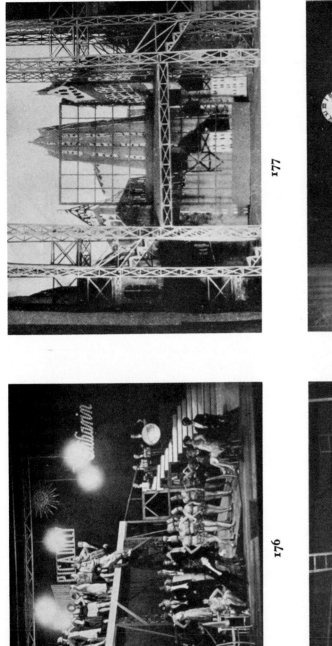

177

179

176

178

176   *Karlheinz Martin, "Franziska" (Wedekind) : Theater in der Königgrätzerstrasse, Berlin, 1925.*

177   *Woodman Thompson, "God Loves Us" (McEvoy) : Maxine Elliot Theatre, New York, 1926.*

178   *Isaac Rabinovitch, "The Sorceress" (Goldfaden) : Jewish Academical Theatre, Moscow, 1922.*

179   *Réné Moulaert, "Tyl" (Vandervelde) : Het Vlaamsche Volkstoneel, Brussels.*

180

181

180 *Boris Aronson, " The Bronx Express " (Dymov) : Astor Theatre, New York, 1922.*

181 *Donald Oenslager, " Pinwheel " (Faragoh) : The Neighbourhood Playhouse, New York, 1927.*

182

183

182 *Eisenstein, " Enough Stupidity in Every Wise Man " (Ostrovsky):
Proletkult Theatre, Moscow.*

183 *Isaac Rabinovitch (Meyerhold), " The Inspector General " (Gogol):
Meyerhold Theatre, Moscow.*

184

185

184 *Vsevolod Meyerhold, " D.E ." (Ehrenburg) : Meyerhold Theatre, Moscow, 1924.*

185 *Vsevolod Meyerhold, " Mandate " (Erdmann) : Meyerhold Theatre, Moscow, 1925.*

IX

| THE MODERN MEANS OF EXPRESSION | LES MOYENS D'EXPRESSION DE L'ART THÉATRAL MODERNE | AUSDRUCKSMITTEL DER BÜHNE |

186

187

186   *Alfred Roller, " Tristan und Isolde " (Wagner) : Hofoper, Vienna, 1903.*

187   *Hans Wildermann, " Parsifal " (Wagner) : Stadttheater, Breslau.*

188

189

188 *Adolf Linnebach, " Gyges und sein Ring " (Hebbel): Hoftheater, Dresden, 1913.*

189 *Joseph Urban, " Le Prophète " (Meyerbeer): Metropolitan Opera, New York, 1917.*

190

191

190   *Eduard Sturm, " Maria Stuart " (Schiller): Schauspielhaus, Düsseldorf.*

191   *Heinz Daniel, " Brunhild " (Ernst): Stadttheater, Altona, 1925.*

192

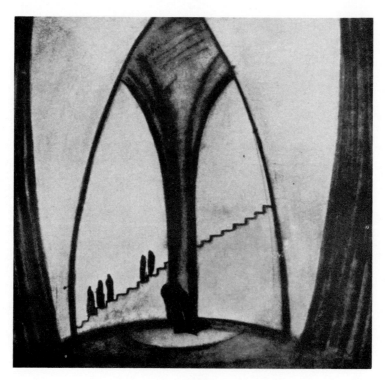

193

192　Oskar Strnad, " Danton " (Rolland) : Deutsches Volkstheater, Vienna.

193　Kurt Gutzeit, " Faust " (Goethe) : Project, Munich.

194

195

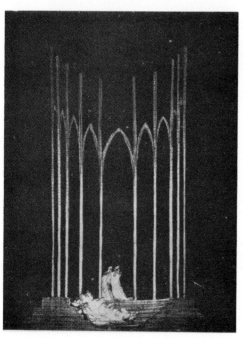

196

197

194-195   *Paul Ott (Medenwald), " King Lear " (Shakespeare): Reussisches
Theater, Gera, 1923.*

196   *Robert Edmond Jones, " The Seven Princesses " (Maeterlinck): New York, 1920.*

197   *Oskar Strnad (Reinhardt), " King Lear " (Shakespeare): Josefstädtertheater, Vienna, 1925.*

198

199

198 *Paul Nash, " King Lear " (Shakespeare) : From the set of designs made for " The Players Shakespeare," Ernest Benn, Ltd., London, 1927.*

199 *Manuel Fontenals, " The Tempest " (Shakespeare) : Project for Théâtre de l'Odéon, Paris, 1926.*

200

201

200 *Georges Pitoëff, " Le Lâche " (Lenormand): Théâtre des Arts, Paris.*

201 *Robert Edmond Jones (Hopkins), " Macbeth " (Shakespeare): Model, Apollo Theatre, New York, 1921.*

202

203

202–203 *Bedrich Feuerstein (Hilar), " Edward II " (Marlowe) : National Theatre, Prague, 1922.*

204

205

204 *Robert Edmond Jones, " Pelléas et Mélisande " (Maeterlinck–Debussy) : New York.*

205 *Ludwig Sievert, " Don Juan " (Molière) : Schauspielhaus, Frankfurt.*

206

207

206 Ludwig Sievert, " Trommeln in der Nacht " (Brecht): Schauspielhaus, Frankfurt.

207 Ludwig Sievert, " Mörder, Hoffnung der Frauen " (Kokoschka):
Schauspielhaus, Frankfurt, 1921.

208

209

208 *Walter René Fuerst, " L'Homme et ses Fantômes (Lenormand) : Théâtre de l'Odéon, Paris, 1924.*

209 *Stanislas Sliwinski, " La Malédiction " (Wyspianski) : Teatr Maly, Warsaw, 1926.*

210

211

210–211 *Svend Gade, " Traumspiel " (Strindberg) : Barnowsky Bühnen, Berlin.*

212

213

212–213 *Jonel Jorgulesco, " Caesar and Cleopatra " (Shaw) : Boston*
Repertory Theatre, 1926.

214

215

214 *Gerhard Buchholz (Hagemann), " Salome " (Strauss): Staatstheater,
Wiesbaden, 1925.*

215 *Gerhard Buchholz (Hagemann), " Elektra " (Strauss): Staatstheater,
Wiesbaden, 1925.*

216

217

216 Georges Pitoëff, " Le Juif du Pape " (Fleg) : Théâtre des Arts, Paris, 1924.

217 Heinrich Heckroth, "Alexander Balus" (Handel) : Stadttheater, Münster, 1926.

222

223

222 *Isaac Grünewald (André), " Samson et Dalila " (Saint-Saëns): Royal Opera, Stockholm, 1922.*

223 *Walter René Fuerst, " Faust " (Goethe): Théâtre de l'Odéon, Paris, 1925.*

X

THE PICTURE STAGE	LE DÉCOR	MALEREI
AND THE	PEINT	UND
PAINTED SETTING		BÜHNE

224

225

224-225 *Joseph Urban, " Pelléas et Mélisande " (Maeterlinck–Debussy):*
Metropolitan Opera, New York, 1925.

226

227

226 Paul Shelving, " The Immortal Hour " (Broughton) : Regent Theatre,
London, 1922.

227 Aubrey Hammond, " The Rose and the Ring " (Thackeray) : Wyndham's
Theatre, London, 1925.

228

229

228 *T. C. Pillartz, " Hassan " (Flecker): Hessiches Landestheater, Darmstadt, 1923.*

229 *Walter von Wecus, " Die Freier " (Eichendorff): Stadttheater, Bonn.*

230

231

230   *Léon Bakst, " Lâcheté " (Bakst): Théâtre Kousnetzoff, Paris, 1922.*

231   *Léon Bakst, " Le Martyre de St Sebastien " (D'Annunzio): Théâtre du Châtelet, Paris, 1913.*

232

233

232 *Nicolas Benois, " Boris Godounoff " (Moussorgsky) : La Scala, Milan, 1927.*

233 *Simon Lissim, " Tsar Saltan " (Rimsky-Korsakov) : Liceo Theatre, Barcelona, 1924.*

234

235

234   *Vassily Schoukhaeff, " La Pastourelle " : Chauve-Souris, 1924.*
235   *Vassily Schoukhaeff, " La Traviata " (Verdi): Chauve-Souris, 1924.*

236

237

236 *Boris Anisfeld, " The Love for Three Oranges " (Prokofieff) : Chicago
Opera, Chicago.*

237 *Serge Soudeikine, " Petrouchka " (Stravinsky) : Metropolitan Opera,
New York, 1927.*

238

239

238 *Stanislas Sliwinski, " L'Échange " (Claudel) : Teatr Maly, Warsaw, 1925.*

239 *Vincent Drabik, " Le Songe Argenté de Salonica " (Slowacki) : Teatr Polski, Warsaw.*

240

241

240 *Vlastislav Hofman (Hilar), " Žižka " (Lom) : National Theatre, Prague, 1925.*

241 *Vlastislav Hofman (Hilar), " Les Esclaves " (Fischer) : National Theatre, Prague, 1926.*

242

243

242   *Robert Edmond Jones, " Till Eulenspiegel " (Strauss) : Ballets Russes, Chicago, 1916.*

243   *Vlastislav Hofman (Hilar), " Adam the Creator " (J. and K. Čapek) : National Theatre, Prague, 1926.*

244

245

244-245 *Bedrich Feuerstein (Hilar), " Le Malade Imaginaire " (Molière) :*
National Theatre, Prague, 1921.

246

247

246 *Alexander Vladimir Hrska, " Der Kreidekreis " (Klabund): National Theatre, Prague, 1926.*

247 *C. Jandl, " El secreto a voces " (Calderón): Svando Teatr, Prague, 1922.*

248

249

248-249 *Ludolf Liberts, " Judith " (Hebbel): National Theatre, Riga, 1925.*

254

255

254-255   *Otto Reigbert, " Spiel des Lebens " (Hamsun) : Kammerspiele, Munich, 1922.*

256

257

256–257   *Jean Hugo, " Roméo et Juliette " (Shakespeare–Cocteau) : Soirées de Paris, Théâtre de la Cigale, Paris, 1924.*

258

259

258 *Nathalie Gontcharova, " Foire Espagnole " (Chabrier) : San Sebastian, 1916.*

259 *Irène Lagut, " Les Mariés de la Tour Eiffel " (Cocteau) : Swedish Ballet,
Paris, 1921.*

260

261

260 *Fernand Léger, " Skating Rink " (Canudo) : Swedish Ballet, Paris, 1922.*

261 *Fernand Léger, " La Création du Monde " (Cendrars–Milhaud) : Swedish Ballet, Paris, 1923.*

262

263

262   Pablo Picasso, " Le Tricorne " (de Falla) : Ballets Russes, Paris, 1919.

263   André Derain, " La Boutique Fantasque " (Rossini) : Ballets Russes,
Paris, 1919.

264

265

264 *Ljubo Babić, " Diogenes " (Brezovački) : National Theatre, Zagreb.*

265 *Walter René Fuerst, " Candide " (Voltaire–Vautel) : Théâtre de l' Odéon, Paris, 1923.*

266

267

266 *Walter René Fuerst, " Le Bourgeois Gentilhomme " (Molière) : Théâtre de l'Odéon, Paris, 1924.*

267 *Walter René Fuerst, " The Taming of the Shrew " (Shakespeare) : Théâtre de l'Odéon, Paris, 1923.*

268

269

268   *Rostislav Dobujinsky, fils, " L'Enlèvement du Serail " (Archangelsky):
Chauve-Souris, 1926.*

269   *Johannes Schroeder, " Kaffeehaus " (Zoff): Kammerspiele, Hamburg.*

270

271

270 *Vlastislav Hofman, " Hedy " (Fibich): National Theatre, Prague, 1923.*

271 *Vlastislav Hofman (Hilar), " Le Jeu de l'Amour et de la Mort "*
(Rolland): National Theatre, Prague, 1925.

272

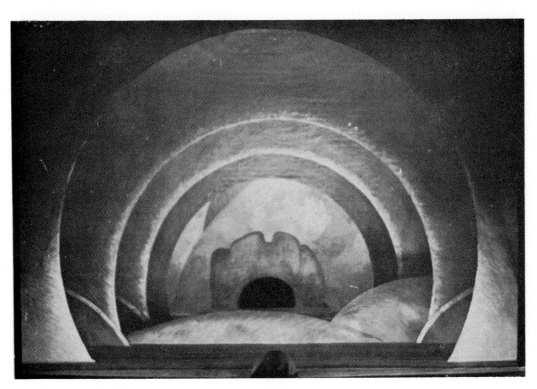

273

272 *Vlastislav Hofman, " L'Échange " (Claudel) : National Theatre,*
Prague, 1922.

273 *Josef Wenig, " La vida es sueño " (Calderón) : National Theatre, Prague, 1923.*

274

275

274 *Josef Čapek, " Le Pain " (Ghéon): Municipal Theatre, Prague, 1922.*

275 *Hermann Krehan, " Der Bauer als Millionär " (Raimund): Deutsches Schauspielhaus, Hamburg.*

276

277

276–277 *Paul Thiersch, " Kabale und Liebe " (Schiller): Altes Theater,*
Leipzig, 1926.

278

279

278 Curt Herwig, " La Bottega di caffé " (Goldoni) : Stadtbühne, Madgeburg, 1925.
279 Curt Herwig, " Salome " (Strauss) : Stadtbühne, Magdeburg, 1925.

280

281

280   *Edward Suhr (Piscator), " Sturmflut " (Paquet) : Volksbühne, Berlin, 1926.*

281   *Karlheinz Martin, " Razzia " (Rehfisch) : Lessingtheater, Berlin, 1926.*

XI

COSTUME	LE COSTUME	KOSTÜM
AND	ET	UND
MASKS	LE MASQUE	MASKE

282

283

284

285

282–283   *Boris Bilinsky, Costume designs.*

284   *Michel Andreenko, Costume design.*

285   *Mario Pompei, Costume design.*

286

287

286–287 *Karl Walser, Costume designs.*

289

288

288–289 *Aubrey Hammond, Costume designs for " The Pilgrim of Love " (Irving) : Repertory Theatre, Liverpool, 1923.*

290   *Léon Bakst, Costume design for " Syrian Dancer."*

291   *Léon Bakst, Costume design for Queen's Guard in " La Belle au Bois Dormant " (Tchaikovsky).*

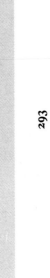

293

292

292 *Simon Lissim, Costume design for The King in " The Love for Three Oranges " (Prokofieff).*
293 *Simon Lissim, Costume designs for Le Pain in " L'Oiseau bleu " (Maeterlinck).*

294

295

296

297

294–295 *James Reynolds, Costume designs for " Grania " (Lady Gregory):*
Ram's Head Players, Baltimore.

296–297 *Isaac Grünewald, Costume designs.*

298

299

298-299 *Jean Hugo, Costumes for " Roméo et Juliette " (Shakespeare–Cocteau):*
Soirées de Paris, Théâtre de la Cigale, Paris, 1924.

300

301

302

303

300–301 *Michel Larionoff, Costume designs for " Chout " (Prokofieff):*
Ballets Russes, Paris, 1922.

302–303 *Michel Larionoff, Realization of the same costumes for " Chout "*
(Prokofieff), shown in plates 300–301.

305

304

304 *Nathalie Gontcharova, Costume design for The Apostle John in "Liturgie": Lausanne, 1915.*
305 *Nathalie Gontcharova, Costume design for The Apostle Mark in "Liturgie"; Lausanne, 1915.*

306

307

308

309

306–307 *Fernand Léger, Costume designs for " La Création du Monde "*
(Cendrars-Milhaud) : Swedish Ballet, Paris, 1923.

308–309 *Enrico Prampolini, Costume designs for " Chitra " (Tagore) : Rome.*

310-311

312-313

310-311 *George Grosz, Costume designs for " Methusalem " (Goll) : Berlin.*

312-313 *Ivo Panaggi, Costume designs for " L'Angoscia delle Machine "*
(Vasari) : Teatro degli Indipendenti, Rome.

314

315

314 *Madame Parr, Costumes and masks for " L'Homme et son Désir " (Claudel):*
Swedish Ballet, Paris.

315 *Nicolas Remisoff, Costumes and masks for " Marionettes " (Satie): Bolm*
Ballet, Chicago, 1926.

316

317

316 *Fortunato Depero, Costume design, Rome.*
317 *Oskar Schlemmer, Costumes for " Das Triadische Ballett " : Bauhausbühne, Dessau.*

318

319

320

321

318–321 *Jean Hugo, Costume designs for " Les Mariés de la Tour Eiffel"*
(Cocteau) : Paris, 1921.

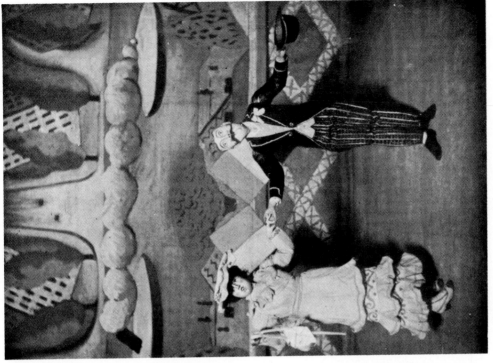

323

322

322–323 *Jean Hugo, Costumes and masks for " Les Mariés de la Tour Eiffel " (Cocteau) : Swedish Ballet, Paris, 1921.*

325

324

324–327   *Hildo Krop, Masks for " The Only Jealousy of Emer " (Yeats) : Stadschowburg, Amsterdam, 1924.*

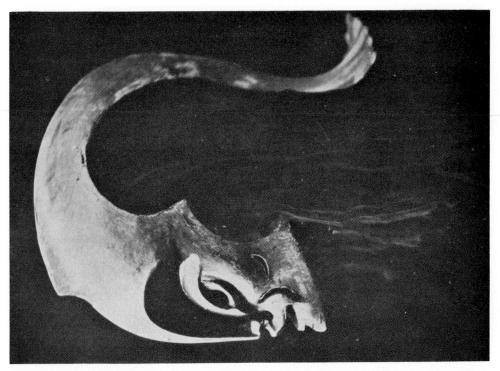

327

326

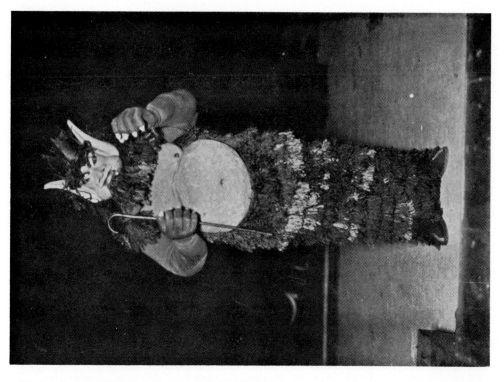

329

328

328 Oliver Messel, Mask and costume, London, *1927*.

329 Walter René Fuerst, Mask and costume for " Peer Gynt " (Ibsen) : Théâtre de la Porte St.Martin, Paris.

330

331

332

330 *W. A. Benda, Mask, New York.*

331–332 *Theodore Weidhaas, Masks, New York.*

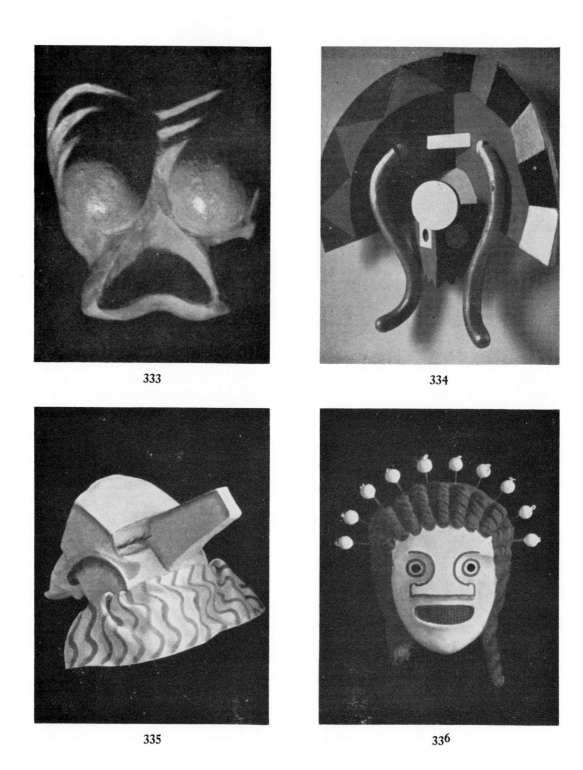

333

334

335

336

333 *Norman Bel Geddes, Mask for Dante's " Divine Comedy " : New York.*

334 *Enrico Prampolini, Mechanical mask for " The Psychology of Machines "*
(Mix) : Rome, 1924.

335-336 *Oliver Messel, Masks, London, 1927.*

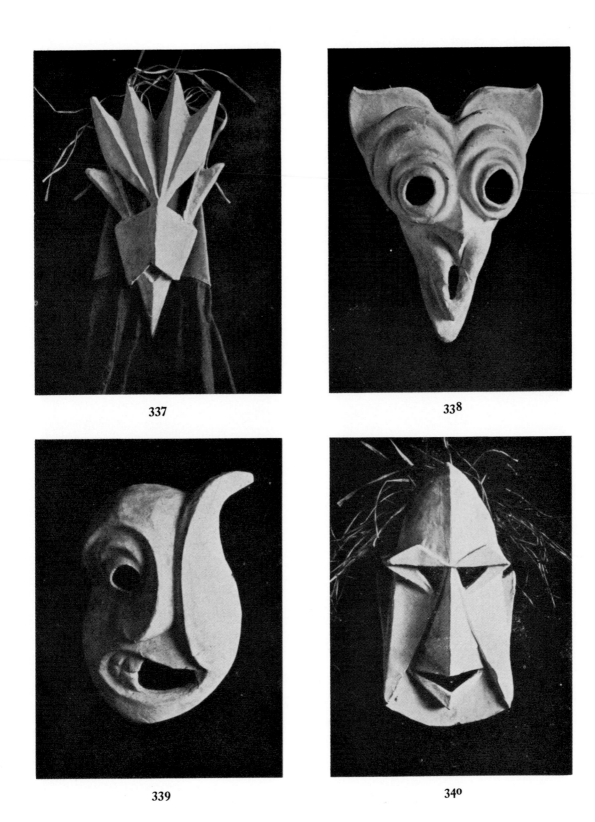

337

338

339

340

337–340 *Emil Pirchan, Masks, Berlin.*

XII

TECHNICAL
DEVICES

LES MOYENS
TECHNIQUES

MODERNE
BÜHNENTECHNIK

341

342

341 *Adolf Linnebach, View of the elevator stage, Opernhaus, Hamburg, 1926.*

342 *Adolf Linnebach, View of the elevator stage, Schauspielhaus, Chemnitz, 1925.*

343

344

343 *Adolf Mahnke, Satirical sketch of the Schauspielhaus, Dresden.*

344 *Adolf Linnebach, Cross section showing elevator stage, Opernhaus, Hamburg, 1926.*

345

346

345 *Ernst Stern, " The Tempest " (Shakespeare) : Model for the revolving stage, Deutsches Theater, Berlin.*

346 *Adolf Mahnke, " Dame Kobold " (Calderón–Hofmannsthal) : Model for the revolving stage, Schauspielhaus, Dresden.*

347

348

347 *Eduard Sturm, " Kaiser und Galiläer " (Ibsen) : Model for the revolving stage, Schauspielhaus, Düsseldorf, 1924.*

348 *Eduard Sturm, " Manfred " (Byron) : Model for the revolving stage, Schauspielhaus, Düsseldorf, 1925.*

350

349

349–350 *Oskar Strnad, Two designs for a new theatre, known as " Ringbühne." A project.*

XIII

| STAGE LIGHTING | L'ÉCLAIRAGE DE LA SCÈNE MODERNE | MODERNE BELEUCHTUNGSTECHNIK |

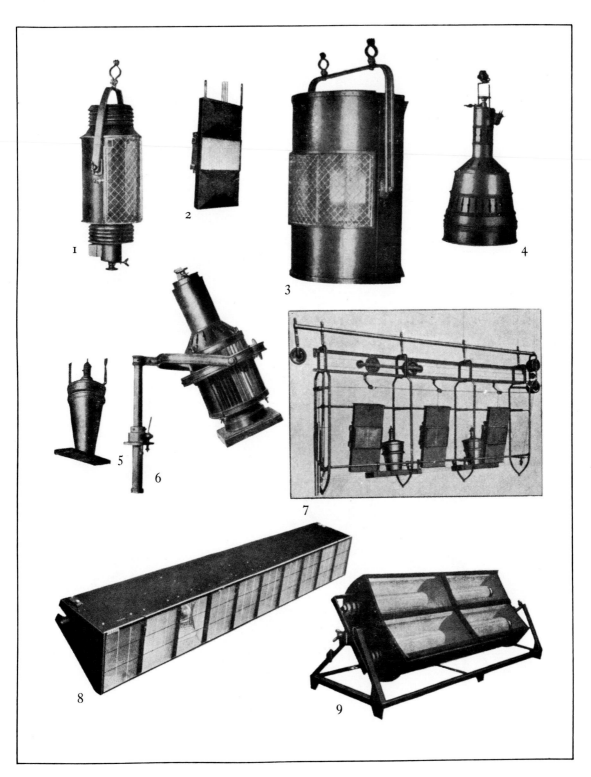

351 *Various light units, Figs. 1–9.*

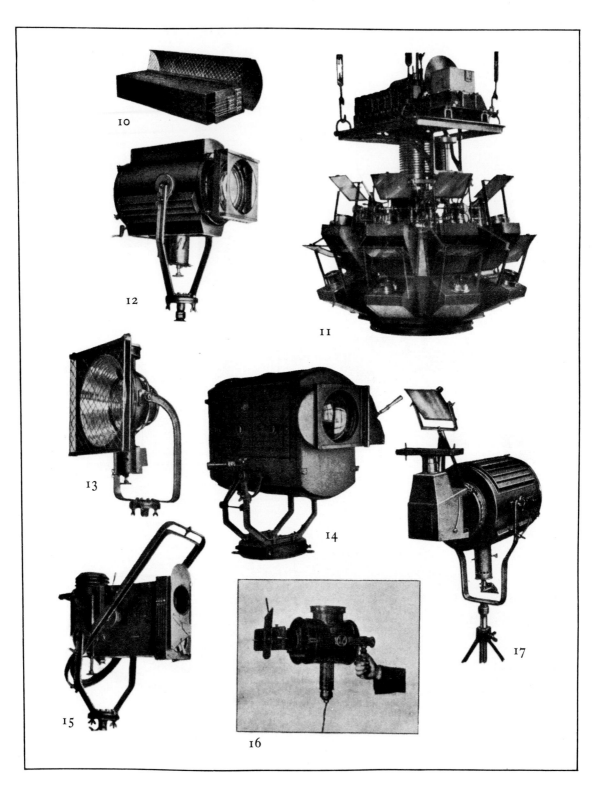

352 *Various light units—projectors, spots, floods, etc., Figs. 10–17.*

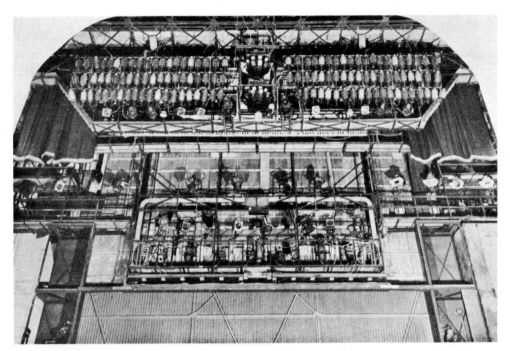

353

354

355

353 Hasait-Schwabe light installation.

354 Ward Leonard, Dimmer Bank, New York.

355 German Altgemeine Elektrizitäts Gesellschaft, Dimmer Bank.

356

357

356 *Max Hasait, Cloud projection in " Turandot " (Puccini) : setting by Fanto,
Staatsoper, Dresden.*

357 *Josef Čapek, " The Insect Comedy " (J. and K. Čapek) : Projections,
National Theatre, Prague, 1922.*

358

359

358 *Traugott Müller (Piscator), " Gewitter über Gothland " (Welk): Volks-bühne, Berlin, 1927.*

359 *Remigius Geyling, " Peer Gynt " (Ibsen): Projections by the Gekape process, Burgtheater, Vienna.*

360

361

360 *Jonel Jorgulesco, " The Adding Machine " (Rice): Mobile projections,
Boston Repertory Theatre, 1926.*

361 *Jonel Jorgulesco, " Macbeth " (Shakespeare): Mobile projections, Boston
Repertory Theatre, 1927.*

362

363

362 *Vlastislav Hofman, " Wozzek " (Berg): Projected setting, National Theatre, Prague.*

363 *Lee Simonson, " Back to Methuselah " (Shaw): Projected setting, Theatre Guild, New York.*

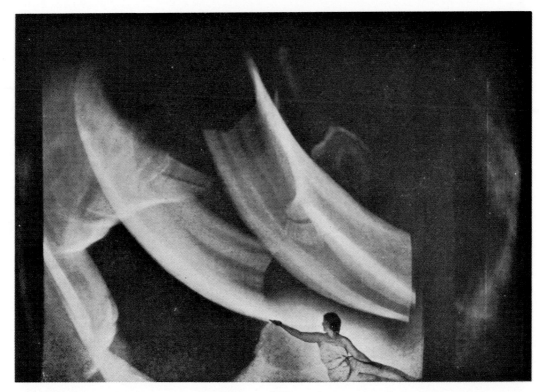

364

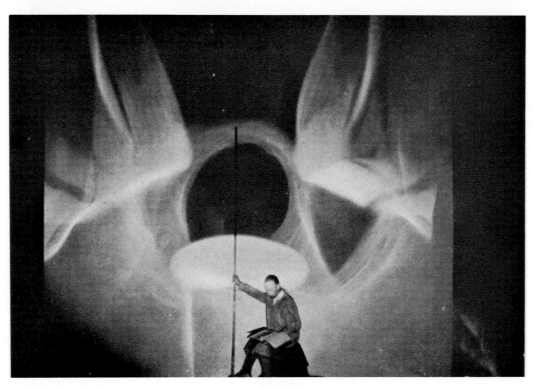

365

364-365 *Thomas Wilfred, Mobile composition produced by the Clavilux:
Thomas Wilfred, inventor, New York, 1927.*

XIV

NEW STAGE FORMS	VERS DES FORMES	NEUE FORMEN
AND	NOUVELLES	UND NEUE
NEW POSSIBILITIES	DU SPECTACLE	MÖGLICHKEITEN
	SCÉNIQUE	DER BÜHNE

367

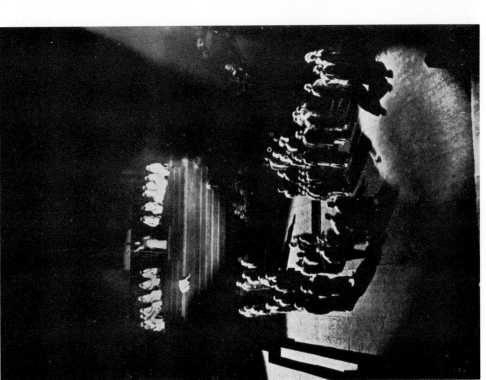

366

366 *Ernst Stern (Reinhardt), " Oedipus Rex " (Sophocles–Hofmannsthal) : Zirkus Schumann, Berlin, 1910.*
367 *Ernst Stern (Reinhardt), " Danton " (Rolland) : Grosses Schauspielhaus, Berlin, 1920.*

368

369

370

368–369   *Alfred Roller (Reinhardt), " Das Grosse Welttheater " (Calderón–
Hofmannsthal): Kollegienkirche, Salzburg, 1922.*

370   *Ernst Stern (Reinhardt), " Lysistrata " (Aristophanes); Grosses Schauspielhaus, Berlin, 1923.*

371

372

373

371   Oskar Strnad, " The Miracle " (Vollmoeller) : Project for Milan.

372   Oskar Strnad (Reinhardt), " The Miracle " (Vollmoeller) : Zirkus Renz, Vienna, 1927.

373   Max Reinhardt, " Jedermann " (Hofmannsthal) : Cathedral Square, Salzburg, 1921.

374

375

374 *Karlheinz Martin, " Antigone " (Hasenclever): Grosses Schauspielhaus, Berlin, 1920.*

375 *Ludwig Kainer (Karlheinz Martin), " Europa " (Kaiser): Grosses Schauspielhaus, Berlin, 1920.*

376

377

376–377   *Norman de Kalb Edwards (Hume), " Oedipus Rex " (Sophocles) :*
Greek Theatre, University of California, Berkeley, Calif., 1922.

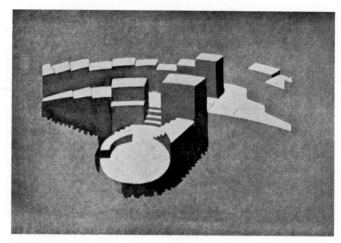

378

379

380

378–380   *Walter Neuzil, Franz Loewitsch and Rudolf Scherer, Plastic stage, Vienna.*

381

382

381 *Donald Oenslager, Project for Wagner's " Ring des Nibelungen " : New York, 1926.*

382 *Ernest de Weerth, Project for a Tri-Arts Temple—Music, Light and Movement, New York.*

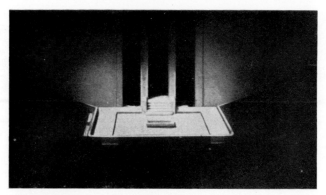

383

384

385

383–385 *Wilhelm Treichlinger and Fritz Rosenbaum, Theatre project, Vienna.*

386

387

386 *Norman Bel Geddes, " The Singing Globe " (Wentworth) : Model for a new stage form, 1923.*

387 *Adolf Mahnke, Spiral stage, Model for a project, Dresden.*